RESONANCE OF SUFFERING

THE INTERNATIONAL PSYCHOANALYSIS LIBRARY

General Editor: Leticia Glocer Fiorini

IPA Publications Committee

Leticia Glocer Fiorini (Argentina), Chair; Salman Akhtar (Philadelphia); Thierry Bokanowski (Paris); Alessandra Lemma (London); Sergio Lewkowicz (Porto Alegre); Mary Kay O'Neil (Montreal); Piers Pendred (London), Ex-officio as Director General; Cesare Sacerdoti (London), Ex-officio as Publications Director

Violence or Dialogue? Psychoanalytic Insights on Terror and Terrorism
edited by Sverre Varvin & Vamik D. Volkan

Pluralism and Unity? Methods of Research in Psychoanalysis
edited by Marianne Leuzinger-Bohleber, Anna Ursula Dreher, & Jorge Canestri

Truth, Reality, and the Psychoanalyst: Latin American Contributions to Psychoanalysis
edited by Sergio Lewkowicz & Silvia Flechner

Verdad, realidad y el psicoanalista: Contribuciones Latinoamericanas al Psicoanálisis
edited by Sergio Lewkowicz & Silvia Flechner

The Geography of Meanings:
Psychoanalytic Perspectives on Place, Space, Land, and Dislocation
edited by Maria Teresa Savio Hooke & Salman Akhtar

Linking, Alliances, and Shared Space:
The Psychoanalytic Approach to Groups and the Psychoanalyst
René Kaës

RESONANCE OF SUFFERING
Countertransference
in non-neurotic structures

edited by

André Green

The International Psychoanalysis Library

**International
Psychoanalytical
Association**

LONDON

Chapter 3, by Jean-Claude Rolland, first published as "La loi de Lavoisier s'applique a la matiere psychique." In: *Avant d'être celui qui parle* (Paris: Editions Gallimard, 2006). Translated by permission. Copyright © Editions Gallimard, Paris 2006.

Grateful acknowledgement is made to Free Association Books Ltd, London, UK, for permission to reprint André Green, "The Central Phobic Position", as published in *Psychoanalysis; A Paradigm of Clinical Thinking* (London: Free Association Books, 2005).

First published in 2007 by
The International Psychoanalytical Association
Broomhills
Woodside Lane
London N12 8UD
United Kingdom

British Library Cataloguing in Publication Data

A C.I.P. for this book is available from the British Library

ISBN: 978-1-905888-01-6

10 9 8 7 6 5 4 3 2 1

Produced for the IPA by Communication Crafts

Printed in Great Britain

www.ipa.org.uk

CONTENTS

THE INTERNATIONAL PSYCHOANALYSIS LIBRARY

IPA Publications Committee

The International Psychoanalysis Library, published under the aegis of the International Psychoanalytical Association, is the product of the editorial policy of the IPA Publications Committee: to serve the interests of the membership and increase the awareness of the relevance of the discipline in related professional and academic circles, and to do so through a continuity of publications so that the benefits of psychoanalytic research can be shared across a wide audience.

The focus of the Library is on the scientific developments of today throughout the IPA, with an emphasis within the discipline on clinical, technical, and theoretical advances; empirical, conceptual, and historical research projects; the outcome of investigations conducted by IPA committees and working parties; selected material arising from conferences and meetings; and investigations at the interface with social and cultural expressions.

This volume condenses the work of a series of research meetings sponsored by the IPA and led by André Green, with participation of colleagues from all regions. We are grateful to the editor and to the contributors for the additional effort in preparing their remarkable material for publication.

Leticia Glocer Fiorini
Series Editor

EDITOR AND CONTRIBUTORS

André Green is a psychoanalyst who lives and works in Paris. He is Past-President of the Paris Psychoanalytical Society. He also served as Director of the Paris Psychoanalytic Institute and as Vice-President of the International Psychoanalytical Association. In addition, he has been co-editor of the *International Journal of Psychoanalysis* and the *Nouvelle Revue de Psychanalyse*. He has written several books, including: *The Tragic Effect; On Private Madness*; and *The Fabric of Affect in the Psychoanalytic Discourse*.

William I. Grossman died on 22 June 2006, while this book was in preparation. In the place of a biographical note, we quote a message to the members of the New York Psychoanalytic Institute by Arnold Richards, which says more than listing his works and the positions he held:

> "With the passing of Bill Grossman psychoanalysis has lost one of its foremost thinkers. Bill was one of a small group of clinical theoreticians who profoundly influenced the development of my own psychoanalytic thinking, a group which included Jack Arlow, Charles Brenner and Leo Rangell as well as Donald Kaplan who was one of Bill's collaborators. He was a mentor and a friend. Our relationship began in 1964 when

we were both on the staff at Montefiore. I was honored to
participate in an analytic course in the psychoanalytic theory
development for the psychiatric residents before I had started
analytic training at the NYPI and the discussions about theory
and technique during our rides back and forth to Montefiore
was an important part of my extra classroom analytic training. Twenty of his papers and a superb introduction to his
work by Arnold Wilson are available on the Internet Press for
Psychoanalysis website (http://www.psychoanalysis.net/ippsa/
grossman."

A valediction from André Green: William Grossman was an active
participant in our group. He had to miss one session because he
already had health problems. I wish to express my regrets about
his death, as he had become a very respected member, whose vast
knowledge and expertise in problems of theory was recognized by
all the other colleagues of the group. Though I had met him before
the creation of the group, our bonds became tighter, and, apart from
being a respected colleague, he also became a personal friend. I consider him as one of the leaders of North American psychoanalysis. I
am deeply sorry for not being able to exchange ideas with him any
more.

Otto F. Kernberg is Director of the Personality Disorders Institute
at The New York Presbyterian Hospital, Westchester Division, and
Professor of Psychiatry at the Weill Medical College of Cornell
University. Dr. Kernberg is a former President of the International
Psychoanalytical Association. He is also Training and Supervising
Analyst of the Columbia University Center for Psychoanalytic Train-
ing and Research. He is the author of 10 books and the co-author of
10 others. His most recent books include: *Aggressivity, Narcissism and
Self-destructiveness in the Psychotherapeutic Relationship: New Developments
in the Psychopathology and Psychotherapy of Severe Personality Disorders*;
*Contemporary Controversies in Psychoanalytic Theory, Techniques and Their
Applications*; and *Psychotherapy for Borderline Personality*, co-authored
with John Clarkin and Frank Yeomans.

Gregorio Kohon is a training analyst of the British Psychoanalytical
Society. Originally from Argentina, he moved to England in 1970,
where he studied and worked with R. D. Laing and his colleagues of
the anti-psychiatry movement. He edited *The British School of Psycho-*

analysis: The Independent Tradition and *The Dead Mother: The Work of André Green*. He is also the author of *No Lost Certainties to be Recovered* and *Love and its Vicissitudes* (co-authored with André Green). In 1988 he co-founded, with Valli Shaio Kohon, the Brisbane Centre for Psychoanalytic Studies in Australia, which he directed until December 1994. Kohon has also published three books of poetry and a novel in Spanish. An English version of his novel, *Papagayo Rojo, Pata de Palo*, [*Red Parrot, Wooden Leg*, and a new collection of his poems in Spanish, *El Estilo del Deseo*, are in press. At present, he works in London in private practice.

Jaime Lutenberg is a psychoanalyst and full member of APA (Argentine Psychoanalytical Association). He lives and works in Buenos Aires. He is a former Scientific Secretary of APdeBA (Psychoanalytical Association of Buenos Aires). He is Training and Supervising Analyst and Professor of the APA Psychoanalytic Institute. He is also Professor in the Master's Programme in Psychoanalysis. He is the author of several books and co-author of others, including *El Psicoanalista y la Verdad*; *La Ilusión Vaciada*; and *Actualizaciones en Psicosomática*.

Jean-Claude Rolland is a full member and former President of the French Psychoanalytic Association. He is Co-editor, with Catherine Chabert, of the *Libres Cahiers pour la Psychanalyse*, a review published twice yearly by IN Press, Paris. He is the author of *Guérir du mal d'aimer* and of *Avant d'être celui qui parle*.

Elizabeth Bott Spillius originally studied psychology and anthropology and is now a training and supervising psychoanalyst of the British Psychoanalytical Society. She was the General Editor of the New Library of Psychoanalysis from 1988 to 1998. Her publications include *Tongan Society at the Time of Captain Cook's Visits* and *Family and Social Network*. She has also been the editor of *Melanie Klein Today*. Her new book, *Encounters with Melanie Klein: Selected Papers of Elizabeth Spillius*, edited by Priscilla Roth and Richard Rusbridger, is in press.

Fernando Urribarri is a psychoanalyst of the Asociación Psicoanalítica Argentina, where he co-chairs with Madeleine Baranger a research group on Contemporary Psychoanalysis since 1998. Since 1989 he has been editor of the psychoanalytic journal *Zona Erógena*. He is director of the two book collections, in Argentina and

France: "Contemporary Theory", EUdeBA (Editorial Universitaria de Buenos Aires). He lectures on French Contemporary Psychoanalysis in the University of Buenos Aires (UBA). He co-chaired international conferences on contemporary psychoanalysis and social theory at Columbia University of New York, at Centre International de Cerisy-France, and at UBA. He has published several psychoanalytic papers in books and international journals in the United Kingdom, France, Italy, Spain, and Australia, as well as the official journals of Argentina and Chile's IPA societies. He is the co-editor of the book *On André Green's Work: Toward a Contemporary Psychoanalysis.*

RESONANCE OF SUFFERING

Introduction:
a unique experience

André Green

As one who initiated the group and organized its meetings, when I try to examine the feelings each of the workshops inspired in me—and I was not the only one to have experienced this—a sense of elation stands out on emerging from the meetings about what had been achieved. I have to say that it was with some regret that our work had to come to an end due to lack of funding to cover the necessary expenses of these meetings.

By and large, the others who participated in the meetings share with me this regret. However, the reader of this work may not be able to detect the sense of enthusiasm that was felt. For when the meetings were all over, the emphasis was less on capturing the atmosphere of the work than in describing the thoughts that these meetings had stimulated in the participants: not just the thoughts that were shared but the thoughts of each individual.

At this stage we may well ask in what sense this work can claim to be the result of research. If research is required to have distinct objectives, a common and well-defined methodology, performing comparative studies, then it is true that the term is inappropriate in our case. However, it will be made clearer if I describe how the group was born, why it met, and the work it was engaged in, even if, at the end of the day, this work cannot lay claim to the name "research". But more about this later. . . .

Ever since I have been taking an interest in borderline personality disorders—that being from around 1975—two questions have preoccupied me. The first of these is the following: does this so-called patient group possess a unity—a structure—that would allow us to treat it individually in a clinically coherent way using only the instruments of psychoanalytic thought and not, for instance, a statistical or a psychiatric approach? The second question is indirectly linked to the first: do all psychoanalysts, regardless of their origin, conceive of borderline cases in the same way? Are we not using a blanket term to categorize what are, in fact, different kinds of patients with separate realities? Once again, it was about determining whether or not the psychoanalytic criteria could be generalized in such a way as to be sure we were speaking about the same thing when we alluded to such cases.

I could only conceive of one way to confront these questions if we did not wish to set out on an extensive research involving millions of cases that would provide us only with superficial data of limited use. Psychoanalytically, some other solution had to be found. Then the idea came to me of bringing together a select number of analysts—two representatives from South America, two from North America, and four from Europe (consisting of two from the United Kingdom and two from France)—for two weekends a year, during which time they could openly discuss the way they saw the problems of technique and of theory and clinical problems. I was anxious that the research group should be open-minded in its attempt to develop an expertise on the subject of borderline cases. The group would include renowned classical analysts, though representing different analytic families: Freudian, Independent British, Kleinian, ego-psychologists, and others. I put forward the following list of names:

Jaime Lutenberg (Buenos Aires);
Fernando Urribarri (Buenos Aires);
Otto Kernberg (New York);
William Grossmann (New York);
Gregorio Kohon (London);
Elizabeth Spillius (London);
Jean-Claude Rolland (Lyon)
André Green (Paris)

Most members of the group did not know one another. It was only after the first few meetings had been held that were we able to speak trustfully and openly together and to become accustomed to different ways of thinking.

After holding the first session in New York, which turned out to be very expensive, the decision was taken, in order to cut spending to a minimum, to make Paris the permanent place of meeting, and we agreed to meet at my home. Moreover, the IPA grant (of $8,000 a year for three years) having proved insufficient, one of the group members managed to find a private donor who agreed to support us with up to $4,000 dollars a year for three years. He supported us willingly the first year; however, during the second year he had to be reminded a number of times. Because of the difficulties, it was decided to renounce on this funding for the third year. It should be kept in mind that the funds being sought were limited to covering the travel and accommodation expenses of the participants, as well as any secretarial costs, such as transcripts of the clinical material and of the group discussions. Soon the need for saving led to the decision to confine ourselves to the notes taken during the meetings rather than running the costs of producing transcripts of the meetings by deciphering recordings, often difficult to make out, although the recordings remained available to help clarify obscure points. However, being unable to rely on an increase in subsidy from the IPA, we were obliged to cancel some of the meetings and in the final year to confine ourselves to a single reunion. There was, however, full participation at all of the meetings (with the exception of one occasion, when one member was absent due to illness).

After a final get-together, which lasted three days instead of two in order to make up for the one that was cancelled because of a lack of funding, the group separated, with each member promising to write a chapter for a collective work that would treat freely of the subjects that we discussed.

Fernando Urribarri volunteered to coordinate the information. The programme for each session was as follows: we opened the meeting with a clinical presentation, given by one of the group members, the content of which had been communicated beforehand to the rest of the group. Presentations were given, successively, by: André Green, Jean-Claude Rolland, Otto Kernberg, Jaime Lutenberg, Elizabeth Spillius, and Gregorio Kohon. For reasons of confidentiality we cannot publish some of the material (Kernberg, Lutenberg, Spillius).

In the course of the discussions, each participant gave his or her opinion on the clinical case study being presented or on certain fragments of the material that were focused on. Often the discussions led to theoretical views being expressed regarding the points of discussion. It was on such occasions that each of us discovered just how inaccurate—even erroneous—were our ideas concerning the points of view of the other participants: for instance, the notions of ego psychology as seen from the European perspective, unfamiliarity with the ideas held by all the South American analysts and, to the same extent, the lack of knowledge of the French way of thinking.

The discussions were pleasant and served to enrich our knowledge. On no occasion did we feel the need to resort to amalgamations that would have been schematic and misleading. Generally speaking, the concern to emphasize the psychoanalytic point of view outshone every other consideration. In particular, the need to clearly distinguish the psychoanalytic point of view from the psychiatric one resulted in lively debate (as regards diagnosis). The majority of the group wished to keep to a purely psychoanalytic discussion, although there was no prior intention to be univocal.

It may be seen why, strictly speaking, this was not research. It would be more appropriate to describe what took place as: "an international discussion group involving inter-analytic exchanges on the notions of borderline personality disorders: from clinical, technical, and theoretical points of view." This title would better reflect the content of our exchanges.

Was it or was it not research? *Sensu stricto* it was not; but how might one qualify the exchange or views if it is not in reference to a standing point that addresses a problem among psychoanalysts? As far as I am concerned, it may be called research, both clinical and conceptual. If one adds to this the critical comments that are to be found on the usual way of conducting research in psychoanalysis, this work opens the debate about the future paths to explore in the various types of research in psychoanalysis.

Nothing can replace the exchanges between psychoanalysts when it comes to debating an issue that is a constant theme of discussions, often of a passionate nature, among them. This is why I said the reader might be unable to experience the same sense of enthusiasm the meetings offered—which allowed spontaneity, constant liveliness, and sometimes arguments. But we must not look for the impossible. I, personally, am delighted with the success of these meetings, and I could not more strongly encourage their pursuit. They seemed to me to offer, in a more satisfactory way than the congresses of the IPA, a certain freedom in psychoanalysis, tempered always by the need to understand and to be understood by one another. I hope this effort in understanding reaches out to the readers of this work, which the IPA publications made a point of publishing.

I can only once again express our regret that lack of funding for the group did not permit proper transcripts of the discussions—always lively and passionate at times—which would have been of considerable benefit to the reader. We had to confine ourselves to a collection of articles exposing the point of view of each participant on a particular problem or general conception. This is highly regrettable, despite the importance of the collected contributions.

Non-neurotic structures: a continent

Any psychoanalyst who knows a little about the history of psychoanalysis will know that the so-called "borderline" cases ("borderline personality disorders", according to Kernberg) were not seen as such when psychoanalysis was in its beginnings. Without getting involved in a detailed critical review, we do know that Freud himself was unaware of this category of patients. However, a thorough scrutiny of his work does reveal certain indications he left that allow us to apply his observations to what would later come to be a category that is almost universally acknowledged by psychoanalysts. (Interested readers may refer to my work—Green, 1977).

However, certain psychoanalysts (particularly, Lacan and his followers, in France), probably because they avoided the problems these kinds of patients presented, refused to individualize their states. In their opinion, the neurosis/psychosis split does not have any intermediate stage. Yet the great authors of contemporary psychoanalysis (especially Winnicott, but also Bion) acknowledged implicitly if not explicitly the existence of this category of patients: for example, one may refer to Bion's (1957) article, to mention but one, concerning the neurotic and psychotic elements of personality and to the entire work of Winnicott.

If our group chose to study this category of patients, it is because from the point of view of the indications for treatment and from the clinical, technical, and theoretical perspectives it concerns a great number of problems about which there is no consensus, nor is there agreement regarding the technique to adopt and even less about which theory would lead to a unified conception. This will become apparent to the reader of the present work.

I would like to state that the borders of the collection are not well defined, as indeed the name suggests. Rather than another regional diagnostic category to add to the list, it is more like a continent of varying landscapes. Initially, I used the general terminology, calling them "borderline cases", which had originally stood for "cases bordering on psychosis". My knowledge of the various types encountered, however, made me give up on this term in favour of the wider designation of "non-neurotic structures". Indeed, it appeared to me that it is no longer appropriate to define them as being on the border between neurosis and psychosis. We may well have considered certain clinical cases that lie on the borders of perversion, melancholia, or a psychosomatic illness. The only thing I felt the cases had in common is that none of them could be called "neurosis" in the sense Freud used the term in his descriptions, treatments, and theory. I refer, of course, to the transference psychoneuroses. It is a designation that will suffice for the time being: it will be left to the future to find a more satisfactory way of naming them.

I believe that the metaphor of the continent will be reinforced by reading the résumés of the clinical presentations and of the discussions in this collection. Thus we have one case presented as obsessional neurosis considered by others to be, in fact—and without the shadow of a doubt—schizophrenia. Another case, presented as hysteria (unpublished for reasons of confidentiality), was considered borderline by some of us. Nevertheless, many balked at the idea of requesting a prior diagnosis. It is difficult for the notes to render the richness of the discussions. Some are transcribed in detail. If the requirement for a prior diagnosis—supported by the indications regarding the type of therapy (psychoanalysis or psychotherapy)—most of the participants avoided forming any hasty conclusions rather than use the nosographical references. This involved postponing the results to await the development of the treatment, even when a strong opinion was held during the first encounter. By and large, the psychoanalytic process and the setting also allowed us to reveal the structure better than any other approach (mental, systematic, or statistics-oriented tests).

It is, on the whole, an unexpected application of the transferential and countertransferential exchanges in the light of clinical psychoanalysis not being subject to psychopathological or psychiatric thinking. We may affirm that this way of proceeding is more or less directly linked to the degree of analysability of the patient, taking into account the registers belonging to different theories: the erotic and destructive drives of pulsional life, the ego and its defences, the object relationship, the self, intersubjectivity, and so on. The most important thing here will be to remain psychoanalytic without requiring psychoanalysis to assume some general theory that goes beyond its own set of criteria.

One might suspect this notion to be biased; however, it only arises from the need not to lose sight of what makes psychoanalysis relentless in the defence of its originality. On the other hand, acceptance by most of us of this general principle helped us to understand the differences in our reference criteria, which no longer centred on Freud's theory. Hence the need for certain clarifications of what induced a particular colleague to adopt a particular theoretical approach, often in relation to the authors traditionally honoured in the analyst's country. Such was the case, for instance, with Bleger's theories, focusing on the notions of symbiosis and ambiguity, which are held in high regard in South America but were almost unknown to analysts outside, despite the fact that some translations of his works did exist. This indicates the scattering and the fragmentation of the psychoanalytic concepts with which one had at first to become familiar. However, some of the authors were known beyond the borders of their own countries, although not everyone understood them in the same way.

However that may be, all members of the group acknowledged that Freudian nosography relied too much on the psychiatric nosography of the time, despite certain innovations that Freud himself had proposed. A psychoanalytic nosography was required. Many authors made the attempt but none of them were given unanimous acceptance. We found that our exchanges raised more questions than obtained unanimous answers—not necessarily a bad thing.

The psychoanalytic setting

Looking back, I notice the following significant fact: that there was no substantial discussion focusing on the psychoanalytic setting. In the cases we referred to, some of the patients were in hospital, while most of them were seen in private practice. In certain cases—psychosis, obsessional neurosis with suspected schizophrenia—some adjustments had to be made, such as having preliminary interviews in conjunction with the family or having to respect institutional procedures. Apart from the old controversy about the frequency of visits, some analysts (especially in France) seeing patients three times a week while in North America and in Great Britain they see them four times a week or even more often if the patient is lying down, the frequency varied also for others; however, nobody, as I remember, contested anyone else's practice or their indications for whatever choice of technique. However, as I mentioned already, there was often controversy over matters of diagnosis: on the requirement or not for having one, on the need for basing the diagnosis exclusively on the clinical interview or, in the case of institutionalized patients, by availing oneself of the means of *ad hoc* tests and questionnaires.

Apart from this problem, choices regarding the setting were not contested, with no one criticizing the method the speaker had adopted. On the other hand, understanding what took place in the setting led, in some cases, to rather different interpretations. The importance of the setting and the respect owing to it were rightfully upheld, and the relationship between setting and material was well illustrated. Never did any one of us say: "I would have had this patient lying down in a strict psychoanalytic setting" or "I would have taken this patient in face-to-face sessions". When the question was raised, each of us tried to understand the reasons that prompted our colleague to adopt a certain technique. Of course, it is clear that whenever we were dealing with a patient near to psychosis, with the possibility of interruptions—such as suicide attempts, hospitalizations of various duration, changes imposed by parents—being more or less frequent, the original setting could no longer be maintained and naturally face-to-face sessions were preferred.

I did state, however, that the setting—which according to Winnicott is a facilitating environment—was experienced in a traumatic way by the borderline patient, who can neither stand free association nor perceive the therapist. The associative process was affected by it, and the containing of anguish was difficult to ensure or to analyse. On the other hand, the setting did enable the psychoanalyst to better analyse her/his countertransference by virtue of the distance so established and the detachment it afforded the psychoanalyst.

It seems that in their day Winnicott and most of the French psychoanalysts attached great importance to the setting, giving various interpretations of its meaning, while others took it less into consideration. While British psychoanalysts saw the setting as a metaphor for maternal care, French psychoanalysts tended to attribute multiple meanings to it, such as the prohibitions of incest and parricide or the dream metaphor, among others.

Among patients in institutions, the setting—as well as the analyst who guards it—is for various reasons severely attacked. It may be concluded that no general theory arises from this situation. Once again it shows how borderline cases represent more a continent of varying landscapes than a regional category, confined, uniform, and coherent. All thematic modes may be envisaged. In our group, we rarely encountered changes of setting once the treatment was under way, from psychotherapy to psychoanalysis or vice versa. Patients were treated according to the same procedure from beginning to end, which may be interpreted as being the result of a well-developed diagnostic intuition on behalf of the psychoanalyst. No doubt the face-to-face setting is more taxing for the analyst than is the classical one. But this situation is more and more frequent. Generally speaking, whatever stance was adopted, the main concern, held in common by the members of the group, was to find a psychoanalytic approach as close as possible to the classical treatment. Adaptive methods usually found in psychotherapy—encouragement, support, "presence"—were rarely used. Still, we cannot ignore or lessen the differences between the analysis of neuroses and that of borderline cases. We should speak, rather than of consensus about the sharing of a common psychoanalytic ideal with confidence upheld in the classical psychoanalytic references, even if at times they had to be adapted using versatility and discernment.

Transference

All the group members agreed about the significance of the experience of transference. It is undoubtedly the undisputed parameter

that allows access to the other major ones referred to in the material. Should one go so far as to consider the object relationship as
the most suitable theoretical criterion? Even if some of us had been
taught to think so, others were sensitive to other theoretical references—for instance, referring to the theory of drives, the consideration of language, the way of imagining the role of the past in relation
to the technical line of the here-and-now honoured by the British
school. Others emphasized the interpretation of the ego and of its
defence mechanisms. In short, we found the whole range of views
existing in the theory with varying approaches.

To return to the subject of transference, the following two points
were given general approval: first, the chaotic nature of it often being muddled by the regressions it causes or makes one relive and,
second, the importance of countertransference in either allowing
one—as we think since Paula Heimann—to better understand that
part of transference, inexpressible other than by induction by the
analyst, which the patient is unable to communicate, lacking words
to express it or in showing not only the vulnerability of the analyst
whose limits have been exceeded but also the analyst's capacity for
detachment, which is essential in order to understand the hidden
side of the transference.

In any case, it is inappropriate to speak here of a "transference
neurosis" comparable with the one we find described in the classical cure. Neither can we talk here about a "psychoanalytic process"
in the sense given to it in the classical theory of analysis. For a long
time the analysis of transference appeared strange, progressing like
saw-teeth with ups and downs, with contrasting phases in which persecution and idealization dominate the scene, holding on to unpredictable mechanisms of repetition appearing suddenly without any
direct link to the traumas that provoked them or to the spontaneous
accentuations of transference. It seems that clarification "after the
fact" (*après coup*) is the rule. Often the motives enabling us to understand the "storms" in transference only become apparent afterwards
when the patient, a long time later, provides details that serve, in
hindsight, to elucidate the shocks of the therapy.

Interpretations should vary according to the responsiveness—
which is very unsteady—of the patient. When the patient shows a
willingness to work by herself/himself in a "transferred" (Donnet),
transference interpretations could be kept to a minimum, when

the need arises to give new impetus to an associative process in fear of running dry. In certain instances, when the patient seems overwhelmed, a response of silence on the part of the analyst would be a mistake in technique. It is on such occasions that the analyst should "lend" her/his psychic apparatus to the patient and elaborate her/his understanding on behalf of both of them, even at the risk of making a mistake. An error at this stage is less serious—indeed, it should be recognized afterwards, when the analyst has time to reflect—in comparison with the mortifying effect of the silence confirming the patient's anxieties of having destroyed the object.

Some insisted, during certain sessions, on the need for continuous interpretations as the free associations of the patient unfold. These interpretations should have a richly imaginative potential in order to reach the layers of the psyche that would otherwise remain inaccessible. A real "interpretive process" develops in parallel with the psychoanalytic process—often so fragile—of the patient. In such situations we have the impression that analysis is a mutual development, woven together by patient and analyst: thread by thread, as we have said, in the weft and woof of a common cloth. Subject and object alike participate—or, we may prefer to say, interact, are linked together. The object emerging from this relationship is indeed the analytic third, as described by Green (1986a, chap. 1, p. 19) and Ogden (1994). Its aim is the transformation of the psychic realities of patient and analyst, which, some maintain, have the same sense of symbolization as described in psychoanalysis.

In the progression of the transference we rarely speak about healing in the way we usually use the term in neurosis, although in some cases it does happen. Ordinarily, what follows is more than just a lessening of the symptoms: a greater level of tolerance is reached of the form the conflicts take, bringing about less "disastrous" masochistic reactions. For some time progress may be blocked because of active or psychosomatic regressions. Suicide attempts may occur at unexpected moments. However, in a significant number of cases the results of the therapy involve noticeable benefits. If is of great satisfaction to the therapist to hear one fine day the banal phrase: "I am well."

All these trials may be understood in the light of different interpretations. However, all of the members of the group felt that their role as analysts was to be "tested" by the patient, who tries to find out through this how much the object can withstand and often replays conflicts, past or present, originating within the family unit that are unbearable to the patient.

The role of the environment is felt even more in borderline cases. However, one should avoid reactions of countertransference in which the analyst is tempted to objectify the words of the patient, going even so far as to be invested with a collusive sympathy for the patient, sharing the patient's hostility towards the "defective" parents, which sometimes leads to a death wish being aimed at them. The analyst should be wary of losing control and should try to examine the unconscious organization underlying these echoes in the countertransference, which to the patient are more alienating than beneficial.

The task is not easy for the therapist, who has to adopt a dual role: on the one hand that of trying to discover the intimate world of the patient, and on the other, as if viewing it from a height, above the intra and inter-family relationships, that of trying hard to grasp the threads the intricacies of which are like Gordian knots. As the therapy progresses, the patient will be better able to identify the interactions at the nodal points in these family relationships. The therapist can then proceed to an intrapsychic analysis of the material without being concerned with the rest, which can be handled by the patient herself/himself. The gain will be the restoration of the psyche to its rightful owner: the patient.

The environment

The discussion is endless concerning the role of the environment: its effects, its importance, its etiopathogenic qualities, whether referring to the identifications it brings about, to the countertransferential reactions it induces, or to the unconscious demands connected with the desire of the patient not to be cured or even to die—whatever the case may be, we cannot fail to recognize it.

In most of the cases discussed during these meetings it was rare not to be tempted at some point to put the focus on the parents, who influenced the patient's illness either by exhibiting some personal pathology—and here the discussion regarding the nature of the trauma was pushed further and extended far beyond its traditional meaning: seduction as mentioned by Freud—or by their attitude towards the treatment, or by the way in which they interpreted the cultural (religious) norms of their own society. We know that for a long time many authors asked themselves: "Who is mad": the symptomatic child or the parent totally unaware of the significance of her/his influence exerted on the child? Whatever the case, our discussion was centred on the following question: "How did the patient react to what was channelled by the parents?" We did not tackle the problem from the point of view of family interactions, placing ourselves, as it were, "above" the psychopathology of the patients. Neither did we seek to consider their role as determining factors. Our stance was always the same: trying to analyse the psychic life of the patient without ignoring any of the numerous parameters, of which parental influence only formed a part.

One important aspect—we might say, almost an unavoidable one—concerns the effects of the countertransference. These effects—whenever they occurred—were subjected to an auto-analysis on the part of the analyst when subsequently re-examining her/his psychoanalytic function. All of us acknowledged the importance of the post-session role in taking the time to elaborate and to calmly reflect on what happened during the session once it is all over, away from the anxiety of the session's disturbances, which can often be traumatic for the analyst. One thing seemed to be evident: we were dealing with situations vastly different from the kinds psychoanalysis had encountered among neurotic patients.

We should be wary, however, of establishing oppositions that are too clear-cut. The main difference is that in neurosis the parents are always approached indirectly through the words of the patient, raising questions about the projections of the latter, of her/his interpretive and subjective efforts, and so forth. Not that these aspects were lacking in borderline cases—but there was always, to a certain extent, some component either directly or indirectly perceived, that carried its weight. But even if the analyst did not directly witness the parental pathologies, their imaginative recreation by the patient gave them the strength of reality, which arose less from the objectivity of the words of the patient than from the sense of sincerity felt by the analyst, as if the latter had been led to believe: "That cannot be invented: it must be true"—an opinion that, like any other, calls for analysis and should not be taken as gospel. Indeed, it was as if the analyst was driven to an identification with the patient that was strong enough to suppress any other reflections. In such cases, the analyst "lends credence" to the words of the patient—which cease being just words and become real. Of course, countertransferential reactions—such as hostility, condemnation, even "parental homicide"—allows the affects of the patient to be reflected in the countertransference of the analyst.

Theoretical differences

When Robert Wallerstein went searching for a "common ground" (Wallerstein & Green, 1996) to address the fragmentation of psychoanalytic theory, his reflections led him to the conclusion that it was not on the theoretical side but on the practical side that one should look for it. At first glance this assertion may seem right. However, on being more deeply considered, it would appear that things are not so simple. Indeed, if we were able to spend more time examining the different clinical presentations and the interpretations that flowed out from them, we would better grasp how the understanding of the material and of the adopted attitudes to technique greatly depends on the basic theoretical options available to each one, which are not directly referred to but which underlie, more or less implicitly, the analyst's understanding of what the patient leads the analyst to understand and which other analysts—especially those belonging to a foreign tradition—understand in different ways. The crisis of psychoanalysis may not lie only in the decrease in numbers undergoing analysis but also in the psychobabble that gives a very bad impression to the public: "If they aren't able to agree among themselves, how can I be sure the analyst I choose is on the right side: that of truth?" These remarks have since encouraged analysts to search among themselves for points at which they converge as well as diverge. But here also the points of agreement and disagreement may be seen as very weak, and, instead of searching for unanimity, the aim has been for precision, nuance, and postulates and axioms that may be radically different.

We noticed in our group different affiliations depending on the point being discussed and, in particular, on the relative knowledge we had of one another. Sometimes the groupings that emerged were surprising. Sharing a common language, for instance—such as the English-speakers (British and American)—did not necessarily mean having the same opinion. We also noticed that those who criticized ego psychology, who were not from the United States, knew in fact little about it because they were unaware of the modifications made to the theory since the death of Hartmann. On the other hand, Bleger, who is a major reference in South American psychoanalysis, is practically unknown outside its borders: his theories have not penetrated to the United States or to Britain and he is only slightly known in France, although his work has been translated. The Kleinian position, as represented among us, did not show clearly the difference between the analysts of the Independent group of the British Society and generated a certain interest—indeed often of a critical nature—among the French participants. There were as many differences to be found among US analysts, depending whether or not they worked exclusively in private practice or in institutions, than between the analysts of different origins. We will not mention the influence of Lacan in France, regarding which the ideas held abroad often showed complete ignorance and were at best an approximation. Analysts outside France seemed unfamiliar with the post-Lacanian movements. We might as well say we waded in mutual ignorance. But the chance was given to correct our mistakes, to ask questions, and to listen to the answers from the mouths of interviewees or, even better, to listen to one another. From this point of view the meetings held by the group were a total success.

The meetings brought together all the researchers (except for the one previously mentioned absence, which was due to illness). The atmosphere was one of open friendship, with the impression that everyone was benefiting from the exchanges. Without doubt, if suitable financial means had been available, we would have wished to go on thinking together. But the sum allocated was not enough to meet expenses (travel, accommodation, food), despite drastic cutbacks. With no extensions to the funds being possible, we finished up with a deficit of €4,000.

We all felt privileged to have had the chance to participate in a unique enterprise of great importance. Did the result have to be a summary of our exchanges? Apart from one member of the group, who felt it was essential, encouraging us to send our recommendations to the analysts of the IPA who had provided us with funding, the other members thought that forming a consensus was not as important as a precise understanding of our differences. In any case, we were far from reaching a consensus. That being said, it was advisable to wait until the experience was over before giving our opinion.

When finally the end was reached, we felt even more strongly than
before that it was better to abstain from any conclusion resulting in
compromise and, instead, to apply ourselves to improving our understanding of how we viewed our own experience by confronting
it with that of others.

We were unable to inventory the discussions (inaudible recordings, notes difficult to decipher). I would like to thank those who accepted the difficult task of making resumes of the debates, requiring
many hours of hard and often unacknowledged work.

So we took our leave, with each one of us promising to contribute
a chapter to a collective work we intended to publish. Thanking the
IPA for having provided us with part of the necessary funding, at the
same time we regret having to put an end to our collaborative reflection, which we consider to have been of use to the psychoanalytic
community. We believe that were the IPA to encourage this kind of
research, based on clinical experience and on the critical examination of theoretical concepts, our results with difficult patients would
only be improved.

Psychoanalysis will not survive its crisis through administrative
measures or through changes in the rules, but only through the
enthusiasm of its analysts in seeking new answers to problems, some
of which are starting to take on a certain age. I would like to thank
all those who kindly accepted my invitation and who, with humility,
passion, and a strong sense of critical investigation, joined with us to
further the advancement of psychoanalysis.

NOTE

Translated by Hélène Boulais and Bernard Holland.

1

Psychoanalysts doing exploratory research: the borderline patient, the borderline situation, and the question of diagnosis

Elizabeth Bott Spillius

The focus of this chapter is primarily the experience of taking part in a small exploratory research group of psychoanalysts whose aim was to study countertransference in work with borderline patients. It was what is usually called an "exploratory" rather than a "scientific" research, meaning that its purpose was to develop hypotheses rather than to test them. In a sense every psychoanalytic treatment is a little piece of exploratory research, but this group research was different from that sort of solitary pursuit because it involved eight psychoanalysts belonging to at least four psychoanalytic traditions: those of France, Britain, the United States, and Argentina. There were two psychoanalysts from France, André Green and Jean-Claude Rolland; two from Britain, Gregorio Kohon and myself; two from the United States, Otto Kernberg and William Grossman, and two from Argentina, Jaime Lutenberg and Fernando Urribarri. André Green introduced and chaired the six weekend discussions, which were held from January 2000 to September 2003, and Otto Kernberg did most of the organizing and liaison with the International Psychoanalytic Association, which funded the work.

Our first meeting was a bit uncomfortable, because we hardly knew each other. André Green and Otto Kernberg were, of course, very well known, and it was obvious that they knew each other. Gregorio Kohon and I knew each other because we belong to the same Society. I had met Bill Grossman but did not know him or his work very well, and I knew nothing of Jean-Claude Rolland, Jaime Lutenberg, and Fernando Urribarri. I had assumed that all the others were specialists in the treatment and understanding of borderline patients but soon realized that this was really true only of André and Otto. All the rest of us had worked with borderline patients at one time or another, but for us it was not a special interest. I was puzzled about why I had been asked to join—actually, why any of us had been asked to join. Much later I came to the conclusion that it must have been because André and Otto knew something about all of us and thought we would be able to work together, which indeed proved to be the case.

I had been a little uneasy about working with André Green, because he has a formidable reputation and not only as a theorist. He did not much like Klein's ideas, I was told, though Bion and Winnicott were important to him. He certainly, I had heard, did not suffer fools gladly. But none of these supposedly ferocious attributes emerged in the research situation. He was extremely helpful and friendly towards all of us, very insightful about our clinical work, a good chairman, and a welcoming host—not to mention his wife, Dr Litza Guttieres-Green, who put up with our periodic invasions with grace and generosity.

I already knew quite a lot about the method of exploratory research because I used to be a social anthropologist, and exploratory research is what most social anthropologists do. Many anthropological field situations are so novel that even knowing something about other similar societies does not help much—one feels thrown in at the deep end. And so it was with the borderline research group: quite overwhelming at first, and then gradually things began to take shape. Nevertheless I thought then and still think now that if our aim was really to understand countertransference in work with borderline patients, it would have been better if all of us had been especially experienced in work with borderline patients. If that had been the case, we would have been able to control this one variable—familiarity with borderline states—at least to some extent. To carry out an exploratory study with *two* main variables that were not at all fixed, the two being expertise in borderline states *and* school of psychoanalytic thought, seemed to me to be asking for trouble.

It soon appeared that there was considerable variation in our interests and in the type of patient we presented for clinical discussion. André and Otto presented patients who were clearly borderline, but the rest of us presented three more-or-less psychotic patients and two more-or-less neurotic/normal patients. Because our interests and the sorts of patient we presented were quite varied, our discussions ranged over many ideas and issues. This diversity led to a change in our task: our implicit aim came to be to understand one another and the patients that were presented, not just to understand countertransference in borderline states. At first there was some pressure, especially from Otto, for us to reach a consensus, but the dominant sentiment seemed to be that our views were too different for us to reach a natural consensus. We would try to understand one another and see what came out of it. I felt how familiar this sort of open-ended resolve was, how similar to the way one feels at the start of an anthropological field trip.

I think all of us found our group meetings immensely interesting and enriching. The experience did a great deal to challenge the stereotypes we held about our respective points of view, and each of us learned valuable ideas from the others—far more, at least in my experience, than one ever learns at psychoanalytic Congresses. And gradually, especially towards the end, our ideas began to come together, even our ideas about countertransference with borderline patients, although I do not think we produced any very precise hypotheses that could be tested by more "scientific" methods. Nevertheless I think that by the end we were all satisfied with the work we had done. We had some new ways of looking at borderline states; we had acquired some specific ideas about psychoanalysis in general and about our own work in particular; and, perhaps most important, we had come to feel for each other the same sort of curiosity and respect that is at the heart of the psychoanalytic approach.

Most of the other contributors to this book about the research focus mainly on their own clinical and theoretical contributions, but I have decided to describe the research itself and the gradual development of our interchange of ideas. I am doing this partly because I think this sort of small exploratory research is a suitable way for analysts to do research and to learn from each other, and partly just because I found it very interesting. I will try to give an idea of the main topics we discussed at each of our six weekend meetings and some of the practical problems we ran into in trying to keep a record of our discussions; but I will also describe my own personal reactions, so as to give some idea of the shifts in interest and feeling that the work induced as our meetings went on.

The first seminar (January 2000)

André Green presented his paper, "The Central Phobic Position", and associated clinical material (Otto Kernberg took notes, and the seminar was tape-recorded.)

As I have said above, this first seminar was rather overwhelming. The combination of the paper, the clinical material, our not knowing each other, and eight people all having different ideas about the material was difficult to grasp at the time or to think about coherently.

My first and lasting impression was how insightful and familiar André's clinical material was. It was much easier for me to understand than are his more theoretical papers. It reminded me of something Bob Wallerstein has said about differing psychoanalytic ideas seeming to be much more contradictory and difficult to understand than the clinical material on which they are based. But I was also impressed by what André had drawn from the clinical material—his idea that important experiences, especially traumatic ones, resonate and reinforce one another rather than forming a linear, repetitive causal sequence.

André did not define the term "borderline" on this occasion, but it later appeared that central to his idea of it was the view that "borderline" means people who have never crossed the boundary—as he put it—into depression, neurosis, psychosis, or perversion. Borderline patients oscillate continually, stable in their instability. He mentioned their attack on themselves and how painful analysis usually is for them. Some of what he said sounded rather like John Steiner's observation that borderline patients are in a precarious equilibrium between the paranoid–schizoid and depressive positions—though I don't think I expressed this impression at the time.

I remember that at this first meeting Fernando Urribarri said something about Kleinian analysis that did not sound like any sort of Kleinian analysis I had ever heard of. Should I argue, I wondered,

but decided no, better to wait. I found Jean-Claude Rolland's observations difficult to understand—his English is a little idiosyncratic,
and my spoken French is non-existent—but immediately I also felt
that he was struggling to say something that really mattered. I think
it was that he would not say to a borderline or psychotic patient: "I
don't understand you, you're not understandable": he would try to
explore what motivated his patient to do that. He would say, "You
want me to be in a non-understanding position, and I shall try to
explore why." This focus on the analytic relationship rather than
just on the patient was something that turned out to be a leitmotif
in his contributions throughout the seminars. It struck a chord with
both Gregorio and me, something we thought was important in the
work of many people in the British Society. André Green reinforced
what Jean-Claude had said, adding that one has to give up trying to
understand what happened in the past: what is needed is to understand what is happening in the present, which in this case was that
the patient does not want the analyst to understand. Another point
Jean-Claude made was that diagnosis emerges in the ongoing development of the analytic work—*après coup*, as he put it. This question
of diagnosis was discussed many times later on, as was Bill Grossman's idea that a preliminary map was useful, but that we should be
open-minded enough to change diagnosis as we go along—a point
also made by Gregorio.

   All the rest of us added other contributions from time to time in
this first meeting, with each of us speaking out of our reservoir of
past understandings and seeing how they would fit in with or add
to what André had been saying, each shifting the focus to another
unfamiliar point of view.

The second seminar (July 2000)

Otto Kernberg presented a paper, two videos of a 41-year-old borderline
patient, and transcripts of the verbal interchanges between himself and
the patient on the videos. (He also made notes of the discussion, which
was also tape-recorded. Bill Grossman was unable to be present on this
occasion.)

The woman in the video was subject to a "contract" with Otto, designed, as he put it, "to maintain an ordinary treatment situation

that does not endanger the patient or analyst and his belongings".
But the contract also included the videotaping of certain sessions
and the audiotaping of others. The patient spent her sessions, or the
sessions we watched, trying to subvert and overthrow this contract as
much as she could. She showed very little interest in understanding
herself. She was verbally very insulting and spent much of the session
eating noisily and throwing things around the room, though she did
not actually attack Otto physically. Much of what Otto said to her
was, inevitably, concerned with her breaking the contract, though
he made other interpretations that explained her behaviour in the
sessions by linking it quite explicitly verbally to her internal mother.
Interestingly, in spite of her abusing Otto about everything else, she
did not attack his interpretations about her internal mother.

I thought a lot about Otto's presentation after the meeting. This
seemed to be a very different sort of approach to psychoanalysis
from the one I am used to. Of course, Otto does not claim that this
sort of treatment is psychoanalysis: he calls it "transference-focused
psychotherapy" and considers it the most suitable approach for this
sort of patient. I found it impossible to tell how much of the patient's
aggressive behaviour was because of her own psychopathic nature
and how much was a response to the provocative nature of the
setting. She complained—with some justification, I thought—about
Otto being more interested in his research and his research team
than in her. I wondered whether this sort of treatment design was
really necessary for very disturbed borderline patients, and was it not
possible that it had acted as an invitation to indulge in provocative
behaviour that would make it very difficult for her analyst to think.
After all, I thought, Rosenfeld, Segal, Bion, and others had analysed
very difficult psychotic patients without introducing a contract. But
perhaps they did not try to analyse psychopathic patients. I have no
answer any of these questions. I wish I had asked them during Otto's
presentation, but I could hardly think during the presentation: that
woman's provocations got through to her audience even second-
hand, and, in spite of trying to keep an open mind about it, I was
quite shocked by Otto's research procedure.

By this point in the research, however, there was one thing I was
beginning to become more sure of: the way psychoanalysts think
has complex roots, but a lot of it depends on their external work
situation. Otto works very closely with psychiatrists—in fact he is
(or was at that time) a Professor of Psychiatry at Cornell University

Medical College and Director of the Personality Disorders Institute at the New York Presbyterian Hospital. I think he said in one of our informal discussions that he wanted to make it possible for young psychiatrists to use some psychoanalytic ideas in treating their patients without their having to go through the lengthy training of psychoanalysis. I thought that Otto's close links with psychiatrists must have something to do with his research method, his focus on preliminary diagnosis, and his attempt to be very clear about definitions of borderlines, borderline personality disorder, borderline personality organization, and its distinctions from other diagnoses; the capacity for reality-testing makes borderlines different from psychotics, identity diffusion makes them different from neurotics.

In Britain the social context of psychoanalysis is different. The relationship between psychoanalysts and "orthodox" psychiatrists is rarely close, even though many psychoanalysts were initially psychiatrists and some of them still work as psychiatrists as well as psychoanalysts. But the relationship between the two professions is often one either of antagonism or of indifference. Psychoanalysts do not write for a psychiatric as well as a psychoanalytic audience, and psychiatrists do not write for a psychoanalytic audience. As psychoanalysts, we do not emphasize diagnosis very much, especially diagnosis before treatment, and I think that this is because diagnosis, within broad limits, does not determine the treatment, which is virtually always psychoanalysis or psychoanalytic psychotherapy. And psychoanalytic psychotherapy is not a special system, like Otto's transference-focused psychotherapy. It is as close as possible to psychoanalysis, but on a less frequent basis.

Third seminar (February 2001)

Jean-Claude Rolland (France) presented a psychotic young man of 25, then an older neurotic woman. (Elizabeth Spillius made notes. The meeting was tape-recorded.)

I will discuss Jean-Claude's presentation in some detail, because I think it was at this point that we all began to feel very closely involved in our collective enterprise. The discussion was long and complex, and I have tried to select some salient points, but I cannot convey the whole experience.

(As far as keeping a research record was concerned, I was beginning to be very doubtful about the value of tape-recording. Although we were using a supposedly excellent recorder, it did not
pick up all the voices clearly, there was often something wrong with
the tapes, and transcribing the tapes was very time-consuming and
expensive—the transcription of only part of Jean-Claude's presentation ran to 185 pages. On top of that, the tapes would have had to
be edited before they were used for anything, and that would have
taken still more time. I found the note-taking quite hard work, and
it meant that I was not able to participate fully in the discussions,
though I think it helped me to understand the new points of view.
It also meant that afterwards I had to dictate the notes and a secretary typed them, which was also expensive and time-consuming, but
I think the results were more coherent than the transcripts of the
tape recordings.)

                                  * * *

In his pre-circulated document Jean-Claude stated that there is a war
in the borderline patient between hallucinatory wish-fulfilment and
a struggle between the need to be ill and the desire to be cured. "As
analysts", Jean-Claude said, "we have to struggle to give up our resistance to new experience with the patient, and in this group, we have
to struggle to give up our resistance to the ideas of each other." One
of the important ideas in Jean-Claude's approach, I thought, was that
he thought we should seek the libidinal scene behind the trauma.

My notes of Jean-Claude's presentation describe one episode in
considerable detail. One day his patient, a psychotic man of 25
whom Jean-Claude saw twice a week, said he felt very sad, his doctors
had given up on him. . . . The patient went on to say that he had
had a quarrel with his parents. They had said, "Do you know who
you are? If you fall ill again, if you have delusional crises, you don't
need to come back home: you will find the door closed." Jean-Claude
was very much struck by this and said to the patient, "You were
thinking about your parents when you felt given up by the doctors."
Jean-Claude felt upset. How could the parents say this? And into his
mind flooded memories of other patients and other parents who had
said similar things. Jean-Claude then thought to himself: "Why are
you thinking like this? You know he is a psychotic patient, and his
parents are mad too—no one is responsible for this." He struggled

like this for five or six minutes, not knowing who he was. Then he thought, I must get into contact with my patient. He looked at his patient, who had changed his attitude. He was sitting rigidly, looking at Jean-Claude with an awful look, and looking terrified. Jean-Claude was afraid—he had the feeling the patient was a vampire. (He had not said anything to his patient all this time.) He thought to himself: "Don't be afraid, it is a dream, be calm". The patient drew back and said, "But I am already dead." Then the patient went on to speak of an incident, when he was about 14, when he was upset and cried, and his mother had said, "Don't worry, I am your friend. We will care for you until we die." And from that time the analysis changed from being psychotherapeutic support into being analysis. "Something like a dream had happened in the session", Jean-Claude went on to say. "I had participated in the dream, but I had a discourse too, differentiating what was dream and what was the analytic situation. I thought about Winnicott's "Fear of Breakdown" paper (1963): something happens that has already happened. We come to understand that we are taking part in a situation of repetition of a psychic scene."

The seminar discussion of Jean-Claude's presentation

Most of the rest of the meeting was taken up with an animated discussion of this episode. André noted that "If you come home, the door will be closed" and "We will look after you until we die" really meant the same thing. He said that through combining his view of the objective reality of the parents and the patient's intrapsychic reality, Jean-Claude had begun to think something new.

I [Elizabeth] said I thought that Jean-Claude's terror might have been aroused by his patient's having projected his own terror into Jean-Claude. Then the patient says, "But I am already dead". Is he then being the parents devoting themselves to their son until death?

Gregorio thought that for this patient loving was murdering or being murdered. The vampire is dead but comes alive through killing and sucking the victim's blood. The issue is that for the patient to come alive, the parents must die.

Otto described how these various concrete descriptions fitted his general ideas about the linking of a phantasized relationship between one part of the self and one aspect of the object. In the normal

state, Otto said, there is intrapsychic tolerance of these dyadic relationships. In dissociated states there is intolerance of the affective
state, which then has to be expressed in action and in destruction
of the representation of self and other.

André said that we had got so caught up in this fascinating session that we had forgotten what Jean-Claude had said earlier: that
the parents had murderous thoughts about their son. In the case of
the mother, André thought that her thoughts about death had something to do with her having a fusional relationship with her son in
which there was no room for the development of the child's self. In
the session the patient had said, "I am already dead." This followed
a sequence in which he stared at Jean-Claude who felt depleted
and was terrified. What are the alternative interpretations of this
sequence? One is that it is important for you to die before me. The
second is that if you are already dead, then I can live—the patient's
death would liberate the mother. (Just as Gregorio had thought that
the parents' deaths would have liberated the son.)

Bill noted that Jean-Claude had withdrawn into thoughts about
these parents and other parents. In this he was identifying with the
patient in attacking the parents. The patient perceived Jean-Claude's
absence and felt that Jean-Claude was now dead, and he identified
with Jean-Claude, hence he, the patient, was "already dead".

André thought that for the patient, Jean-Claude was the mother.
It was as if the patient was saying, "You don't have to kill me. I am
already dead." This lead to a discussion between André and Otto,
mainly about the concept of representation, with Otto saying that
any feeling implies meaning and motivation, and André saying that
the meaning was in Jean-Claude, not in the patient. André thought
that Otto was applying the thinking of normal patients to psychotics
and said that only normal—or neurotic—individuals can distinguish
between affect and representation. He agreed with Otto that psychotics have intense affects, but did not think that these affects have
a meaning that the psychotic recognizes.

Gregorio thought that we were reluctant to use Otto's model
because it didn't quite fit Jean-Claude's material—the confusion between birth and death, for example, or the construction of love as
death—so that it was difficult to apply a constructed theoretical approach. "With these patients", Gregorio went on, "I cannot assume
anything, so it is very important to look at the clinical sequence in
which there were no words. It was a major event, the moment when

the analysis started, so it is important to try to work out what happened."

Jean-Claude spoke quite a lot after this, but I did not catch it at the time and could not decipher it from the tape.

Gregorio talked then about the vampire as a libidinal figure and the patient's libidinal attachment to being dead, and linked this to Winnicott's paper "Fear of Breakdown" (1963), saying that the breakdown has to happen in the analysis.

Jaime said that he was interested in Otto's point of view and thought that he was speaking about the processes inside the mind of the patient, whereas Jean-Claude was speaking about "what happens between analyst and patient and in the analyst's mind. . . . In Jean-Claude's way (of analysing, I think Jaime meant) in every session you have the possibility to make a dream that has never happened, because you have an analyst who can have the dream that the patient cannot make for himself."

There was some discussion again between André and Otto about the role of self and object representations in primitive affect states; they disagreed at first and then partially agreed with each other.

Fernando said this was a major disagreement (meaning between André and Otto). When Otto says that the affect has a self and an object pole, this is a very different statement from saying that when you analyse *après coup,* you give a meaning to an affect but you don't think that this meaning is within the affect in its origin. . . . When you say that affect has a cognitive structure from the beginning, you take out the conclusion before it has happened. This also affects technique. You give the impression that even before something happens, you are looking for it. This gives a different direction to the analytic research process.

Otto reiterated that he thought affects had meaning from the beginning, even before the meaning could be named or have motivational sense. Bill added that one of the issues here was, how do we know what the experience is? One view is to take the position that because we see an undifferentiated state at the beginning, we therefore have to act as though we know nothing about the relation of affect and representation. A second approach is that all these things have a developmental aspect, that there is a premature form of cognition that in development becomes cognition.

By this time I [Elizabeth] wondered what Jean-Claude was thinking. All our statements were more or less plausible, I thought, but how could we really be sure what had happened between Jean-Claude and his patient? We couldn't. And I was exhausted by note-taking. Fortunately it was time for tea.

After tea André asked Gregorio whether we were shifting level too much, and Gregorio said he thought we weren't doing justice to Jean-Claude's material.

After a bit more discussion Jean-Claude said that his interest in borderline patients was in face-to-face analysis, to keep the visual stimulus. One aspect of the transference process, he said, is that it is made up of visual images in which the patient brings alive internal objects in the experience of the transference. The second aspect is discourse, and when the patient speaks, he detaches himself. He said he had chosen the patient he presented because it was a transference process without much discourse, though there was some. The patient was having a dream in the session but also narrating it at the same time, and when he spoke, he was somewhat detached from it. "The dream captures his unconscious desires", Jean-Claude said, "but the discourse is an indirect representation of what happens in the transference, in the core of the situation, and through that we can go from transference to memory."

I was impressed, but I still felt I didn't understand it all.

Jean-Claude's second presentation

Jean-Claude then talked about a second patient, a woman married to a well-known man, who had suddenly left her. She had become depressed. Her father had already died. In the session Jean-Claude described, the woman had said that a strange thing had happened when she was in a group of people: she had to introduce herself, and she had forgotten her name (her married name). Everyone had laughed, and so did she. She had had a big struggle with her mother. After her father died, her mother was the only one who had that name. Jean-Claude said, "You were thinking of the death of your father when you forgot your name." She cried. After a long silence, she said, "I loved that chap a lot." Jean-Claude did not know whether she meant her husband or her father. She went on to say that on another occasion, when she had expected to talk about her husband, she had found herself talking about her father's death, and that she had been traumatized not by his death, but by the way he had stopped caring about her before his death.

"At that moment", Jean-Claude went on to say, "she discovered that she was able to separate psychologically from her husband; she had used the loss of her husband as a substitute for the loss of her father. . . . I think that at that moment I detached myself from being the father in the transference, and at that moment the transference substitution suddenly became a memory for her. And also she was able then to separate the reality from the memory. And what I wonder is, for me, where did that interpretation come from?" (Where indeed, I thought.)

Later he added that a crucial link in her discourse had been the ambiguous phrase "that chap", which was a crossroads, making the link between husband and father.

André described a hypothesis to fill in the gaps, as he put it. It could not be just the fact of her husband having left her—it needed the additional meaning, which came from the situation of not wanting to use her maiden name because it was her mother's name. But it was more than that. The patient was hostile to her father and didn't want to use his name. Jean-Claude wasn't consciously aware of the link at the time, but his interpretation was confirmed by the patient's association about intending to talk about her husband but actually talking about her father. Jean-Claude had been an attentive father in the transference, but was also separate from her, and this transformed the experience into a discourse in which she could separate from both husband and father. André went on: "When the patient speaks in this way, there is an activation of word presentations in the Preconscious, and this stimulates thing-presentations in the Unconscious. It is the Preconscious that is structured like a language, not the Unconscious. It is a useful acting out which makes a connection with the Unconscious." (I too thought that the idea of the Preconscious being structured like a language made far more sense than Lacan's phrasing that the Unconscious was structured like a language.)

Otto wondered whether it would be better to call it "enactment" rather than "acting out". Gregorio thought that acting out is an enactment noticed by the analyst, whereas enactment is mutual acting out by analyst and patient without the analyst noticing it. André suggested the term "actualization".

Gregorio went back to Jean-Claude's question of where the interpretation had come from. "From the guts", Gregorio said, "From the unconscious. Those are the interpretations that are most useful."

A little later André said that Jean-Claude was able to function with the psychotic patient, but not when the patient looked at him. Then André said that here we could come to an agreement with Otto. The psychotic patient's look had stopped Jean-Claude from functioning. With the second patient, when she was deeply depressed, Jean-Claude could only support her. So an important issue is the intensity of affect. "If we think of Otto's patient", André said, "Otto was limited because of the intensity of the patient's attack, and all he could do was resort to some interpretation that was supposed to work but didn't because he was not able to think freely."

Otto replied that in his research project (of which the patient he had presented was part) he and his colleagues think there are three channels of communication: (a) subjective, (b) nonverbal—that is, action, and (c) countertransference. The more disturbed the patient, the greater the weight of the second and third channels. He and his colleagues try to see which of these three is operating in any given exchange.

Fernando made a comment here to the effect that with his first patient, Jean-Claude had had a kind of hallucination. With his second patient he was surprised by his own interpretation, but Fernando thought he was working on the level of word process. In Otto's presentation, Fernando thought that it was impossible for Otto to have space for the relationship because the countertransference affect was so strong.

Jean-Claude thought about the word "pain". She was not in such great pain, but suddenly when she spoke of the death of her father, Jean-Claude had been empathic with her pain, and probably with the pain in himself.

André then talked about Freud's "Project" (1950 [1895]), in which he describes pain—something he does not come back to. He develops the pleasure/unpleasure principle, and unpleasure is a warning against pain. In the first patient, pain was obvious: it was linked with terror in the patient and terror he aroused in his analyst. In the second patient there was a phase of melancholic complicity—in the sense of empathy, I think was the connotation here—and Jean-Claude had to wait until she was not in so much pain but was in the domain of the pleasure/unpleasure principle, so that he could think. Freud's system of analysis is built on the expectation of "moderate" affect; he doesn't speak of *jouissance* (Lacan) or pain. Modern psychoanalysis has made us more aware of witnessing pain. Classical analysis is not possible in acute states.

I found this exchange very interesting, but we were all getting tired; at least I was. André and I had an exchange about Joseph Wortis, a rather unpleasant young man who had had an analysis with Freud and wrote a book about it after Freud had died. And then it was time to stop.

The discussion on the following day was more general, at first concerning the conditions of analysis and whether the patient could accept them: the couch, free association. How frequent should sessions be? Should the analyst limit his functioning for a time, as Jean-Claude had done with his second patient? André said that liking the patient and thinking one can help him is important; if there is no benevolence, there cannot be neutrality. Gregorio thinks analysis is really only possible if the person, independently of the severity of his symptoms, can take something in. He also thinks there can be no fixed rule about how many sessions suit borderline and psychotic patients.

At this point Jean-Claude said a good deal more about the almost Fascist parents of his first patient and the un-assimilated mother as an internal object inside the patient. This led to a discussion of the concept of "*subject*" in relation to *alienation*, the "*ego*" and the "*self*". The "*subject*", André explained, is a concept used only in France and Latin America; in other psychoanalytic cultures it would be called "*ego*" or "*self*". André said: "There is in the patient's mind someone to whom he is alienated, someone who is colonizing him." This led to a little protest by Bill and by me that one couldn't talk about "alienated *to*" in English, it had to be "alienated *from*", which didn't convey the meaning that André wanted. You could get around it by saying "someone alienating who is colonizing him". André said, "A patient who has such an internal organization often responds to an interpretation by saying, 'I don't know, ask my mother'. This is what is meant by alienation to the object." Bill and I tried the grammatical point again—not, I think, very convincingly. I then said that in this sort of situation the internal object is what Paula Heimann (1942) had described as "unassimilated" (and for Klein it would be a particular sort of "bad" internal object).

Gregorio said that the problem for the analyst is the difficulty of allowing himself to be used as this alienating internal object that invades and colonizes the patient. If the analyst cannot accept this projection, he will start to use theory. Jean-Claude said to Gregorio that the difficult thing for the analyst is to endure being in the feminine position. He talked at some length about the feminine position and the role of the child. He thinks it is only when the object is lost that sexual attraction appears. André added here that this is an important view in French analysis, this view that it is separation that creates sexual desire.

Bill said that the analyst behaves differently from the parents, and when the analyst goes through the process that Jean-Claude described, he becomes a different object—from the parents, I think he meant. We must include this in our theoretical formulation.

From here the discussion became increasingly abstract, without any reference to clinical material. I got rather bored but dutifully wrote it all down. At one point André and Otto talked a lot about Edith Jacobsen. There was also a protracted discussion of the concept of "subject" in French psychoanalysis and the difference between "subject" and "self". André, Bill, and Otto were the chief participants, with occasional contributions from Jean-Claude and Fernando. Bill managed, I think, to convince André that his view of American ego-psychology was not entirely correct.

In general, I felt that although André's and Jean-Claude's conceptualizations were different from those of British analysis, their way of thinking was easier to grasp than I had expected, especially when they were sticking close to clinical material.

When I got home, I thought a bit more about how much variation there is among psychoanalytic cultures on what sort of patient can be analysed, on how many times a week patients should be treated, and so on. Jean-Claude had said something interesting—namely, that he got his first patient to sit up so that the visual stimulus was retained, which helped to bring his internal objects alive in the transference; but at the same time his patient did speak, there was a discourse, which was a more indirect representation of what was happening in the transference. André had talked a bit about the necessary conditions for analysis, saying that at least some liking for one's patient was necessary for there to be benevolence, and without benevolence there could not be neutrality. Gregorio had mentioned the question of frequency and what sort of patient should be treated in what sort of way, saying that what matters is that a patient should be able to take things in, not the severity of his symptoms, and that for borderline and psychotic patients he does not think it is possible to say how many sessions there should be.

But we really did not discuss the question of how psychoanalysis is to be defined either in general or with borderline patients. I think in Britain most people think of psychoanalysis as happening four or five times a week, so we would not think of Jean-Claude's twice-a-week treatment as psychoanalysis: it would be called psychoanalytic psychotherapy. In France, however, I understand that training analyses take place three times a week, and the sort of treatment Jean-Claude was doing would be thought of as analysis. In the United States Otto calls the kind of treatment in his video "transference-focused psychotherapy", not analysis. Bill didn't discuss the question of what is analysis. I must say that even though I hadn't taken in the discussion either about the "subject" or about Edith Jacobsen, I was relieved just to be thinking about the material and the ideas, not to have to get into arguments about what is and what is not psychoanalysis.

The fourth seminar (September, 2001)

Jaime Lutenberg presented the case of a young man he saw three times a week for five years, still ongoing. The patient was 18 at the start of analysis.

At the beginning of this seminar André summarized something important about our research, saying that it had become a research on ourselves: our technique, our countertransference reactions, how we work, how we think, how we express and interpret our different psychoanalytic backgrounds and our different personalities.

(The struggle with the tape-recorder continued. We did not have these tapes transcribed. I consulted them to check on my notes, but they were rarely of any real help.)

Jaime Lutenberg

Jaime explained that his patient had been diagnosed by psychiatrists as hebephrenic, but at the start of treatment he was on antidepressant medication, which Jaime changed to a neuroleptic. The patient was very obsessional and very preoccupied with his rituals, such as opening and closing doors 200 times, and so forth. The family were religious fanatics, and there was suspicion of sexual activity between the boy and his grandfather. (Jaime knew this from the colleague who had referred the patient.) Jaime had seen the family and had offered them family treatment, which they refused. His feeling was that they wanted him to take the boy off their hands. He thought that the boy's very strange, fanatical family had a great deal to do with his psychic situation.

Jaime saw his patient three times a week, listened sympathetically, but made very few interpretations—almost none for the first two years. His method was to think very hard after each session about what the session had meant, but he did not say any of this to the boy. He said more later on, but his comments were not so much interpretations as ways of helping his patient to make discriminations and to talk more about his activities, including his sexual activities and his grandfather's sexual behaviour. (Earlier in the treatment the patient had openly masturbated in sessions.) Jaime's rationale for not making interpretations was that if he had done so, his patient would have superficially conformed to them, and Jaime's system would have served the same sort of controlling function for the young man as the family's religious fanaticism. Jaime was trying, as he put it, "to make a space where the real ego can grow".

Jaime thought of this case ". . . not as a psychosis but as a case of void. Secondary autism, secondary symbiosis, and also psychotic symptoms are defences against the underlying void." Jaime said that in the void, a person is stopped in his development. It is not that an already formed personality is destroyed, it is that the personality has not evolved. Symbiosis is a defence against the void. Symbiotic patients cannot choose, cannot discriminate. Jaime thinks of symbiosis as a state of mind in which there is fusion and confusion, similar to the blending process of liquids. In André's view, symbiosis means that when two people are together, they have become one, and there is no boundary between them. In primary identification, one is *like* the other; in symbiosis, one *is* the other. Otto asked how one would differentiate between the symbiotic state of mind and the psychotic state of mind. Jaime replied that in symbiosis there is fusion, but in psychosis there is destruction of the mind's components. But Jaime also thought that his patient did not live entirely in a symbiotic state; he was also neurotic.

The young man had improved, but I think most of the group was rather sceptical, either feeling that a central component of analysis—interpretation—was not present in the usual way, or that there was perhaps something perverse about the patient that had not become fully explicit. I think the group felt that they were uneasy and suspicious about the patient, whereas Jaime was more trusting—but I think this is always the case. In an analytic treatment one comes to be more sympathetic to one's patient than one's colleagues are.

There was considerable discussion of the possibility of other diagnoses apart from Jaime's diagnosis of symbiotic defences against the void. Otto thought the patient was a chronic schizophrenic, and he described in some detail the methods of "structural diagnosis" and "dynamic diagnosis" used by his research team at Cornell. Fernando thought that dynamic diagnosis is what we, as analysts, are trained for, and that the crucial question it should ask is whether the patient can work in the psychoanalytic setting. André thought that in the case of Jaime's patient ". . . we might be in the presence of a *huge obsessional structure*—an idea that no one picked up at the time, but having read and re-read this material several times, I find it convincing.

Jean-Claude talked about the method of treatment rather than the diagnosis. He thought Jaime's method of treating this patient was more like a child psychotherapy than an analysis, especially because of Jaime's contacts with the family and his telling them not to allow contact between the boy and his grandfather, and so forth. (I thought, but did not say, that child psychotherapy in France must be different from child psychotherapy in England, for in England if anyone saw the parents, it would not be the therapist of the child: it would have to be a different therapist.) In Jean-Claude's view, and I think also in Gregorio's, this contact with the family had complicated Jaime's relation with his patient and had made an ordinary psychoanalytic approach to him very difficult. Jean-Claude also suggested that fear of losing the patient—there had been four previous analysts—made the analytic attitude difficult to maintain. I think Jaime felt that more work needed to be done on methods of working with "symbiotic" patients, and that not much work had been done with such patients because they normally do not seek analysis.

Gregorio questioned the lack of psychoanalytic interpretation, and was not wholly satisfied by the idea that interpretation would have made Jaime like the family in the patient's mind. Gregorio thought that if you believe that certain conditions are necessary for the treatment to succeed, such as the family being treated in this case, and if you cannot secure those conditions, then it must become difficult to work in one's usual psychoanalytic way.

There was discussion, too, about the lack of a third dimension, of depth, in the thinking of Jaime's patient. Jaime had noticed one particular aspect of this: namely, that his patient had difficulty in using his pockets; he could not put anything away in them, implying a lack of third dimension. I [Elizabeth] talked a bit about the similarity of this idea of lack of third dimension to Esther Bick's belief that there is a very early phase of development in which the third dimension is lacking, and that this phase, which she thought of as the phase of "adhesion", precedes introjection and projection, both of which require the notion of psychic depth. Esther Bick wrote very little herself, but she influenced Meltzer's thinking.

André concluded our discussion by saying that it had been a difficult discussion, partly because the clinical material was complicated and partly because of our trying and not quite succeeding in sharing Jaime's diagnosis and his feeling for his patient. It seemed to be our general view, André said, that the patient was more ill than Jaime thought. André recognized the importance that Jaime gave to healing splitting, and that he thought that this was more important to Jaime than giving interpretations.

I thought—but did not say—that Jaime was probably rather dissatisfied with our general reaction, and I thought, too, that he probably felt, though he did not say, that we did not fully understand his work because we had not worked very much with "symbiotic" patients.

The fifth seminar (February 2002)

Elizabeth Spillius on a neurotic/normal patient, definitely not borderline.

I presented a normal/neurotic patient who had had several traumatic experiences. The comment from seminar members I found most interesting was that since this patient had a somewhat hostile and dismissive attitude towards her father, it was probable that instead of having a relationship with him she had a tendency to *become* him. I think it was André or Jean-Claude who said this first, but others added to it. The discussion also made it clear how very different she was from the borderline and psychotic patients we had discussed—troubled but very perceptive about others, and very much aware of herself in relation to others. In Otto's terminology, she had excellent capacity for reality testing (so, not psychotic) and there was no identity diffusion (so, not borderline).

Following the seminar, I think this patient gradually "improved". I never explicitly put the idea about her father into an interpretation, but it was always around in the back of my mind and no doubt coloured what I thought and said. Gradually she seemed to enjoy life a bit more. She asked a friend whether she had changed in the course of analysis, and the friend said "softer", which I thought .was a good description.

I had made it clear from the start that I would not be able to publish anything about this patient.

The final seminar (September 2003)

(As usual, the discussions were tape-recorded, and, as usual, the tapes were virtually useless. I don't recommend marathons of note-taking, but one incidental thing that has emerged from this research is that tape recordings are not as useful as one would expect.)

We talked about organization and finances, and then André summarized our various presentations and said that borderline personality disorder was a diagnosis with no sharp limits and variable descriptions, so that each of us was very dependent for our usage on our training and background. That was why André had wanted the research group to have the combination of different nationalities and points of view that it had. He said that we had corrected some of each other's wrong ideas—Bill had corrected André's ideas about ego psychology, for example. It was at this time that André made his statement about borderline being a continent, not a country, and that borderline means people who have never crossed the boundary into depression, neurosis, psychosis, or perversion. Because of the concept being so broad, it was inevitable that diagnosis became important. In a few words he succinctly described our clinical contributions so far. He then briefly introduced Gregorio's presentation, and after it he asked each of us what we thought about the seminar as a whole.

Gregorio Kohon

Gregorio asked us to take as read his pre-circulated and very moving account of his long psychoanalysis of a young man originally diagnosed as a paranoid schizophrenic but who might perhaps more properly have been diagnosed, after some psychoanalysis, as someone who had undergone an acute adolescent crisis complicated initially by drug abuse. Psychotic? Neurotic? Borderline? Gregorio then talked about the third part of his paper, which was on diagnosis.

First Gregorio talked about the "global" and the "universal". The idea of the global is simpler, for all one needs to do is to translate the language of the other into one's own language. The idea of the universal is more complex: it is the universality of the singular. The Oedipus complex, for example, only becomes meaningful when it emerges in the particular understanding of the subject.

In relation to the concept of the borderline, Gregorio looked at it not in terms of symptoms but in terms of what is needed to accept such a patient for analysis: first, whatever the presenting pathology, the patient needs to have a certain humility; second, the patient needs to be motivated by an internal conflict that involves suffering; and third, the patient should possess a fairly reliable character.

Gregorio discussed the history of the concept of borderline, which led to a complex discussion between himself, Otto, and André. Gregorio said he had found Otto's distinction between borderline personality disorder (symptoms) and borderline personality organization (adequate reality testing plus identity diffusion) very clarifying. He also talked about French views on borderlines, and Fernando, André, and Jean-Claude joined in. He went on to discuss the "frame"—the "setting" in British terminology—and something of the work of Rosenfeld with borderline and psychotic patients. He ended this part of his presentation by describing seven attributes of the analytic relation with the borderline patient:

1. The patient needs the analysis and the setting but also finds the setting traumatic and humiliating.

2. There is a passionate and extreme transference.

3. There is confusion between love and hate.

4. A malignant impasse tends to develop in the treatment.

5. There is much guilt associated with the mother, and difficulties

arise which involve conflict with the analyst, but it is not quite the same as a negative therapeutic reaction.

6. Patients have difficulty in symbolization, which Gregorio calls "symbolic impairment".

7. He quoted Jean-Claude's distinction between being full of dead objects in contrast to feeling dead. Being full of dead objects has to be a secret that is kept from the dreamer as well as from the object.

There was an animated discussion of Gregorio's presentation from which I will select several main points. I think everyone was both impressed and moved by the patient's struggles as well as by Gregorio's understanding of him.

André emphasized the strong transference and the need for basic trust in the patient. Then he talked about the tolerance of suffering and the origin of the madness, which he thought of as an identification by Gregorio's patient with the ill part of the mother and of the father. Jaime stressed Gregorio's tolerance of the ambiguity of the patient. Fernando raised a point about the "bi-personal field" of the Barangers. Jean-Claude said when we treat borderline patients psychoanalytically, the important thing is our willingness to allow ourselves to be modified by the patient, to become the patient, and yet at the same time to remain outside the patient. It was agreed that he would send some thoughts he had written to Gregorio and me, which Gregorio's wife Valli very kindly translated later on. Gregorio agreed with Jean-Claude's idea about being inside and outside the mind of the patient, mentioning how long it had taken him to assimilate this experience and to be able to write about it.

* * *

Individual contributions summarizing our conclusions are described in Chapters 8, 9, and 10.

2

The central phobic position:
with a model of the free-association method

André Green

From the very beginnings of psychoanalysis, phobic neurosis was described as an irrational fear, often combined with a feeling of disgust, arising in the face of certain objects or certain situations. It combines an attitude of avoidance, a displacement on to the object or the situation which would then become phobogenic, and a projection towards the outside. Ordinarily, this combination of factors constituting the symptom only concerns the psyche in a circumscribed and limited way, to the extent that when the subject succeeds in circumventing the objects or the circumstances giving rise to the phobia, his functioning can even be compatible with normality. This well-circumscribed picture has subsequently been challenged as a result of encountering wider-ranging forms, the analysis of which was rarely based on the mechanisms of symbolization revealed by the displacement. The neurotic framework of the phobia seemed shattered, allowing much more invasive forms of anxiety to appear.

Furthermore, the very nature of the anxiety appeared to be different from the anxiety present in phobic neurosis. I am not referring to the differences established from the outset between anxiety neurosis and phobia, otherwise known as anxiety hysteria, but rather to the relations between anxiety, terror, and fright, which were only referred to allusively, without really being developed, although they were taken into account in psychiatric pathology. Admittedly, one does find mention of them in the theory with regard to a hypothetical appearance, during the childhood of patients, of "fears of annihilation, and nameless anxieties" or "primitive agonies", but their clinical description in the adult has been given little detailed attention in clinical psychoanalysis.

Moreover, the analysis of phobias has primarily consisted in trying to understand the constitution of the neurotic symptom based on deductions derived from information provided by the patient, without, however, imagining that it is possible to demonstrate the appearance of a particular psychic functioning during the session. On the couch, patients speak of the attack of anxiety they have had outside the session—that is to say, of the memory they have kept of a crisis between sessions. What I propose to describe is the analysis of phobic functioning during the session. If such functioning is not to be confined to the limits of a symptom manifesting itself primarily outside the session, the conflict or, at least, the most cathected aspects of it, cannot be circumscribed by the symptom alone.

The patients I am going to speak about may present phobic manifestations. However, their analysis during the sessions brings little in the way of results, for the conclusions arrived at often remain vague and unspecific. They lead to few associations and to the massive mobilization of the solutions of avoidance I have referred to, but they do not prompt the patient to understand what they reveal about his psychic life or to link them up with what they are displacing. Contrary to cases where the phobia is circumscribed, permitting normal psychic functioning, here what results is an extensive inhibition of the ego, often confining patients to an increasing degree of isolation. They very often say they are obliged to adopt an attitude of flight without managing to specify exactly what they are afraid of. The onsets of anxiety do not lead to any significant discussion, even in a rationalized form. We are not, however, dealing with panic attacks where the principal feature is a state of turmoil. In other words, it is as if phobic functioning had become installed within speech itself, preventing the latter from being deployed in the psyche. The analyst is eventually struck by certain distinctive characteristics of the patient's way of associating in the session, without being able to say whether what he notices in his listening is an expression of the same phobic mechanism as those that manifest themselves outside the session. At any rate, although the meaning is not identical, it may

well have a common origin that can be identified as a thought disturbance. It could be said that the only object involved is the analyst
and that the avoidance is directed at the analytic function itself in
the desire to avoid any investigation. In fact, what is involved here is
not so much the analyst as a distinct object as a situation of insepa-
rability between subject and object in which the feared transference
towards the analyst reveals the projection onto the latter of a power
to penetrate the patient's thoughts, so that the only remaining solution is the radical erosion of the intelligibility that could come from
communicating. This aspect of projection, which is limited here to
the analyst's presence itself, in fact disguises the patient's need to
flee from himself as if he were facing a danger far greater than that
consciously feared by the lifting of a repression. Here, as always,
the deeply ingrained fear consists, for the patient, in discovering in
himself something that cannot be accounted for solely in terms of
transgression, even though this fear is also present. When analysis is
nonetheless successful in elucidating the situation, it will be noted
that the avoidance involves not so much fear as a sense of being
caught in a trap with no way out, closing in on itself. It even seems
that the patient imagines the analyst is a victim of the situation in
which he has managed to trap him.

Definition of the central phobic position

By "central phobic position", I mean a basic psychic disposition that
is often met with in the treatment of certain borderline states. I have
chosen the adjective "central" in order to emphasize the fundamental aspect that I want to describe of the mental functioning of these
cases. I am not referring to what is considered to be the deepest level
of the analysand's psychic functioning, the drive or object relation,
nor to the aspect that can be attached to consciousness through the
patient's discourse. Nor is it a question of reaching those levels assumed to be the oldest or the most primitive. I shall be concerned
not simply with the accession to consciousness of certain parts of the
patient's unconscious, but, rather, with the echoes and connections
between a number of themes emerging out of diverse aspects of the
repressed. These are threatening not only in respect of the sanctions
of the superego but also for the organization of the ego. This is why
the full emergence of these contents in consciousness, and their

complete revival, must be prevented. These themes, which punctuate the subject's history, are mutually potentializing: that is to say, they do not simply accumulate but are amplified through coming into contact with each other, affecting his psychic functioning, which can no longer simply avoid that which resurfaces in isolation or prevent the resurgence of the oldest or deepest material, for it is also necessary to prevent the extension linking the themes to each other. The overall result cannot be understood in terms of a particular traumatic event, however deep and intense it may have been, but relates, rather, to the mutually reinforcing relations between diverse events, which, as a whole, create a virtual disintegration arising from the combination of different traumatic situations echoing each other. It is therefore preferable, in the patient's communication, to conceive of condensations of what appear to be hubs, which are alarming because they form the knot of encounters where different traumatic lines intersect. I would like to suggest that it is not simply a matter of precluding the return of the most significant trauma; nor are we dealing with that which has been described as cumulative trauma (Khan, 1974), but with the relations between different traumatic constellations. When they come into contact with each other, the patient has a terrifying feeling of being invaded by uncontrollable forces. If any one of these traumas is awakened, it starts resonating with the others, the composite image of which is unthinkable because it would unleash incredible violence against the patient's ego. It must therefore be supposed that what makes the agglomeration of these themes very dangerous is that they are related to fundamental organizers of psychic life, which are liable to provoke a catastrophe. It is, indeed, the pillars of mental life that are affected, the patient having more or less succeeded, before the analysis, in keeping them separate, or in denying that they were related. The real trauma, then, consists in the possibility of seeing them come together into a configuration in which the subject loses his internal capacity to resist prohibitions and is no longer in a position to safeguard the limits of his individuality. He thus resorts to multiple and sometimes contradictory identifications and finds himself incapable from there on in of employing isolated defensive solutions. This is why the idea of centrality seemed to me to be most appropriate for an in-between situation—that is to say, a situation that is perceived by the analyst intuitively as one where the flow of associations progresses while at the same time being impeded in its progression, its ramifications, its deployment towards the surface as much as towards the depths. This type of functioning, which bears witness to a fragile capacity for self-examination, has such radical consequences that the use of these mechanisms, which are self-mutilating for thought processes, can only be explained by the need to ward off serious internal threats. This is why the reference to fright or panic still seems to correspond best to the patient's experience. If it were possible, one would be justified in speaking here of memory traces of *waking terrors*, deeply buried but still active.

The associative discourse in the session: a model

In order to understand the approach I am adopting, it is essential first to know how I conceive the functioning of an ideally productive session. Let us begin with the scheme of chapter 14, "Introduction of the Ego", in the first part of Freud's "Project" (1950 [1895]) (Figure 2.1). In this diagram, Freud pictures a network of units, assumed to be neurones, the structuring of which he describes in terms of two processes. Their activity is maintained by *quantities in a state of flow*, to use his terminology. On the one hand, a quantity cathects neurone *a* and passes to neurone *b*, linking them by a "wishful attraction". On the other hand, a chain referred to by Freud as side-cathexis starts from *a*, spreading out in an arborescent manner towards other

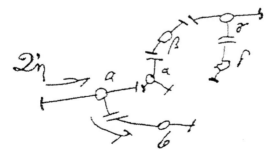

Q'n: quantities in a state of flow. Path *ab*: inhibited direct cathexis.
Path α β γ δ: lateral cathexis

Figure 2.1. Freud's schema from the "Project for a Scientific Psychology" (1950 [1895])

neurones α β γ δ. The side-cathexis replaces the passage $a \rightarrow b$, when the latter is barred, because it is liable to lead to displeasure. In fact, Freud speaks of inhibition, for repression had not yet been discovered:

> It is easy now to imagine how, with the help of a mechanism which draws the ego's attention to the imminent fresh cathexis of the hostile mnemic image, the ego can succeed in inhibiting the passage [of quantity] from a mnemic image to a release of unpleasure by a copious side-cathexis which can be strengthened according to need. [Freud, 1950 (1895), p. 324]

The side-cathexis thus finds an alternative outlet for these inhibited facilitations. *It is my hypothesis that the relation between a and the substitute side-cathexis α β γ δ is more or less closely related to the inhibited facilitation $a \rightarrow b$ so that the analysis of this side-cathexis in relation to a should give us a partial or approximate idea as to the inhibited relation "$a \rightarrow b$".* If we generalize this statement, nearly every principal semanteme produces a side-cathexis α, α β, γ, δ, α' β' γ' δ', except when the transition from a principal semanteme to another is direct, and when it does not threaten to generate displeasure.

I shall consider this schematic outline as a nuclear model combining cathexis, the dynamics of meaning, repression, and resistance, as well as associations as a mode of recognition permitting indirect and partial access to the repressed unconscious. I wish to modify the outline in order to apply it to the type of communication occurring in the session. When the patient is associating freely in a fruitful session, he utters sentences with no logical connections between them. In this dispersed order of free-associative communication, one can see that each idea that has a certain semantic consistency—I call them principal semantemes—is surrounded by circumstantial commentaries, which I liken to the side-cathexes described by Freud in his "Project". Sometimes these commentaries serve as mere developments of the principal semantemes, playing an analogous role to subordinate clauses in grammar, and occasionally indicate a difficulty in allowing a direct link to be established with another principal semanteme. What is important to note is that free association makes use of narrative or grammatical structures without respecting their distinction between principal and subordinate (side-cathexis), the flow of the discourse establishing links by ignoring the categorization between principal and subordinate structures, or between direct facilitation and side-cathexis. Resistance makes a detour necessary, but this, in turn, enriches the possibilities of association! This is shown retrospectively by analysing the meaning emerging from certain relations that stand out from the different elements dispersed in the communication. This supposes that (a) the discourse produced by free association stimulates incidental developments in order to prevent links with the unconscious that are too direct from being established; and (b) that the commentaries that seem secondary or subordinate are liable to play, for the unconscious, the same role as side-cathexes: that is to say, apart from their function of creating detours, the paths followed come into contact by benefiting from the lowering of the rational censorship so as to create new links that appear because the distinct grammatical categories of discourse have been set aside. This is known and accepted by psychoanalysts who, in general, do not go further than this. It has been noted that it is possible for a new system of relations to emerge, but no attention has been given to the ways in which it is formed. Although for consciousness this disconnectedness obscures overall intelligibility, for analytic listening the new network suggests that meaningful relations may exist between *any* of the elements uttered, whether they be a product of two semantically consistent ideas or of one idea that is semantically consistent with any other aspect of the verbalization, present incidentally or contingently, belonging to the side-cathexes uttered, or linked by inference. This follows from the hypothesis I have put forward that the different side-cathexes may be related to the barred pathway that cannot be opened up—namely, that which goes in a direct line from *a* to *b* in Freud's model of the "Project".

This is merely the beginning of what we have to understand. This process of associating invites us to search for the latent meaning by inferring that the comprehension of one element—let us say, element *d*, of the network *a, b, c, d, e, f*—cannot disclose its function simply by its presumed reference to that which precedes it, *c*. To be more exact, it must be added that *c* will be infiltrated, inhabited, and potentially engrossed by the reflexive relations it may have had with one or several contingent elements at some distance from it: either with its side-cathexes or with a previous element, belonging to the semantically consistent series of ideas. The general idea is that, as it advances towards consciousness, unconscious meaning seeks to force its way through and, in order to do so, has to make use of connections that do not bring the elements it is composed of into direct contact; or, that these cannot be inferred simply from relations of immediate proximity or equivalent importance, while neglecting what appears only to have the function of a digression.

Of course, affects—deviations, ruptures or progressions—play the most important role in this diffraction. It would be a mistake to think, however, that the tracing of affects in itself would provide a sufficient pointer towards what should lead to the latent meaning. For affects can well up as a consequence of associative dismantling and merely have the function of connoting an isolated aspect of the discourse that has appeared on the way, without necessarily playing an important role in the network of meaning revealed in the wake of the work of association.

It can be seen that this form of thinking not only seeks a relaxation of moral censorship but induces a form of functioning freed from the constraints of stringing words together sequentially, making use of the attraction—and the attendant repulsion—of the repressed elements that govern the production of the themes presented on the surface. In other words, it also has to free itself from the rational censorship. The requirement of associating freely has a two-fold consequence. On the one hand, it leads to giving up the constraints that ensure the sequence of ideas, the logical coherence required by secondary thought processes, and thus to liberating the flow of thematic ramblings in their various types of expression, concerning both the succession of different ideas emitted and the detours produced by certain of them, which may, at first sight, seem contingent or adjacent. On the other hand, by loosening up the links within communication, this mode of discursiveness, which is at once loose and disjointed, in turn facilitates an activity intensifying the modes of influence at a distance between the parts of the discourse, just as poetry and artistic writing strive to do deliberately, albeit in a controlled way. This means that this radiation, having effects at a distance, seems to be a capacity of the human mind that comes into play when the aim of the discourse cannot be stated without endangering the one who is speaking, or that indirect discourse is richer when it adopts the forms of poetry (Green, 1984). The links between words have a great deal more semantic capacity than does the strict coherence of words. This illuminates the importance of the evocative dimension of language (Lacan, 1977a), which escapes the visibility, continuity, and order obtained from the perceptible links in the logic defining its rules[1] by obeying laws that govern secondary processes.

The tree-like functioning thus obtained helps us to get a better grasp of the originality of analytic understanding. That is to say, in the apparent disorder of communication, it is the effects of a *mutually resonating chain of signifiers* that increases the value of this functioning. It still remains to be determined how this functioning induces the analyst's understanding and interpretation. Thanks to condensations and displacements and other mechanisms, associations make it possible to identify nuclei of *retroactive reverberation*—that is, an element uttered only really acquires meaning if, on the basis of it, retroactive echoes, sometimes convergent and contained in what has been said earlier in the session, are illuminated, revealing how the power of their meaning persists long after the discourse conveying them has finished. Similarly, at other moments, although there is no hint beforehand that it will be the first step of a sequence, certain terms will act as warning signs; they are experienced as such *a posteriori*, although when he hears them the analyst is unable to predict the form of what will follow on the basis of the danger signal. When this comes, it will enable him to infer their relationship with their precursor. The import of these relationships is noticed retrospectively, for the value of anticipation was isolated and could give no precise indication of what was coming. *Retroactive reverberation and heralding anticipation* will thus act either in concert or alternately, helping us to understand that free association gives us access to a complex temporal structure (Green, 2000c) that challenges the apparent linearity of the discourse. This makes us sensitive to a progressive as well as regressive temporality, assuming an arborescent form, and, above all, producing unexpressed potentialities or potentialities generating retrospective echoes. If this is the case, it means that psychic organization is constantly being reshaped over the course of time. Without elaborating on its theoretical implications, Freud alluded to this by speaking of the attraction that is exerted by that which was already repressed (Freud, 1915d). (See Figure 2.2.)

It is clear that such functioning is much more suggestive of the figure of a network than one of linearity, sometimes ramified in the coexistence of different temporalities, linear and reticular. Furthermore, among the ramifications involved in representing the process, certain branches may remain mute because they are subject to a very strong counter-cathexis. They are no less active in the unconscious and are capable of being reactivated or, in other cases, of exciting other branches without expressing themselves explicitly and directly.

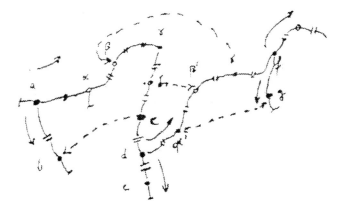

●   *a, b, c, d, e f:* functioning of principal semantemes
○   α, β, γ, δ, α′ β′ γ′ δ′: functioning of subordinate semantemes
      (side-cathexes)
←   retroactive reverberations
←   heralding anticipation

Figure 2.2.   Diagram of associative radiation

Other branches will appear absent, since meaning never develops from them, but they suggest to the analyst's mind the idea that they are necessary for arriving at a minimal understanding, which is nonetheless always hypothetical. *If meaning is indeed arborescent, it is in the sense that one can go from one branch of the tree to another by a recurrent route, then returning to the subsequent bifurcations of the branch from which one set out.*

Consequently, one must stress that the nature of the associations reveals a characteristic that, to my knowledge, only belongs to psychoanalysis. We have just been questioning the linearity of associations generally found in linguistic theorizations. Linguists readily affirm that the relations between the terms used are much more important than the is the meaning of the terms themselves. Moreover, owing to the infiltration of the conscious discourse by the unconscious—which means, in addition, by the indirect, invisible, mute effect of the cathexes of unconscious thing-presentations on word-presentations as well as the pressure exerted by the quanta of affects connoting them and commanding their dynamic progression—the associative discourse is marked at certain moments by what I call the *effects of irradiation.* Thus certain terms—or, better, certain moments in the discourse—occupying a strategic position that can often only be understood after the event, are vehicles of dynamic effects in such a way that once pronounced, and even before they are pronounced (even though they are still only unarticulated thoughts), they irradiate and influence the discursive intentionality. Moreover, it is often the same ones that, defensively, engender side-cathexes. It is then that they will have the tendency to start resonating retroactively either with the terms already stated or—and sometimes simultaneously—with terms still to come, *not thought of as yet*, but potentially generative of themes that enable one to note new connections with what has been expressed. They therefore function as *indicators* under the effect of an internal vibration. We have seen this in the movement, both backwards and forwards, in the flow of communication during the session, in relation both to what has already been said as well as to what still remains to be said, suggesting a *virtuality of existence* or a potential form of meaning. This conception, which I propose to call the *associative radiation*, traces, by means of the manifest discourse resulting from free association, lines of force running through it, which constitute the veins of the discourse. This makes it possible to follow, to resonate, to retroact, to gather in advance the richness of meaning circulating along the pathways, the plan of which is based on the coordinates of the unconscious, marked by the hyper-cathexes and counter-cathexes accompanying them. Moments during which there is a suspension of association are of interest in that they point to the knots of resistance and allow the analyst to get a feeling for the reorganization that is underway. This description enables us to get a better understanding of the preconscious modalities of the analyst's listening to the discourse in the session, with all its transferential connotations and countertransferential recurrences.

Within such a perspective the analyst adopts an approach in line with his perception of the way the patient is expressing himself. He tries to draw out the meaning conveyed by the analysand's words, in the light of what he has already heard him saying during the session, which will undoubtedly echo themes already touched upon in earlier or current sessions. Furthermore, he will also be listening attentively for what he is expecting to hear regarding the development of themes that have already arisen in the discourse. It is a disjointed process in which past and future are mingled, involving exploration back and forth in the midst of the present. This movement of waiting for a meaning to emerge is usually not confined to a single anticipation or to just one hypothesis waiting to be realized, but to several simultaneously, one of which may be selected to stabilize the meaning. In certain cases, none of them will be validated, all of them having to give way to an unforeseen hypothesis, arising extemporaneously, which is a product of the connections already established by the discourse. The earlier invalidated hypotheses will not disappear completely; most of the time they will remain latent, resurfacing from time to time, or becoming obsolete if they are not reactivated.

But, in any case, the movement of the session seeks an equilibrium between the holding back of resistance and the progressive thrust towards consciousness, training the ear to be receptive to a polysemic and temporal complexity, at once open to the conjectures of prospective and retrospective connections and participating in the construction of a dialectical semantic process. Process means movement, the act of moving forward.

Finally, in speaking of the organizers of the patient's psychic life, I am alluding to the key concepts around which the patient's mental universe is organized. They are for psychoanalysts what referents are for linguists. It is quite deplorable to have to observe that there is still no agreement among psychoanalysts with regard to the categories they represent. One of the tasks of the future will surely be to come to an agreement on this subject.

First steps towards understanding associative avoidance as a manifestation of the negative

It is a long time now since I was first intrigued by the associative behaviour of certain analysands who, at different moments in the session, seemed to turn their backs on the entire process of thought that had brought them to a certain point in their discourse, even though the conclusion of what they were saying seemed almost predictable. At the time, I had made these observations with neurotic patients, and I attributed to resistance what seemed to me to be a flight from becoming aware of a prohibited desire.

Subsequently, I was struck by Bion's account of a slightly different situation that I could not help relating to the preceding observation (Bion, 1967a, 1967b; 1970). Bion was speaking of those cases in which the material presented by the patients seemed extremely meaningful for the analyst, although it made no sense to the analysand. But he was speaking here of psychotic patients, whose mental functioning was clearly deeply impaired. Along with other remarkable facts, this was at the origin of the conception of *attacks on linking* with which Bion's name is associated.

The comparison with the earlier situation highlighted the fact that, whereas in the first case repression was directed mainly at the offshoots of the sexual drives, in the second the activity of destructive forces against the ego was in the foreground. Subsequently, my interest for the work of the negative sharpened my ear for forms of negativity that could not be interpreted in terms of their direct relationship with the destructive drives (Green, 1999a; Winnicott, 1971b).

What the analyst is mainly faced with in the transference with "borderline" patients is destructivity that is directed, *first and foremost, at the subject's own psychic functioning*. Destructivity is made use of by negativistic defences of which Freudian splitting is the subtlest form. Analytic communication contains essential contradictions that coexist, without one dominating the other, obliging the analyst's thinking to elaborate the product of his listening according to unusual, disconcerting, and strange registers. I have referred on more than one occasion to the uncompleted work of Freud, "Some Elementary Lessons in Psychoanalysis" (1940b [1938])—an alternative English version of his *Abriss*—in which he anticipated that analysis would in the future be confronted with modes of psychic functioning increasingly remote from those ordinarily met with. This probably also means increasingly remote from what he had learnt from the psychoanalysis of neuroses constituting the basis of the "Papers on Metapsychology" (Freud, 1915d). *The Work of the Negative* (Green, 1999b) was an attempt to develop their clinical, technical, and theoretical implications.

In this chapter, I am dwelling on certain "negativistic" manifestations in the cure which can present themselves in such a way that it takes the analysand a long time to recognize their function, and which do not stop once he has recognized them. I am alluding here to the behaviour of an analysand who came to see me because of chronic anxiety. He had tried various forms of treatment, which, among other things, revealed his difficulties in tolerating the relationship and silence. Shortly after starting treatment with me, which he had apparently wanted very much, and following a number of interventions on my part that seemed all the more necessary to me in that he had been unable previously to tolerate the silence of his therapists, he replied, as he had done before with his previous analyst: "I can't hear you, I've got shit in my ears." He clearly spoke of this deafness in terms that suggested he was refusing to hear me. During a recent session, ten years later, he again repeated, in connection with an interpretation I had made that happened not to please him: "I can't hear you." I did not understand that he was expressing the same opposition as in the past, and I really thought that my voice was not sufficiently audible. This was astonishingly consistent; he had simply suppressed the metaphorical anal contraction of his ear. In the following session, he nonetheless showed a remarkable capacity for integration. However, this switchback understanding remained a characteristic of his functioning, even after considerable progress had been made. The difference lay in a capacity for re-establishing insight, the progress of which was not illusory, but its exercise had to be preceded by repetition compulsion, fortunately now of a transitory nature, designed to make me lose my footing in order to ward off the imminent danger that the deeper vision he had acquired of his past conflicts might represent anew.

Today, it seems to me that this behaviour, the defensive aim of which I had understood, needs to be related to phobic manifestations (a defence against anal penetration or against the fear of losing one's boundaries). But it remained for me to move beyond the level of behaviour, however symptomatic it might be, to that which gave it its specific character and stood in the way of analytic understanding. That is to say, to the situation in which the meaning emerging from free association in the transference relationship becomes subject to jamming and quasi-systematic asphyxiation.

Description of the central phobic position

The analysis of the transference of a patient, Gabriel, brought me understanding that I was lacking. This analysis, often stormy, is teeming with all sorts of incidents and heuristically fruitful discoveries. It is currently at an advanced stage, after a long development. Some previous therapeutic experiences had been terminated by a unilateral decision due, probably to uncontrolled countertransference reactions. This had increased Gabriel's sense of abandonment, at a moment when he particularly needed to be supported. For many years the sessions were taken up with complaints about constant anxieties, and what he had to say was particularly confused. At times, when I managed to follow them, themes of considerable interest also emerged, regularly accompanied by the impression that I was sighing with weariness, irritation, and boredom, all signs of what was going to happen, according to him—that is, that I was going to throw him out. "I don't know", "I'm not sure", "I can't remember", "It's not very interesting, what I'm saying", and so on, interspersed the sequences of his discourse. I had no precise information about his history. He later recognized that these expressions had the power to kill representation. Facts, never dated in a manner that provided a chronology, were situated now at one age, now at another, rarely accompanied by memories that could be recalled which would have given an idea of the psychic position of the patient regarding the events related. Revisions were lost in the resurgence of the events related. He had had a disrupted life, marked by great solitude, that was aggravated at the age of 12 by his parents' divorce—after the discovery by the father of his wife's unfaithfulness—which meant that Gabriel had to share his life with a depressed and inaccessible mother, prisoner of her moroseness and lack of zest for living. When he was 15, his mother disappeared one day, not returning from a cure at a spa. His resistance to his father remained unrelenting. No longer knowing to whom turn, the father, who had remarried, decided to consult a psychiatrist who concluded that his son hated him, without proposing anything beyond that. Soon afterwards, he left the country, and his son refused to follow him. He was in permanent conflict with his stepmother and found himself completely isolated after their departure, having already been abandoned by his mother. Chaotic studies at school and a stormy adolescence marked by political agitation and transgressive behaviour revealed his vulnerability. After failing his *bac* [A-levels], he spent some time abroad, experiencing isolation, solitude, and distress. He came back home and, on the initiative of a friend, decided to go to University—after a special examination—for studies that had no relation to his present occupation. It took me some time to understand that the feeling I had of periodically losing the thread of what he was saying to me was due to potentially meaningful ruptures of association. Rather than interruptions or changes of theme—which are part and parcel of associating freely—it was a discourse that seemed to be kept at a distance, developed at length on the basis of generalities expressed in broken speech that gave me the impression that I was trying to find my way in the fog. I thought at first that I was faced with an attitude stemming from a massive and extensive repression. But then I understood that if he needed to stop himself associating freely in this way, it was not owing to a lack but rather to an excess of potential associations.

In other words, the more he continued talking, the more he felt in danger, because the communication between the parts of his discourse was not sufficiently watertight. He was speaking in a broken or muddled way, as if he was trying to avoid an outcome towards which he would have been pulled irresistibly had he let himself go. The outcome he feared was none other than that of somatic illness or madness, and he subsequently succumbed to the latter. Many clues helped me to understand that the danger of madness was related to the idea that he was linked to his mother by a tie that nothing and nobody could break, leaving no room for any other cathexis that risked taking him away from her. By coming to his session, he had the impression that he could hear her voice calling him. On the other hand, it was accompanied by the recollection of his father's constant disapproval in the past.

A major event in Gabriel's childhood was being sent away to be nursed, but at what age? It took me about eight years to find out that this had taken place between the ages of 1 and 3. Why? It was a mystery—the reasons given were not very convincing. But a further trauma compounded the separation: although his father apparently came to see him almost every week in the country 300 km from Paris, his mother never did, except to collect him. Predictably enough, he did not recognize her when she came and called her *"Madame"* during the journey home. Then, a few hours later, he would remember who she was. This mother, who was living in the provinces, never visited him, wrote to him, or telephoned him, disconnecting her phone from time to time and going for long periods without answering calls. She never saw anyone, refusing his offers to come and see her, yet addressing herself passionately to him when he conversed with her by telephone, complaining about this and that and adding that he was the only one who could help her. Nevertheless, all the suggestions and proposals that he made were repeatedly turned down. I had realized from very early on that she was probably a very disturbed person, but it was more difficult to tell what the nature of this disturbance was. I eventually realized that her strange behaviour could be explained by the fact that she preferred not to see people because she could not bear separating from them, fearing that she would fall ill once they had left.

Gabriel had learnt that, before he was put out to be nursed, his mother had had an abscess of the breast while she was breast-feeding him. As she felt nothing, she had gone on feeding him—which gives an idea of how narcissistic and masochistic she was. She did not realize that her baby was crying like mad, visibly wasting away, and only absorbing the contents of a purulent and empty breast. His father eventually intervened, calling the doctor who separated the mother from the child and prescribed "marine water injections"—in other words, I suppose, a physiological serum to re-hydrate him.

One day, during his tenth year of analysis, he was recalling for the umpteenth time the period when he was put out to be nursed. Whereas when I alluded to it he preferred to trivialize the event by saying, for example: "not all children who have been put out to nurse are affected by it like me", this time he said: "Yesterday I was thinking again about the visits I expected from my parents on Sundays. *I saw myself again as a child, racked by an indescribable state of anxious tension, drawn body and soul towards the entrance of the farm in expectation of their arrival and in the hope of seeing them appear.*" He was speaking in fact of the disappointment at not seeing his mother: "*My face wore a terribly tense expression, so dreadful that I told myself: 'It's not possible, it can't be me'.*"

I was moved by this movement combining a traumatic resurgence with the non-recognition of an image of himself, perceived and represented yet disavowed. I was also at a loss to know whether it was a recollection or a revival. But I was sure it was not a fantasy. A creation of the cure, certainly, but one laden with truth. If, in addition to the repeated disappointment of not seeing the figure of his mother appear, one adds the fear of letting his father see his sadness lest he, too, should stop visiting him, one can understand that this situation, which may have echoed the dual relationship of the baby at the breast that was starving him, had, under the circumstances, indeed acquired a dimension of thirdness, not to mention the possible fantasy that it was also the father who was preventing the mother from coming to see him in order to keep her for himself, just as in the past he had deprived him of the breast which, albeit deadly, was nonetheless his possession. It was some time before he admitted that this interpretation was plausible.

From then on I understood that this was the key to my patient's attitude. He was in a permanent state of torment, but to a certain extent he was not the one who was experiencing this. Or else, the explanation for his anxiety was to be found in the way others behaved towards him. This defensive movement was facilitated by numerous temporary confusions of identity: between him and his mother, between him and the deceased paternal uncle whose first name he shared, an uncle whom he had never known but whom he apparently greatly resembled, according to his father, and, more recently, between his wife and his mother, and, finally, between his son, not yet 3 years old, and himself. What is more, his mother had fostered similar confusions during his adolescence, to the point of introducing him to the local people as her brother, or even as her husband by modifying their common family name. These were not identifications but temporary suspensions of his identity. At one point in the transference he said: "I like to think I *am* Dr Green", which entailed a sense of usurpation precluding any possibility of identification.

Some time after evoking the expectation of seeing his mother who did not come, he came back to the episode of the abscess of the breast to report some words he remembered her saying to him: "And you pumped, and you pumped, and you pumped". And I said, to myself: "And nothing came!" This was not simply a movement of identification with my patient, nor even a reconstruction. Suddenly, I realized that I had made the link between the two events: the abscessed breast and the absence of the mother during his stay at the farm. Between the first and the second there were many differences. But establishing an associative bridge was indeed the consequence of the radiating effect to which I have referred, which I had already experienced while listening to what he had to tell me. As for Gabriel, much of what he did seemed aimed at preventing the possibility of being caught out: he did this by taking pre-emptive action and by making others experience the void he was creating by actually disappearing or withdrawing. On the other hand, he was extremely regular in coming to his sessions, which, he said, were important for him.

The meaning of my patient's behaviour now became even clearer. I had completed a sequence in which he had been content to describe the action of the other person—that is, his mother—without imagining with me what he may have felt, but prompting me unconsciously to pursue to its end what he was feeling. The only solution left to him was to cut off (to split?) mental activity for fear of the resonance that might be attached to the different traumatic situations. I shall pass over other situations related to more familiar psychoanalytic themes such as castration anxiety or the feeling of not being understood by one's current companion or the betrayal of a friendship or love affair. I am mentioning them, without developing them, simply to underpin the idea that he did indeed feel a great sense of insecurity when faced with the key signifiers of psychoanalysis.

I was struck by certain characteristic aspects of his behaviour. Thinking that he had paid enough with all his sufferings, he decided, while suffering the shock of an emotional setback, to stop paying his taxes, effectively disappearing as far as the Administration was concerned. Of course, the tax department caught up with him after a few years, and he feared much harsher penalties than are usually applied in such cases. Or, for example, he tried to get involved in certain professional activities entailing a selection process, and, after overcoming this hurdle, would turn up once and then disappear. In analysis, he could not offer the slightest explanation for this dodgy behaviour. Likewise, he avoided seeing his close relations for fear of being accused of causing them trouble. He was very anxious at the slightest sign that his son might have a health problem, and the only way he could deal with this was by exerting absolute control over his wife, expecting her to get rid of the symptoms, even those of a benign nature. He could not stand it if she replied that she did not know what was wrong. As he was extremely concerned to establish an unclouded relationship with the child, he was very unreceptive to the son's manifestations of oedipal jealousy, being unable to imagine its existence.

What seemed perfectly clear to me, however, was the reason for his way of associating, at once blurred, vague, often elusive, out of step with the events related. At times he acknowledged the correctness of certain interpretations, acting as if they had never been made in previous sessions. I thus understood that what stopped him from associating, causing this multidirectional progression to stagnate and to be unproductive, was the *anticipation* of where it might lead him, which he desperately tried to avoid. In the end, it was as if all of the interpretations might lead to the cascade of traumas echoing each other. I realized that the effect of repression was not enough in itself to explain what was happening. In fact, a certain degree of decathexis from the arborescence of the chains of association extinguished the radiating power of the thematic moments. To put it in another way, his discourse lapsed into linearity. His capacity for associating retrospectively was as limited as his capacity for imagining what could follow, thus impeding new avenues of meaning from emerging. The talking, even the associating, did not stop. Sometimes it was fragmentary, but, in any case, the associations were flat, without interest, without depth, and without flashes of insight. They were not generative, and there was no hope of any solution through interpretation of the traditional kind.

But why the central phobic position? Why was there this need to avoid pursuing the path of associations to its end? Was it to make me experience the disappointment of not seeing him conclude, of not seeing him get there, just as he had never seen his mother arrive? No doubt, but what the distress reveals above all is *the murder of the representation of the mother who does not appear, or of the breast that does not appease hunger but increases excitation. Subsequently the subject who carries this out denies the existence of his own psychic reality*: "No, that isn't in me, it can't be me, it isn't me." Here, then, we have a new variety of the work of the negative concerning *the subject's own negative hallucination of himself*, consisting less in a non-perception than in a non-recognition. By not seeing his mother, Gabriel reactivated *nachträglich* the no-breast of the mother. Not the absent breast—since it is a breast that is supposed to be there nourishing him—but a breast that is *there and empty*; that is to say, deprived of its functions, nonexistent as a breast, pushing to get rid of him, to make him disappear, even though he is very noticeably there, in flesh and mouth, as it were, with nipple between his lips, which were sucking nothing of any value. Nor could he imagine receiving anything at all from a paternal image desiring to transmit something to him that could be of use for his own development in life. The path of associations should therefore have awakened the links between his mother's absence when he was 2 years old, the breast from the period when he was 6–7 months old, his incapacity to be cathected by his mother when he found himself alone with her, the sense that his father was disappointed in him, the desertion of mistresses with whom he was in love, leaving them before they left him, and, finally, the feeling that he had been abandoned by his therapists. The complete revival of all this in analysis threatened to be devastating. Each time he was reminded of one trauma, it divided him even further, making him incapable of using his affects to see what his ego could do with them by trying to find the meaning that might emerge from becoming aware of the connections between these events.

I would like to emphasize that it does not seem right to me to trace everything back to the earliest trauma—that is, the abscess of the breast. I have tried to show, on the contrary, that what is important is the grouping together of various traumas that intensify each other, and the fact that the subject attempts to deny the connections they can establish mutually within the psyche. This is because they do not so much suggest an integrative evolution as they assume the form of a repetitive persecution involving, ultimately, the denial of the subject's own psychic reality or self-image, leading to some form of emptiness and, subsequently, depression. This explains why the phobic position is at the centre of psychic organization, keeping watch, at each instance, over all the paths leading to it and away from it: for the emerging picture would oblige him to accept his rage, his envy, and, more than anything else, his destructivity, forcing him to see himself in the depths of distress, subject to an omnipotence that can only find an outlet in transgression, overwhelmed by endless excitement.

Some consequences of the central phobic position

What are the effects of the central phobic position when the conflicts cannot be contained by it?

> I have already mentioned the blurring of the discourse, a sign of *associative avoidance* more than an attack on linking. In order to exist, the latter always seems to me to come after this avoidance *when it has not been successful in preventing links from being established.* It engenders in the analyst the feeling that the analysand is confused and that he himself is also in danger of becoming confused.

> *Projection.* Its aim here is one of objectivization. It sometimes happens—Gabriel was a case in point—that these subjects find themselves plunged into situations in which third parties behave in a really hostile manner towards them. This does not prevent the subject from making use psychically of this genuinely spiteful

behaviour to blind himself to the role that it plays in his psychic reality by providing him with a screen. In the same way, the perception of inadequacies and shortcomings in loved ones, real as it may be, is nonetheless aimed at taking his mind off self-reproaches of a much more serious order.

› *Masochism.* Masochistic traits infiltrate the entire clinical picture: sometimes they are linked with identification with the maternal object, sometimes with mechanisms of reparation or, more fundamentally, with the sense of unconscious guilt, which is *immensely* deep. As for sadism, it is less related to the pleasure of causing suffering than to the desire for mastery in a bid to gain vengeful control over an object that is particularly elusive, unpredictable, precarious, and evanescent.

› *Repetition.* This plunges the subject back indefinitely into the same situations overwhelming the ego's capacities to defend itself against them; its role here is one of insistence, marking, discharge, familiar reassurance, and self-blinding.

› *Provoking the object.* The masochistic pseudo-aggression aims at repeating the injustice of others, at inciting the object's desertion in order to confirm a sort of inexorable malediction.

› *Wounded narcissism.* The consequence of the humiliations of masochism, repeated failures and desertions sapping self-esteem and triggering depression.

› *Denial.* This should no doubt be distinguished from negation; we have seen that it took the form of a denial of self-recognition, to which I return later in greater detail.

Taken together, the above constitute a second line of defence, brought into play unconsciously by the subject when the central phobic position has been overwhelmed, with the affects of depression and anxiety gaining the upper hand.

All these modes of psychic functioning, whether they belong to the erotic, narcissistic, or destructive order, are designed to protect against a sensation of being overwhelmed, repeating the earliest traumas.

Speaking of his current relationship with his mother, whom he has seen once or twice since the beginning of his analysis and with whom he has not communicated for several months, Gabriel told me: "I act as if she didn't exist, saying to myself: now I can live in peace. And yet I cannot stop myself from recalling those rare moments in the past when she was attentive and warm, and from hoping to find her again like that."

It is only very recently that he has been able to recall his mother in this way, with a fragile halo, enabling one to understand, retrospectively, what has been erased by her loss. He was unable to renounce the hope of her resurrection. However, the potential excess that could take hold of him thwarted this hope. He was in terror on the couch when he recalled a moment of intimacy with her on vacation, in the father's absence, when he was 10 years old. He remembered the mornings in the winter sports hotel where they were served breakfast in bed. "I remember the tea and toast very well." But the memory of finding himself in the same bed as his mother raised in him the retrospective fear that they may have had incestuous relations, apparently forgotten, the eventual reminiscence of which he was terrified by. At the age of 3 he had accompanied his mother to her native country and had been welcomed in her family like a little prince. Here it seemed that the whole family environment approved of his being alone with his mother, whereas at home there were constant disputes and he had the feeling that his father condemned him for his closeness to his mother. He thought he could read in his mother's expression: "You and I are agreed that your father is a damned nuisance." But usually she looked at him smiling, without saying anything, with an expression full of innuendoes. In the end he admitted that his mother had left him when he was 16 because he had made life impossible for her. He had, in fact, pushed her unconsciously to go away because he was extremely worried about her excessive tolerance of his transgressive behaviour at the time, although she herself was never the object of a misplaced gesture. A few years before, he had returned to visit her; it was their last meeting. It was summer, and he was wearing sandals. She said to him: "You've got lovely feet." The following day he left abruptly for Paris.

The network of meaning and radiating associations

Gabriel received alarming news about his mother from her doctors. She had a serious illness, which she had neglected disdainfully, obliging her son to look after her, though he had been unable to do so up to now owing to her resistance. He now arranged for her to be hospitalized in Paris. It was a very moving time of family reunion. In particular, it provided an opportunity for his wife to get to know his mother, whom she had never seen before, and for his son to get to know his grandmother. Contrary to all expectations, his wife liked his mother very much, managing to have exchanges with her that astonished Gabriel. She thought his mother was "exceptional". During the entire period of hospitalization, the staff on her ward were struck by the patient's intense resistance, her refusal to let herself be treated, and, above all, her anorexia, which had already appeared many times in the past and risked hastening her end. Gabriel did everything within his power to bring her the food he thought she liked. It has to be said that this final hospitalization brought back the memory of an earlier attack of anorexia that his mother had had, against which Gabriel had battled in vain, and also the memory of having received a call, years after his mother's sudden disappearance, from the person he called his "uncle", who was, in fact, none other than the mother's former lover. Their relationship had brought about his parents' divorce, even though the "uncle" had not left his own family to live with Gabriel's mother. The "uncle" had asked him to come urgently and see his mother, whom he discovered in a clinic at death's door, with "tubes coming out of her everywhere". He was overwhelmed by this spectacle of physical and mental catastrophe, for she was clearly depressed as well. It was as if the nightmare had returned, reminding him in an inverted form of his illness following the abscess of the breast. On the couch, now, he was able to feel very intense affects and, for the first time, to express his love. He would have liked, he said, to take all her suffering upon himself—a common enough fantasy in this kind of situation, but one that gave a new meaning to the earlier manifestations of fusion. It seemed, however, that all the problems raised by the sight of his mother's body in the hands of doctors had awoken the memory of his own bodily experiences when she was the one who exercised control over his health.

I recalled the writings of Joyce McDougall (1989), who, describing different, but not unrelated psychic structures, speaks of "one body for two". It was when he was having treatment in his childhood that a very intense anxiety was aroused of seeing their erogenous zones confused, causing the spectre of an impingement to loom up which would have led to a complete feminine identity that went beyond a simple identification. This appalled him all the more in that it was accompanied by an experience of intrusion, suggesting that a real invasion was progressively taking possession of him—all the more so because his father, whom he continued to see intermittently, had little tolerance for the most benign manifestations of homosexuality, which reduced them when they met to remaining silent for long periods. This was compounded by the fact that Gabriel's mother disapproved of these meetings and reproached him for them. Alongside sessions in which the same complaints and the same litanies succeeded one another regarding his mother, there were others in which he expressed his surprise at rediscovering, finally, a mother as he had dreamed she might be. I sensed that a change was taking place within him so that he could accept an image of her that was less rigid than that which he had presented hitherto.

Yet he returned at length and repetitively to his mother's anorexia and his inability to get her to eat when he was a child. He re-experienced with intense feeling the profound irritation this had caused him. I was struck by a remark he made without understanding what it meant. He told me that even at the hospital where she was staying, where he had himself brought her things to eat which he hoped she would find appetizing, he made sure that he was not present when she was eating. Soon afterwards he was able to recall a period in the past, which he had never mentioned before, when his mother, now over her depression, had taken a degree and led an active life for a time before falling seriously into depression again for unknown reasons. Moreover, Gabriel found it difficult being subjected to the consequences that certain family conflicts had for him, reacting to objectively trying situations by splitting and trying to extract himself by denying problems that affected him, although he was in no way responsible for them. During the same period, and as a result of conversations with his mother, he returned in his sessions to his childhood memories. She reminded him how they used to live in premises of 25 square metres, which also served as a workshop for the father. He had slept on a camp-bed in the workshop, his father in the bed in the bedroom, and his mother on a sofa; he could not remember whether the sofa was in the same room that the father slept in or in the one he slept in. His mother was equally incapable of remembering this detail fraught with psychic consequences. He himself insisted repeatedly that he had never seen his parents sleeping together, except once one Christmas morning when he had received gifts.

Shortly afterward, again speaking about his mother's anorexia, an idea suddenly came to him. He still could not remember her eating, but he could recall an occasion when she was drinking near him. While drinking her tea, she emitted certain noises from her throat, which made him extremely irritated. He would have liked to be able to stop these unbearable noises her body was making. I suggested that these noises obliged him to imagine the inside of his mother's body, which he accepted, but without any real change ensuing.

In the following session, after mentioning his son's problems and the plans for separation, as well as steps he had taken to open up professional opportunities for himself which he imagined I disapproved of, he expressed the wish to come back to his memory of his mother drinking tea. After a period of reflection, he realized that in the parents' maternal tongue the word for "cup" was "*gluss*" [glass], which was reminiscent of the French word "*glousser*" ["to chuckle, to cluck" (translator's note: a very common French expression uses "*glousser de plaisir*" to express strong sexual enjoyment)]. He came to the conclusion himself that it was the idea of a pleasure in his mother's body, which he had found intolerable and would have liked to be able to stop there and then. It can be seen how this association came to him in the context of separation–closeness with an implication of a primal scene, supported by the idea that the mother's desire was to sleep with him. Later in the session, he related his anger and his irritation at these bodily noises to similar feelings of anger he had when his mother would go out in the evening with a female friend. Here we were once again dealing with separation, but with the implication of an absent third party. The irritation he felt when she was drinking tea, on the contrary, was related to the fantasy of a mother excited in his presence, as if she was trying to seduce him, expressing a desire for closeness that he experienced as incestuous. He himself identified with this projected excitation, which engendered anger in him that he then attributed to his father. But the result was the projection of the absence of maternal prohibition, which turned her tolerance of it into an excitation destined to drive him mad without being satisfied, just as he could not help thinking that the wife's insufficiently prohibiting attitude and excess of proximity was dangerous for her children. I reminded him that his mother had passed him off as her brother and as her husband. In fact, he admitted later that his mother had only alluded to the brother–sister relationship, and that he might very well have been the one who had thought that she could have gone as far as to say that he was her husband, and that he had then attributed this alarming idea to her. But the essential issue was not his fantasy, which he recognized as such, but the idea that his mother had consented to such a possibility.

It is important to note this meeting of extremes—as if apathy, depression, anorexia and dissatisfaction, protests, and complaints simply served to mask these cruel expressions of unrepressed fantasies that had the power to drive him mad. He had seen his physically powerful father in a rage upon discovering his wife's infidelity. It was as if the representation of an object that was too absent created in his mind an excessive lack, awakening a degree of excitation that could not find any outlet. In the course of a session in which I tried to present this clinical picture to him, he replied "death instinct" [*pulsion de mort*], without adding anything further. Then he said: "I was thinking in fact about what I had read about alcoholics speaking of an insatiable and inconsolable internal object." We were on two converging lines of association. On leaving the session, he said to himself, "I have a companion."

In this case report, I have sought to reproduce the path of associations provided by the patient. Certain central themes reappeared through different series of associations, some of which were even liable to carry out reversals, but all of which took place in the space of two or three sessions. I have had to regroup the associations to report them for the purposes of this chapter in order to give a better illustration of what I think of as a kind of radiant functioning out of a central hub, which, I consider, we have finally been able to observe. However, this can be so rich that one has to accept that one can only give an idea of it with a few examples. It is extremely difficult to re-establish the integrity of associative functioning during the sessions, for in such cases the analyst's mind is itself constantly solicited by what I shall call unstable movements towards greater closeness—that is to say, these relations cannot easily be grasped consciously. The analyst must himself function by overcoming his own phobia of thinking—that is, by being animated by retroactive reverberation and heralding anticipation in whatever ways they can be followed. In my experience, it is only on this condition that the patient can notice in himself the reflection of psychic functioning that follows the same process as I described when accounting for movements of thought in the session, and can overcome his blockages and inhibitions by recognizing the transformation of the psychic forces within him, replacing destruction with a freer circulation of his affects and representations.

This interpretative construction is only possible if each element, produced as a return of the repressed, preserves a capacity for resonating with others, the key to which resides in the meaning alone. In my opinion, there is no other outlet for the emergence of truth than that of the prior period of the separating out of elements that have been consciously experienced and of the search for possible cooptation with other isolated elements. Regrouping them allows their contradictory condensations to appear: the fury of separation, the danger of closeness, the fear that sexual projections onto the object will return to the subject, appearing in a form that is all the wilder since they are supposed to be even more barred in the object than in the ego. These are permanent attempts to disrupt continuity and to hinder the tendency of the flow of associations to build a more complete vision of the situation.

Metapsychological perspectives

How are we to understand metapsychologically what the central phobic position reveals in these patients? While working on my clinical description, I was re-reading, for a different reason, the "Wolf Man" (Freud, 1918b) and once again came across the well-known quotation on castration relating to what Lacan called *foreclosure* (1977b). "This really involved no judgement upon the question of its existence [castration] but it was the same as if it did not exist" (Freud, 1918b). This resonated with me just as Gabriel's words had: "I'm on the edge of a breakdown because my mother still hasn't come. I don't have that in me. It isn't me." And also: "My mother abandoned me; which mother? I don't have a mother any more. She's no longer there. She doesn't exist." These denials highlight the paradox of a sense of guilt calling for interminable reparation even though the subject puts himself in the position of a victim who has been sinned against more than he has sinned. The guilt is the consequence of the *primary murder*, the aim of which is to carry out an "*excorporation of the abandoning object*" (Green, 1997b). Autoerotic activities are an attempt to fend off the void left by this evacuation: addictive, alcoholic, bulimic, or based on compulsive seductions—anything will do to prove to others or to oneself that the object can still be substituted, and thus that it is destructible. This rarely deceives the superego, which knows that there has been a primary murder. Another paradox of this object, the trace of which is manifested by the hole of its presence, is that these patients "are completely empty-headed", as other authors (Khan, 1983) have already pointed out. So here we have the characteristic of this maternal object: it is only revealed in the void in which it leaves the subject and if, on the contrary, it happens to manifest its presence, its ghost occupies the whole space—it "drives one mad", so to speak. Corresponding to the primary murder of the object there is the idea, whenever it is resurrected, of a paternal power that has no choice but to give way, all the while deploring its inability to free the subject from this fascinating imprisonment.

What kind of judgement is involved here? "Negation" (Freud, 1925h) presents us with two kinds: the judgement of attribution, which determines the property a thing possesses, and the judgement of existence, which, faced with a representation, has to decide whether it refers to a thing that exists in reality (Green, 1997b). Neither of these is applicable in our case. It is not just a matter of attributing the thing with the quality of good or bad. The act of suppressing it testifies to how bad it must be, but, as I have pointed out, the unwavering attachment linking it to the subject inevitably suggests that it is considered as irreplaceable emotionally. What are we to think of its representation? It no doubt refers to an object that exists: the mother; but, on the other hand, this representation claims that she is dead—not only because there is a death wish but because her representation has been evacuated, declared nonexistent, put to death, as if the process of mourning had occurred instantaneously and immediately once and for all, when in fact there was none. The disappearance of the representation in the psyche is just as brutal retroactively as its non-perception in reality. This situation is due to the fact that the negative judgement of attribution does not aim, in this case, at repressing—which is yet another way of preserving—but at erasing, uprooting from the inner world. And, similarly, the negative judgement of existence is not confined to the relation with external reality but to a recourse to omnipotence that would like to disconnect itself from *psychic* reality. It is worth noting, from the point of view of this remarkable psychic reality, that when the patient is attracted by something to which he could aspire, he rarely seems to form a fantasy allowing one to get to know what his subjective position is. He does not so much fantasize as let the thing happen as if already realized—not in the sense of a realization of the subject, but of an emergence into reality that puts him in the position not of one who desires but of one who has already acted. In other words, this should call for a sanction, not for having desired something he should not have desired, but for finding himself in the position of one who has transgressed in actuality.

Here, the superego does not play the role Freud attributes to it, as the heir of the Oedipus complex; it promulgates a punishment that is the very one transgression signifies. Thus, his stubborn determination in being the mother's possessor who is punished by being sent to the psychiatric hospital accomplishes the separation, the segregation, the exile, but also involves the fact that, once among the mad, he will belong among those who have never accepted separation from their mother—a situation that madness would perpetuate. It is possible to speak of a denial of psychic reality to the extent that such patients can only conceive of their inner world as being shaped by the actions and reactions of others towards them, with any demand on their behalf for recognition simply leading to the unmasking, which is always perceived as a consequence of the way they have been treated, of a destructive rage or sexuality that is transgressive towards their primary objects, interpreted by others as a sign of madness necessarily resulting in their being set apart. What is paradoxical is that the task of the central phobic position is to prevent what might have been surmised about all this from appearing, and, at the same time, it reproduces this feared situation, the subject himself acting in a similar way towards his own psychic productions which could not find their way into his own awareness. We can say that he did them violence by considering that the connections that were forming in his mind had to be excluded, thus prohibiting them from being included in wider contexts necessary for thought activity. In this case denying means suppressing that which, through being perceived internally, violates the subject's existence: in order that he can continue to exist, it is necessary that the object, which is not there, be totally nonexistent, without worrying about the consequences of its loss. And if the threat to the subject returns, breaking through the barrier of defences, then the cathexis of the traces it has left behind must be withdrawn. The foreclosure, which will be followed by the denial of this part of the subjective psyche, will have survived in spite of everything, contesting that it is this wounded ego of the past that comes back to haunt the precarious ego of the present. It is thus constantly necessary to avoid the gaze of anyone who can notice in the subject's expression the traces of a mother who reduces him to impotence because she is no longer anything more than a phantom object or a source of excitation, without there being any desire to give her meaning.

In his article on "Negation" Freud writes: "thus originally, the mere existence of a presentation was a guarantee of the reality of what was presented" (1925h, p. 237). In the case we are concerned with it would be better to say: the non-existence of the representation, its suppression, is a guarantee of the non-reality of that which has been foreclosed, as if the object's non-representation sufficed to free oneself of the threat it represents. If necessary, it is the subject who will exclude himself in order to avoid the new murder suggested by the reappearance of the object that has been killed. In this way, he will at least have suppressed the pain that is in danger of returning, attached to the initial, original, basic, primordial cathexis. All that will be left is the mere semblance of a subject who will remain the victim of the object's deaths and resurrections.

To return for a moment to foreclosure: what Freud describes concerns the analytic session and what he says relates *not only to what occurred in childhood but to what re-emerges from it. I infer from this that foreclosure occurs when the experience returns permitting one to infer it after the event—that is, retrospectively.* Like the central phobic position, foreclosure belongs to the analytic process. It blocks the process of generating associations, which allows the development of psychic causality.

We too often entertain the idea that the importance of pregenital conflicts could lead us to regard the Oedipus complex as a negligible factor or as one of secondary importance. It is true to say that the Oedipus complex is not a centrally organizing factor for personality in this case, but it is equally true that it cannot be considered as negligible. For example, one can observe that *castration anxiety* is very present and that it cannot be reduced to the superficial form of a deeper conflict of which it is merely a false semblance. On the other hand, one cannot speak of a *castration complex*. We have seen, in the course of this paper, that the father can give rise to the fantasy of having, so to speak, sequestered the mother. And yet, the adult subject never accepts maternal attempts to keep the child away from his father. It is very clear that the latter incarnates prohibitions. His importance is recognized, and his efforts to facilitate individuation are the object of gratitude. The fact remains that the feelings of hostility belonging to the oedipal setting are experienced here less in terms of the child's rivalry with the father than in terms of the mother's desire to exclude him from the psychic world—an attempt that will be a source of painful regrets later on—so that the child is in a situation of consonance with the mother. Even when the subject is reconciled with the father, whom he cherishes dearly, the latter will not be able to help him get a better understanding of the relationship with the mother. As well as the oedipal father, guardian of the law and respectful of the ancestral line, there is another father who has the function, in the psyche itself, of recognizing the ruses of thought, the distortion of truth, the activity of displacements by relating them to himself. He is the source of a process of thinking, searching for its truth, that knows the relativity of prohibitions, their inconstant, variable and questionable character, making use of him to criticize and to contest them, but who makes himself the herald of their recognition as well as their fallibility. Such is the compensation for not having been able to inscribe himself in the infantile psyche with the incomparable power of participating in the construction of a mental universe by bringing into play all the forms of the deepest intimacy, that of bodies in dialogue.

When these patients are traversing critical moments, one is struck by the *simplicity of causal situations—disappointments, experiences of being abandoned, affective traumas, narcissistic wounds—and by the dissimulation deployed when faced with the contents and affects mobilized, even when these seem "natural", and, finally, by the extremely complicated nature of psychic processes and modalities of the work of the negative* (Green, 1999a). *The clearer it is, the more it has to be disguised, and the more it appears incomprehensible.*

In fact, these patients know that analysis is the only place where they can express their madness and experience it without fearing reprisals that are too serious. Beyond their denial, their energetic attempts to ignore what is concealed by this old material that periodically resurfaces, and beyond their struggles in the transference against recognizing the truth, where all means of defence are used— such as acts of forgetting, contradictions, blaming the analyst, repudiations, distorted reasoning, and so on—the transference remains positive because they are indebted to analysis for the fact that they have remained safe, if not sound, thanks to the experience. Freud reminded us that no one can escape himself.

Post scriptum

Additions have been made to this chapter since its first presentation, taking into account the evolution of the analysis of the patient. Before concluding, I would like to make a few last remarks.

The treatment of Gabriel has followed a course that shows that he has made steady progress. He was finally able to "meet" his mother and to rediscover her, not only as she was in his memory, but as he had always wanted to see her; and, moreover, he realized that she had in fact also been like that. I can now say that, with the help of the transference analysis, the maternal imago has really been internalized, without excessive idealization but with a full recognition of the positive aspects that she had transmitted to him (particularly in sublimation). The mourning process took place in an entirely normal way. Other signs that he is on the path to recovery have appeared. Gabriel has shown evidence of his capacity to confront and to overcome successfully situations from which he has hitherto recoiled. He has been able to tell me not only that he is happy with his successes but—something that seems to me to be even more important—that he now feels as if he is "almost" a free man. And who can be said to be totally free?

NOTES

Translated by Andrew Weller.

This paper was given at the Paris Psychoanalytic Society on January 7, 1998 and was published in the *Revue Française de Psychanalyse*, 3, 2000. The present translation corresponds to the original French text. A somewhat different version was published in the *International Journal of Psychoanalysis*, *81* (2000): 429.

1. Lacan has shown that, as far as psychoanalysis is concerned, the most important aspect of language, as poetry displays manifestly, is its metaphorical function, which addresses meaning obliquely and allusively.

3

Lavoisier's law applies to mental matter

Jean-Claude Rolland

It is Christmas Eve. The five-year-old boy whom the psychoanalytic tradition now knows as the "Wolf Man" is expecting his presents. On account of his current psychological constellation, no gift would be more valuable for him than one that would show his father's love. The child falls asleep and dreams: "Suddenly the window opens and, to my great terror, I see, on the big walnut tree in front of the window, several white wolves sitting. They were six or seven of them. . . . They had big tails, like foxes, and their ears pricked up like dogs when they pay attention to something. A prey to a great terror, obviously of being eaten by the wolves, I shouted. . . ." From this account, helped by the associations of the patient (who is now an adult) and following step by step the shifting movements, condensations, and inversions that led him to this manifest content, Freud pieces together what the dream of this celebration night must have been—the dream that was dreamed: the child, identifying with a woman (his mother), has pictured himself sexually penetrated by his father. The violent defence mechanisms arising in response to the irruption of this homosexual desire turn the acquired satisfaction into anxiety, the father, who was the single object of desire, into a horde of wolves, and the wish to be loved by him into a terror of being devoured (Freud, 1918b).

But how was this original dream constructed? Freud, in *The Interpretation of Dreams* (1900a), partially answers this question: the dream anticipates, by realizing it in a hallucination, the fulfilment of a sexual, infantile, and unconscious desire. A strong and loving attachment for his father dominated the sexual stage the child was living through at that time. But what this young child's ego—or, rather, the numerous psychological agents that contributed to the making of the dream—did not know then is exactly what form a sexual satisfaction coming from his father would take. It therefore had to be that, moved by this ignorance and this curiosity, the dream should explore the tracks able to inform it. That is how the memory was discovered of a scene the child had witnessed passively when he was 2 or 3 years old, as he was sleeping in his parents' bedroom on a summer afternoon: the scene of an intercourse between his parents in a position that clearly showed the different genitals of his father and mother. The dream makes nothing up, it just disguises, in its manifest content, the representation of the latent content, which comes exclusively from the earliest memories of childhood, the reality and the nature of which Freud attempts to establish and study in this extract "From the History of an Infantile Neurosis" (1918b). Of this "primal scene", each detail has settled, with devilish precision, in the outlying—deepest?—areas of the mind's apparatus, areas that it is difficult to call "mental" because they contain mere perceptual or sensory inscriptions that are not naturally accessible to thought itself. Let us consider them as places of memorial inscription, from which mental matter, under certain conditions (notably of dreaming), and in certain circumstances (carried by the force of infantile desire), a dream is born.

"We know", Freud says, "that towards their origin all the characters we use to build our distinctions tend to blur." He also adds, questioning the nature of unconscious fantasy: "It would look like the promise made by the three witches to Banquo: not necessarily sexual, not even sadistic, but the matter from which both must arise." The same confusion could characterize, in the deep strata of the mind, the nature of the material of memory: not mental yet, but the matter from which some psyche will be born. To understand this unusual fact, let us imagine the situation of ruins not yet excavated and belonging to unknown civilizations: mankind recognizes them but must wait until they are properly discovered for the representation of itself to be adjusted. Remembering is a complex operation that involves categories both of time and space. Freud had already had an insight of it in the *Interpretation of Dreams* (1900a): "*Träume sind Erinnerungen*", he said there, which can be translated as "dreams are remembrances"—granted that the English words "remembrance" and "remembering" do not do justice to the semantic complexity of the German word "*Erinnerung*". The latter means literally to put inside—that is, inside a system of interpretation that, in the case of archaeology, is the pre-existing cultural order and, in the case of the individual, is the mental system already organizing the tendencies and forces it contains.

That is why Freud, in the *Interpretation of Dreams*, explored methodically and accurately this remembering function of the dream; but in the text about the "Wolf Man" (1918b) he goes one step further: he assumes that, more than a simple condition of the dream's production, remembering is its basic activity: it is the effect of the mental system's curiosity, or epistemophilia. The dream thoughts filter slightly into the *terrae incognitae* of the mind's apparatus, into these normally inaccessible territories, unknown and hostile, and bring back pieces of information. These thoughts proceed like the antennae that Freud attributes to the living vesicle in *Beyond the Pleasure Principle* (1920g): "Immersed in this external world full of the most powerful energies, this undifferentiated piece of excitable substance asks for information about the direction and the nature of the external excitations, and with this purpose is pleased with a selection of little samples and the tasting of minimal quantities." Thus the dream thoughts, crossing the established borders of the psyche, capture what answers their needs in the perceptual sediments, and import them into the mental system in a form that is certainly not their original form but that uses necessarily the support of the final material . . . that transforms them. The system of the mind is wider than the mental system: the sites of memory where, for example, the memory of the primal scene is stored, are supported by material that is still unknown and unthinkable by us, material about which we can only speculate, and very roughly, about its perceptual origins, whereas the mental material of which the dream thoughts are the model is familiar to us because it is made of the same sort of stuff that we use to describe it: language.

If we follow the new interpretation Freud gives of dreams in the text of "Five Lectures on Psycho-Analysis" (1910a [1909], we are bound to notice that dream thoughts have a sensory insight, a perceptual accuracy, a penetration that waking thoughts do not have. have. Out of the sexual scene between his parents, whose trace is kept by the child in his unconscious memory, out of this factual and immediate datum, made of an irreducible and indivisible materiality, the dream captures something, builds a representation that is necessarily indirect, fills it with sexual significance, and transfers it to a topic that brings about new and very complex perceptions. That is why the child, during the progress of the dream, simultaneously takes part in the scenario by identifying sometimes with the father's sexual position, sometimes with the mother's, and at the same time acts as a watcher, observing *in effigie* the development of the scene, giving himself by this means a way to remember it and to build a narrative of it afterwards.

Facts here are difficult to describe, for this inner perception reached by the dream is inseparable from the movement of the driving force that accompanies the inner perception and probably determines it, and this explains why Freud introduced the analysis of this dream in the meticulous clinical analysis of the sexual difficulties encountered by the child in his development. The dream takes over a driving activity that has not managed yet to become a neurosis: it is a substitute for infantile sexual activity, a substitute that resolves the enigmas and fills the gaps faced by the little boy. If indeed the dream retains, among the mass of all the available memories, the information concerning the question of sexual difference, it is because of sexual curiosity, painfully frustrated, in which the child finds himself at that time; similarly, it is because of the passive homosexual desire that the memory of the mother "offering herself to the father" is privileged in this dream-scenario; and, finally, it is from the narcissistic ideal that the reality of castration is recognized as the price to be paid for this hallucinatory (imagined?) enjoyment.

Through the original perception—an external and passive perception—the child receives, under the effect of parental seduction, the germs of adult sexuality in the most primitive and outlying depths of the mind. The inner perception of memory produced by the dream proceeds differently: it chooses, in the deposit of infantile memories, the representations that fit the need of the driving force to find satisfaction and release, and on which the ego, *in fine*, depends to maintain its homeostasis. The inner perception that the dream realizes with so much subtlety, unlike ordinary perceptions that just register new data, is an active operation with two sides: it extracts some memories from the store of infantile memories and then immediately articulates them into partial driving forces.

This operation is complex and concerns the foundations of mental functioning, for the representation that results from it is jointly and necessarily the representative of the driving force *and* of the object so that its representation is retained by memory. Repression acts precisely, but afterwards, with this original double function, it separates the driving force from the object, submitting the former to a slow mental working-through and constraining the latter, the object, to move towards false substitutes. The inner perception of memory realized by the dream when afterwards it captures the real event and links it to the driving force, creates the conditions of repression. These two mental operations, the movements of which are opposed—one links, the other separates—both contribute, though indirectly, to psychological progress: repression desexualizes what the first operation has sexualized. The latter, indeed, sets up a junction between two immediate realities that would never enter spontaneously into negotiation: the external reality, where the future subject's destiny takes root—his singular history, his own environment with its excess or lack of care, excitation or seduction—and the reality, in fact so mysterious but nevertheless so heavy, of the driving force. From this conjunction, the new reality of the fantasy arises, which is no longer an absolute reality, but is reality anyway—the time, for instance, of the dream, whose words, if we keep the polysemy inscribed in its popular meaning, expresses accurately the flimsiness and fleetingness of the experience, the reality of the conviction it leads us to and the power of the incarnations it reveals to us.

* * *

The inner perception of memory and the concomitant linking of memory fragments with partial driving forces transfer these two elemental and immediate realities into a new area of the mind's apparatus: the mental scene. Thus, they deprive the driving forces of their savagery, their tendency to blind repetition, their flesh, introducing them to the new order of representation, negation, and signification. The passive sexual desire for his father, which moves the child without his knowing, finds in the representation of his mother undergoing intercourse the matter of a feminine identification. But

if, on the scene itself of the dream hallucination, the child adopts
such a sexual identity in an intense way—which will persist in the
latent homosexuality in the adult he will be—the observing ego that
watches the hallucination contributes essentially to the making of a
scene, a *Schauplatz* [a place we look *at* and a place where we look
from]. From this process a censorship will develop, which carries
within itself the rudiments of criticism and judgement. This censorship is a perception of perception: the little boy's ego pictures the
boy actively in a passive identification with the other sex. Besides, it is
because of this censorship that the dream will turn into a nightmare
and come to an end. The discrepancy between the act of identification and the representation of the identification is analogous to the
discrepancy between the driving force's reality and its attaching itself
to the mental scene, analogous also to the discrepancy between the
historical determination of the individual's destiny and its subjective
development. This discrepancy, which creates the space of fantasy,
is a shifting movement.

   Mental reality gathers together, by shifting them, all the realities
that originally confront the human subject. That is why the designation of "mental scene" is so meaningful, provided that its restrictive
aspect is not overlooked, for shifting is not enough to constitute a
scene. An economic change must be added, which the dream also
accomplishes when, regaining a certain fragment of memory and
articulating it to a certain driving movement, it brings about a new
destiny for the driving force. It *is* indeed in this link to an object that
the driving force is sexualized, but it is also because this object is no
longer a contemporary object but an anachronistic one, an object
of memory, that the driving force is psychosexualized: the object is
then regained, afterwards, by the lifting of the infantile amnesia, in
the depths of the mind that escape the ego's jurisdiction—an object
regained, although also lost. All the difference between sexuality
and psychosexuality lies in this threefold transformation—temporal,
spatial, and "mourning-like"—that the workings of remembering in-
flict on the object and on the driving force: an object discovered as
lost, regained as a mental representation, invested by an affection
reduced from then on to an emotion. Through this threefold transformation, memory produces a scene. Psychosexuality, this energy
that belongs to the mental apparatus, is born from a disembodiment
of the driving demand that springs constantly and in successive waves
from the depths of the mind's apparatus.

Some psychotic states indicate this process *a contrario*. Among the many determinants leading towards the outbreak of psychosis, one of the most frequent and easily perceptible—for those who have access to an analytic or psychotherapeutic cure—is the inhibition of the essential functions provided by the dream process: the remembering and the driving link, the construction of the ego and of relating to objects and the institution of the mental scene are lacking in psychotic mental functioning. This failure of the dream process limits at the same time the range of the psychoanalytic process. This calls for two comments. The ability to dream is the first condition for analysis to be possible: *a prerequisite for the analysis of the psychotic patient consists of restoring a dream scene through a "listening activity" which leads the analyst to take part more actively than usual in the transferential hallucination. Such a listening activity, taking over the patient's ego when it fails and providing the absent function which observes and tolerates the development of the hallucinatory scenario, is likely to turn the hallucination into a scene.* If he cannot dream, and faced as he is with a driving force that remains changeless and an object without representation, the psychotic patient's only resort to protect himself against homosexual irruption is "negativism"—a negativism the verbal translation of which would be, "No, I am not a woman." The case is very different for "our" little boy, faced with the same homosexual drive. Thanks to a dream that can be considered partly as failure, partly as success, he concludes, through his growing anxiety, with an operation of negation whose translation would be: "I don't want to recognize myself in my desire to be like my mother." The manifest content of the dream ("not being eaten by the wolves") denies its latent content ("being loved by the father"). The syntactic complexity of this formula allows us to anticipate the part that is played in the process of symbolization by a certain activity of discourse concerning the semantic material itself and its grammatical articulations—comparisons, negations, conjunctions, affirmations—which affect the word's flesh with the same transubstantiating effect as that of a representation on the reality of the memory and of the driving force.

* * *

The reader will understand that by explaining this extract from the "History of an Infantile Neurosis" (Freud, 1918b), I want to draw attention to the renewal of the dream theory proposed rather than explicitly expounded by Freud. The progress he describes concerning the mental functions provided by the dream is implicit, it has to be discovered, to be read between the lines, for Freud's purpose concerns first the study of infantile neurosis, and only secondarily the study of the psychoanalytic process through which the infantile neurosis has been reconstituted. But although the new theory of dreams is implicit, it is not incidental: in Freud's latent thoughts in this work, there may already be the idea of an analogy between the mental dynamics of the dream and the dynamics of the psychoanalytic cure. From this point of view it can be said that this text is situated midway between *The Interpretation of Dreams* (1900a)—where the two immediate functions of fulfilment of desire and guardian of sleep have been firmly established—and *Beyond the Pleasure Principle* (1920g), where going back to the unresolved enigma of traumatic dreams, Freud really discovers the function of the dream in the transformation of the driving force and in the excess of stimulation of the mental apparatus in an economy directed by the pleasure's principle.

This infantile dream, which psychoanalysis brought back to consciousness through a lifting of infantile amnesia, has itself regained (and internalized, in the nascent matter of the infantile neurosis) a block of reality powerful enough to determine the compulsive behaviour of the young man this child became—especially his sexual behaviour. The psychoanalytic work, taking over the dream work, perfected its exhumation. About this dream, Freud speaks precisely of a process [*Vorgang*] realizing a progress [*Fortschritt*]: under its influence the child will give up a disturbed state, dominated by the attacks, fits of fury notably, to enter the infantile neurosis and its required consequence: anxiety. The reason Freud talks about a "process" is perfectly clear: in addition to this "memory link", which, we have seen, the dream produces, the dream experience operates a reversal of the driving forces, and this reversal leads the child to identify actively with a passive and feminine position, and to constitute actively his father as an internal object. The dream proceeds both to the constitution of the ego and to the institution of an object relation that produces an elementary mental structure in which the mental apparatus is only an indefinite extension. At the end of its fulfilment the dream leaves this mental structure in the mind. Other dreams will adopt this structure and complete it, and later the transferential experience of psychoanalysis will operate in the same way.

The inner perception of memory, the linking up of the remembered matter to the driving force, will lead to symbolization, to the constitution of the ego and of an internal object. To these different steps of the dream process should be added the building of a new perceptual surface: the one that allows the sleeper to separate from the dreamer, or the spectator from the actor of the dream. In this way a discrepancy develops between the perception of the dream and the representation in the dream, and this discrepancy calls for a narrative. A question arises immediately: what material does the dream use to achieve this task, which leads indeed to the constitution, from the rough materials of the external reality and the driving force, of a mental scene. But the construction of a mental scene does seem at first sight to require many specific mechanisms and materials, because it involves many mental activities: remembering, inner perception of memory, libidinal thinking and representation, constitution of subjective and objective stances, endopsychological perception.

***

What Freud calls the *working through* of the dream is familiar to us: it turns the latent content—the hallucination to which the *dream process* has lead—into the manifest content, then into a narrative. Let us try now, *a contrario*, to piece together what this dream process must have been like for the child, helped by the associations that the adult provided in his psychoanalysis for its evocation. These associations—and the narrative of this analysis is without ambiguity on this subject—only use the semantic material available to the child before he fell asleep; Freud describes meticulously its constituents—for, far from being ordered in a single homogeneous and coherent discourse, it is made up of several discourses, with different origins, which do not hold the same semantic status in the field of language and which contain different affective connotations. Freud distinguishes them with care: there are the discourses that the child heard from the mouths of grandfather, sister, nurse, housekeeper, which are generally strictly connected to a sexual content; there are those he read in a book of tales and which are articulated to categories of anxiety and terror; and, finally, there are the discourses linked by the child himself to some moving or puzzling circumstances, like the visits with his father to flocks of dying sheep, or like the moment when he was surprised to hear his mother complain, during her conversation with her doctor: " I cannot live like that any more!"—discourses that obviously referred to his oedipal objects.

Whether they are passively received from the world and its objects or actively built and stated in preconscious thought, these discourses constitute the matter from which the dream found a way to represent its latent thoughts. Before proving this assertion, let us take for granted that neither the driving force nor the memory traces have their own representations—the driving force because it is only a pressure, a force demanding a work, without content or container; the memory traces because they are excitations of the mind's texture, a "crossing". It appears, indeed, that it is only through contact between the appropriate representations and the driving force and memory traces that the selection of representations will occur. But because of its outlying position in the threshold of memory, the memory traces cannot have any representative autonomy: they are basically only pre-forms, organizers of representations. Thus, if the same verbal material has helped in the making of the dream process and then comes back in the associative working through, we only have to compare the state of this material in the manifest content of the dream with its state in the content of the associations to discover which specific signifiers have "covered" the hallucination and proceeded to its representation. Three signifiers, essentially, are common to these two steps of the dream experience: the "white" of the sheep and goats, which evokes the parents' nakedness, the "tail" of the foxes, recalling the father's penis and the missing and terrifying mother's sex organs, the "climbing upon" of the wolves, representing their coitus. Shifted to the outskirts of Memory and Psyche, these signifiers taken from the preconscious semantic field must have shown themselves to be the most suitable to link the driving force and to represent the constituents—especially exciting or traumatic—of the memories.

The activity of psychoanalytic listening attributes to some words a signifying value because of the fact that words conserve, through their presence in the manifest associative discourse, the marks of their participation in the dream or the transference experience—excessively glittering or, conversely, reserved, notably detached or delayed in their enunciation, loaded with strangeness, tending to double themselves through various analogies. All these aspects subtly modify their significance, their colour, and their sound. These transformations of discourse "indicate the change that the ego had

to undergo because of its participation in the hallucinatory experience—a change that is an integral part of the psychoanalytic process
as well as the dream process. Just as negation is "an intellectual substitute of repression, its marking sign", the fact that a common word
becomes a signifier is the proof that it is now loaded with an infantile
representation, which marks it as a "certificate of origin comparable
to the sign 'made in Germany'."

We can see language becoming significant in the following way:
after the mental regression generated by sleep has removed some
words from their ordinary context and has isolated them, they will
be invested, thanks to the hallucination, both with some fragment of
real memory, because the memory finds there a way to be reflected,
and, similarly, words will be invested with some partial driving force,
because the driving force can seize the word as its own object. The
process of words becoming significant remains fundamentally arbitrary: it depends entirely on the encounter, prepared by the process
deep inside the mind's apparatus, between the material from the
individual's history and of the driving force. The material form, now
much more evanescent, expresses itself in the language in which
the individual defines his subjectivity. There are no structural or
universal signifiers, as Lacan used to believe: there are only singular
signifiers, transient, opportunist, and ephemeral, between Mind and
Psyche, which give language a power of infinite significance and create the surprise and wonder of speech.

The dream process—like its analogue, the analytic process—
therefore expresses the constitution of a word representation from a
thing representation. In this operation nothing is really lost from the
present forces: the driving force, the object, the context of memory
are all preserved, albeit gathered into a new unity of fantasy. However, everything changes: the object, replaced by the signifier, gives
up its material and incestuous reality; the driving force, being transferred from the oedipal object to its representations, is inhibited in
its tendency to fulfilment for the benefit of a delayed economy of
investment; the original memory, released from the compulsion to
repeat, is satisfied from now on by the evocation, remote as it is, as
long as no rupture disturbs the continuity between the signified and
the signifier.

A single condition, which excludes the arbitrary, is however required of the word for it to become significant: its root must be wide
enough to extend its polysemy, its multiple meanings. The birth of

the signifier proceeds from a transformation of the sound, of the word, of its power to reverberate in images; these plastic qualities of language, born of the sensorial kinship between visual and the acoustic experiences, are present in the signifier's structure and are brought back to the level of the regression inflicted by the dream. It is because of this physical materiality of words that the reality of the parents' desire and seduction is transferred to the mental scene. Without appropriate perceptive tools, this material expression escapes us; so that we refuse to consider language as what it is: a piece of nature. It must be granted anyway: fantasy, as soon as it is constituted, is supported by a discourse. This discourse is, at this step, reduced to a juxtaposition of isolated words; no syntax is here to temper the fever of the driving force and crudeness of the representation by introducing the negative obstacle, the comparative discrepancy or the affirmative resistance. But it is already a discourse because, thanks to the dream work that will convert this latent content into manifest content, and then thanks as well to the working through that will transform this elemental fantasy into a communicable fiction, and then finally to the narrative of the dream, this semantic magma [doughy mass] will find a place in common language. . . and will transform it. We can see here the first form, the concrete matrix of the "inner discourse" that, at the interface between ego and of unconscious, provides a homeostatic function of rejection or of integration and, in the preconscious, regulates the narcissistic and the object-related economy.

This inner discourse, which replaces the driving force's demand and the remembered object (released from its permanence and its force of attraction while becoming a representation of the concept), must be identified as the support of what Freud called the "dream process." Although this hypothesis is not easy to accept, this is not a reason to give it up. It is not easy to accept it because of the obviousness of mental realism, which the dream, more than any other mental formation, persuades us of very strongly. At the time of its production, the dream appears to the ego as the real fulfilment of desire; therefore, it restores the traumatic reality of the memory that the unconscious formation has imposed on the ego. Then the realism of this dream disintegrates under the effect of the narrative and associative discourses. It is through the activity of speech that the tension created by the process fades and the dream can appear to the ego, afterwards, as a fiction. Actually the driving force's demand, like the reality of the memory, has shifted to the weight of the words, with their evocative power. Language does not only represent fantasy: its nature consists in replacing it totally. But for some reasons that remain unknown to us, the human mind hardly considers language as its specific reality, its proper place where all the forces that structure the mind converge. An ultimate question arises: how can we represent to ourselves the economical transformation provided by discourse, and, more specifically, the transformation accomplished by the inner discourse, thanks to the regression performed by the dream?

* * *

Actually, this discourse, which is the core of the dream process, already contains a negation: at this stage it does not yet wear the syntactic form by which the patient anticipates the analyst's interpretation, saying, for example, after the narrative of a dream: "My mother? No, that's not her!" Symbolical expression belongs to the most organized layer of the linguistic apparatus; it is not present yet in the language of the narrative, it appears only in the outer and delayed language of the associations that still take part in the dream process. Therefore negation, at this first step of the inner discourse, is not yet signified: signification is a late step in the process of discourse. But it pre-exists actively, involved in the naming activity to which the words coming from the preconscious proceed. Once removed to the place of memory, words increase their polysemy to represent the fragments, without their proper identity, without the vestiges of the memory and of the driving force. When the little dreamer calls "climbing upon" the act of the parental coitus, whose memory haunts his mind, by this naming he erases the intrusive status of the memory trace and neutralizes its excitation. He cuts himself off from it. Naming and designation are elemental activities of discourse that deprive the unconscious formation of its substance, while conferring on language its extent and its depth: the expression "to climb upon" in the child's vocabulary will be enriched after this dream with a new sexual meaning. This means that dreams are one of the places where the polysemy of personal idioms is constructed.

This surplus of reality that the inner discourse gives to language is only an abstract of the reality of memory and of the driving force. Lavoisier's law, based upon the Newtonian principle of economy, describes mental as well as natural reality: "Nothing is created, neither in the operation of art, nor in the operation of nature, and it is possible to give as a principle that, in any operation, there is an equal quantity of matter before and after the operation; that principles of quality and quantity are the same, and that there are only changes, only modifications." The inner discourse activated by the dream process proceeds to a shifting of energy that "loads" the semantic structure and "unloads" the unconscious experience. With this precise economical perspective, we must isolate in the working of negation a first step that precedes and conditions the advent of a syntactic negation of which the symbol of "No" is the paradigm: this *"Vorarbeit"* is provided by the semantic game of naming and designation that converts the memory representation and the driving force into an extension of the signifying structure of language.

Negation itself comes, afterwards, to stabilize this structure, in the same way as Gothic architecture, raising more and more audacious diagonals, had to add to its cathedrals ever more sophisticated flying buttresses to re-enforce their structure. Freud repeats it firmly: everything that concerns the syntactic articulation in the apparatus of language, as in this symbol of negation, must be dissociated from the semantic material it confirms, supports, reinforces, or lightens, always with the identical purpose, which is to provide the word with the essential mental task it has to assume: to deny the reality it evokes.

The complexity of this work of negation, its harshness, its difficulty, are proportional to the force of attraction operated by the oedipal objects, first of all the mother. She is the primary object of all the driving forces, as illustrated, following the prototype of the tragedy of *Oedipus the King* in the "History of an Infantile Neurosis". She is also the ultimate object of all renunciations, as Freud implies it, when he considers the mother's imago as that which we must, inexorably, deny.

4

Mental void and the borderline patient

Jaime M. Lutenberg

It is the intention of this chapter to expound the relationship between mental void and borderline personalities. This was the core of the paper and clinical material I submitted to our work group for discussion.

The main axis of such discussion ran through the clinical level, taking into account transference, countertransference, and framing aspects. It allowed us to theoretically specify our clinical and technical agreements and disagreements. It also helped us to see more precisely how psychoanalysis was considered and how borderline patients were treated in each of our different regions of the world.

In this chapter I am proposing a new view of the ideas contained in the paper I shared with my research group partners entitled "Mental Void and Psychic Reality".

Given the limited space available, I have decided not to include here the pertinent clinical material and restrict my exposition to the theoretical level. I expect that the contents I include in the psychopathological and clinical levels will help the readers approach their own personal experience.

I must point out in advance that we should, in principle, differentiate the feeling of void that may be directly reported by the analysands from the concept of the theoretical "structural mental void". The feeling of void is an empirical reference that may or may not be linked to the structural mental void. Structural mental void may be temporarily defined, from a metapsychological viewpoint, as the hiatus occurring in the psyche between the symbiotic background and the individual's narcissistic structure. In the present communication I will summarize the technical prospects stemming from this problem. The study of the mental void opened up before me the prospect of achieving edition through the psychoanalytic process.[1]

Let us turn to the privacy of the transferential link, where the psychoanalytic truth is conceived at all levels (Lutenberg, 1998). For Freud, the interruption of the associative flow has been an empirical indicator of the resistance put up by the analysand to the work agreed on in the analytic contract. His technical conceptualization defined resistance, and in the field of theory it fixed the limits of repression. Thus, associative silence, resistance, and repression became a classical triad that was explored quite fruitfully by Freud and his followers.

According to my personal experience, when patients consulting nowadays remain silent during the session, they are simultaneously showing two different phenomena: sometimes silence derives directly from effective repression, but at other times it is directly caused by or derived from the underlying mental void. There is nothing but mental void underneath their associative silence.

The clinical difference between one silence and another is of great significance, since they lead to quite different technical approaches. When the absent word is a direct inference of repression, the technical approach is one derived from the analysis of resistances and the contents of their conscious and unconscious fantasies. When silence is the expression of mental void, the technical approach focuses on transferential edition (Lutenberg, 1993).

Usually, the "structural mental void" appears as a basic primary configuration that is secondarily compensated for by other psychopathological structures. Borderline conditions, clinically stabilized as "borderline structures", as described by Otto Kernberg (Kernberg, 1975, Chapter 1), are among them. Secondary psychopathological structures simultaneously neutralize and conceal them. Mental void is a "non-structure" of virtual existence.

In order to clinically recognize the mental void, it is imperative to previously accept the hypothesis that the ego can be split into several portions and that each of said portions may function in an autonomous manner, disconnected from the others. One of the split portions lodges the mental void; its existence is virtual due to the fact that it is neutralized and compensated for by the symbiotic bonds that give rise to the "secondary symbiosis" (Bleger, 1967b).

Each separate ego portion lodges a mental conception of the inner world and the outer world that is incompatible with the others. In fact, *the structural mental void is unthinkable if not conceived as corresponding to a portion of the split ego.*

Symbiotic bonds constitute the most usual form of a balanced compensation of mental void, and it is in this web, at the core of the symbiotic bond itself, where the virtual structure I am describing is lodged. Only when a subject undergoes the threat of parting—either physically or mentally—from those objects or institutions with which his/her ego was previously united (symbiosis), does the feeling of nameless terror that expresses the existence of the void become evident or "positive" (Bion, 1967d).

In the human being, perinatal linking symbiosis is the matrix at the basis of psychosexual development, which leads, in turn, to the differentiated structuring of the psyche. For the newborn, said link constitutes an undifferentiated totality from which the infant's mind starts to distinguish itself. Such symbiosis is normal in the newborn (Mahler, 1967). As the human being develops, his/her autonomy increases.

More particularized studies on the problems of symbiosis and defensive autism, such as those performed by Bleger (1967b) in Argentina and a number of European and American authors—Margaret Mahler (1958, 1967, 1984), Bion (1957, 1959, 1965, 1967d), Green (1983, 1996, 1999b), Meltzer (1975a, 1975b), Searles (1965), and Tustin (1968, 1981, 1990), among others—contributed new theoretical aspects to the original psychoanalytic postulates. This expanded the frontiers of present knowledge.

The clinical and psychopathological definitions I am expounding here are based on my agreement with the theory of original symbiosis, which I understand to be the basis of the whole subsequent individual development, which may be considered a differentiated outcome of said symbiosis. May I point out that in my opinion the original engram of said primary—symbiotic—aspect of evolution is never lost. The human being always keeps a symbiotic anchorage, not with its parental figures, but with its sociocultural environment.

When there exists a firmly differentiated psychic structure, said symbiotic link with the outer world nourishes inspiration at its foundations. The strong sociohistorical turbulences thus open new creative paths, by means of the interplay between the individual "needs" and the changing "needs" of the social environment.

From the psychodynamic viewpoint, mental void is the hiatus occurring in the psyche between the symbiotic background and the human being's narcissistic structure. I am using the word "narcissism" in a very particular way, not according to the theory that conceives it as a psychopathological alteration but as the unique destination of libido, as its first station, as expressed by Freud (1914c). That is to say, I am referring to "normal" or "trophic" narcissism.

It may be inferred from the foregoing that I postulate that a potential void normally occurs around every structural developmental leap of the psyche. This peculiar "void" is generated when we traverse the way extending from symbiosis to discrimination. In Freudian terms, it corresponds to the developmental transformation of a portion of the "id" into an "unconscious ego" or superego.[2] I understand mental void as being born as a "real image" every time the individual tries to distinguish himself from his symbiotic link with the surrounding world; the initial process is aborted due to the sudden irruption of the unbearable de-structuring experience (terror). The borderline structure belongs to a new defensive equilibrium that prevents the appearance of underlying terror.

From this secondary fight against the feeling of terror there also arise new "traumatic fixations" that fit in the polymorphous nature of this secondary mental void defence. This is the reason why we can find quite a large number of complementary features between the mental void and borderline, neurotic, and/or psychotic structures. The mental void may arise as a "normal feeling" during the sublimation processes.

At the moment immediately preceding a creator's synthesis, when he has already broken inside him every link with his prior thinking as well as with his inner "intellectual parents", a feeling of void informs him that he has been—temporarily—"orphaned" of the semantic support arising from his preceding overall link with knowledge. At any time in the development of a personality, different alternatives in the container (mind)–contents (psychic change) relationship may occur.

Definition of mental void

Void comes from the Latin term *"vacivus"*, an adjective that literally means *"devoid of contents"*. It acquires different meanings depending on the area of application. As a personal quality it means—according to the dictionary—"vain", "wasted", "a fruitless personality". It is also used in colloquial language to designate something that is unoccupied. Another meaning of void is *"the concavity or hollowness"* of certain things or objects.

Although I naturally resorted to the dictionary for defining the word "void", it is not so simple to use a single text for defining what we call "mental" in psychoanalysis—particularly if we seek to differentiate this concept from the term "psychic".

It was Winnicott, in an article written in 1949, entitled "The Mind and Its Relationship with the Psyche Soma", who showed most clearly the differences existing between the psychic and mental levels. In addition to defining each conceptual level, he established a developmental continuity of all three along his whole work (Winnicott, 1958, 1963, 1965, 1971a).

The mind concept has a virtual existence. From the epistemological point of view, when we assign it the "virtual" condition, we are comparing it—as a nosological entity—with the qualities of brain tissue, which is "real" from a positivistic perspective.

For Winnicott (1949), *"the mind is then nothing but a special case of psyche soma operation"*; for him the word "psyche" refers to the *"imaginative elaboration of the somatic parts, feelings and functions, that is, to the fact of being physically alive"*.

As regards the psychic apparatus in general and the "psychic" level in the strict sense, practically every psychoanalyst agrees on the definitions given by Freud in that respect. Such concepts are contained in the articles selectively written while elaborating his first and second psychic apparatus topic theories (Freud, 1915e, 1920g, 1923b, 1940a [1938], 1940e [1938]).

If we accept the existence of a psychic structure consisting of an "id", an "ego", and a "superego", as postulated by Freud (1923) in his topological theory, and that the ego can be split into several parts, as postulated by Freud (1927e), and evidenced by the clinical practice itself, we can assume that the mental phenomena derived from the splitting of the ego are of a highly complex nature and different from those occurring in neurotic conditions, which result from the pathological effects of repression.

Having explained my conceptual reference to the terms "void" and "mental", I will define my conception of "mental void". It should be pointed out that, based on my clinical experience on the one hand and on various psychoanalytic theories on the other, I separate my definition of mental void into two different concepts: "emotional mental void" and "structural mental void".

This conceptual differentiation is justified by the fact that they possess different clinical evidence, psychopathological references, and theoretical interpretations. It is convenient to take into account that such discrimination gives rise to different therapeutic approaches as well.

1. *Emotional mental void* (feeling of void):

This corresponds to a feeling of inner hollowness, of having nothing inside. The lack is experienced at the emotional level. This feeling emerges in the present but involves the past (historic memory) and the future (hope, the project). It must be distinguished from depression.

Many a time it is the only mental evidence that tells us about the analysand breaking off from his/her prior manner of conceiving the world, reality, science, and art. Every creative act implies breaking away from the inner and outer "establishment" (Bion, 1970).

2. *Structural mental void:*

If the mind is defined, as seen above, by the products originating in it, does the reference to an empty mind imply that we are talking about a "non-mind"? In that case, it could be said that there exists no "empty mind". If we take into account the splitting of the ego, the mental void notion tries to recognize and typify what happens with a portion of the mind split off from its overall structure.

The structural mental void corresponds to what happens in just one portion split off from totality of the mind. Inside such a portion a delay has taken place in the id differentiation process towards the construction of the ego and the superego. It is, according to Freud's theory, a deep psychic disturbance of the process of generating representations and identifications inside such a split portion that involves the ego and the superego.

Due to such a peculiar phenomenon, in this split portion the id can only achieve the fulfilment of its drives through symbiotic bonds that express it. The empty portion leads a life conditioned to the personality of another individual—the individual with whom the subject is fused. The subject does not register this otherness because of the ego splitting.

To understand this peculiar phenomenon more specifically, we must go back to the human being's perinatal period. The newborn experiences a total fusion with its surrounding environment. Such fusion is achieved through the mother with whom the baby is symbiotically united from its birth (Mahler, 1958, 1984). The binding symbiosis allows the mother's mind to perform the specific functions—for the newborn's psychic apparatus and mental development—that her body performed for its somatic (and psychic) development during the baby's intrauterine life.

There emerges, from this original fusion, a psychic apparatus that will always keep a portion fused with the universe (oceanic experience: Freud 1930a [1929]). Generally speaking, for Freud the "id" is a psychic instance that lodges all drives. It opens towards the outer world through the unconscious ego. But the concept of the "oceanic experience" indicates that the id is an open psychic instance, fused with the infinite universe: we always keep a portion of the id available for differentiation.

In his unfinished work entitled "An Outline of Psychoanalysis" (Freud, 1940a [1938], chapter VIII), Freud speaks about quite precocious ego splits, generated as a defence from far more primal anxieties than that of castration. This new hypothesis redefines the one stated by him in 1927 with respect to fetishism (1927e). This precocious splitting of the ego leaves an indelible mark in the adult mind for it conditions its lability to frustration. The latter sets off in these individuals a tendency to the appearance of terror or automatic anxiety instead of signal anxiety.

We can then assume that, during the life of an individual, a series of psychic traumas may occur in which the experiencing of inconceivable terror—nameless terror, according to Bion—characterizes different moments of his/her existence. Each subsequent developmental stage will give the terror experience a peculiar morphology that will accompany that of the corresponding anxiety.

When, due to the analytic work, this latent void condition becomes evident during the session, we must necessarily foresee the fact that, at the end of the session, the patient may not be in a fit psychic condition to leave the clinic and wander in the streets alone. Some patients, who are more acutely warned by their own unconscious, manage to balance such vulnerability by going to a bar near the clinic after the session.

Others systematically avoid regression during the session. If we pay attention to this diagnosis, we will be able to differentiate such resistance events from "neurotic resistance"; doing so is of crucial importance, since often the analysand's future life may depend on it.

When there is no discrimination, in the analytic link, between the risk born from castration anxiety and that generated by terror, the release of destructive impulsive aspects that maintain a dynamic balance with the rest of the personality is facilitated. When we summon the unconscious phantoms linked with castration fantasies, its conscious expression is particularly risky if, due to various obstacles, borderline patient sessions are held once or twice a week.

This is particularly evident when, instead of respecting their (secondary) neurotic defences, they are invited to "remove them", as if such personalities were merely perturbed by a structural neurosis (called characteropathy) instead of being affected by a compensation of the underlying mental void. If we are emotionally connected with the analysand, it is always possible to detect (through the analysis of the transference and countertransference dynamics) this lability, which facilitates the immediate passage from signal anxiety to terror.

The phenomenon that led me to study structural mental void was the clinical proof that, underneath the silence of some analysands, there was just that: psychic silence, void. It helped me to continue to perform clinical work with deeply perturbed patients and those whose perilousness could contraindicate not only a psychoanalytic but also a psychotherapeutic approach to said nuclei with classical psychoanalytic approach techniques typical of "neuroses".

Symbiotic links with persons and institutions are the outstanding characteristic of such patients. Any break occurring in their links causes the appearance of an experience of terror, which is often imperceptible for it is automatically cancelled by a wide range of secondary defences.

The articulation of the theories expressed by Freud, Bion, Bleger, Mahler, and Winnicott allows us to draw up a theoretical hypothesis as regards the specific traumatic situation concerning the origin of structural mental void. I summarize this below.

There exist potential developmental psychic transformations that are "aborted" in the course of the infant's life due to the fact that during the first few months of its life the child has experienced severe failures generated in the environment supplied by its parental figures (*holding*, according to Winnicott; *maternal reverie*, according to Bion). Under such circumstances, the baby is unable to transform (Bion, 1965) what it perceives into suitable elements for "thinking thoughts" (alpha elements). Due to such peculiar traumatic processes, these persons lack psychic memories of said events.

We can therefore say that structural mental void pertains to a split portion of the ego that has not undergone the structuring evolution of the psychic apparatus. It relates to the rest of the ego often being equivalent to the concomitant defensive structures that were generated at the time of the psychic disarticulation.

Once the ego is split into different structural modalities, the interplay of forces structuring and de-structuring the psychic apparatus starts. This overall movement gradually crystallizes into defences that determine the final aspect of the psychopathological condition.

In our circle, David Liberman (1970–72) has elaborated an original theory that permits a reading of the double psychopathological structure, based on the patient's discourse. Once the relationship between the analysand's verbalization style and the underlying psychodynamic structure was defined, he recognized a "predominant style" and "stylistic sub-components" in the discourse of any analysand. His view helped me to better understand the dynamic relation between an analysand's edited and unedited material—that is, between the structural void and the different structured portions of the psyche that determine the configuration of each individual personality.

The application of this concept to the psychoanalytic praxis does not override prior ones. At times, the analysis faces the task of turning the unconscious into conscious, but there are other times when it is necessary to condition the total link to edition: that is, to the birth—from the void—of an aspect of the personality that has remained split off from the rest.

Mental void: clinical and theoretical background

The interruption of a neurotic patient's associative flow within the psychoanalytic process led Freud to theoretically conceptualize resistance. As I have proved through my clinical practice, the associative silence of an analysand cannot always be exclusively accounted for by the alleged operation of resistance and repression. This happens particularly when we are working with borderline patients who carry a narcissistic pathology without suffering evident clinical psychosis. I have managed to approach these patients in a different—and more operative—way by assuming that their silence in the session could also arise from the mental void they suffered and, consequently, not exclusively as an expression of their resistance to a favourable evolution of their analysis. This has introduced a change in the technical management of these seriously ill patients during their treatment.

From the structural viewpoint, we usually refer to a psychopathological pattern by describing it as predominantly phobic, hysterical, obsessive, psychopathic, or psychotic. But when mental void is to be typified, it is impossible to conceive of it as a single "structural" existence without taking into account the compensating "sub"structures that go with it. During the course of a borderline patient's analytic regression, they can get in touch with the portion bearing the structural mental void.

For Freud (1920g), repetition beyond the pleasure principle came to typify and define a particular kind of turbulent clinical experience; I am referring to the negative transference and the negative therapeutic reaction. My personal interpretation of Freud's theoretical–clinical conceptualization gave rise to the curiosity that led me to observe the clinical phenomena typical of mental void. Under different transferential circumstances, the patient wasn't concealing anything under the absent word. This was the way in which the "psychic holes" occurred within the analytic relationship.

I also found in the absences of some very labile analysands a number of details that turned out to be very important for my investigation. I was surprised to realize that when I told such patients after their absence that they had missed the session, they showed great surprise, for they had not registered their absence. This also surprised me.

It is quite different to consider that a patient did not psychically register his/her own absence than to infer that he/she "forgot" to come. Such absences and silences not registered by their protagonists only occurred in one particular type of patient, and not in any other. By witnessing these clinical events, I was inclined to think that, rather than being a known resistance phenomenon, it was a nameless mental void.

Bion's hypothesis concerning the fact that a mind may not contain all of the contents it tries to store gave my observations a different significance. The study of his work has taught me that a personality may bear a number of problems related to the manner in which its mind tries to be the "container" of mental contents.

Green's hypotheses (1983, 1986b, 1990, 1992, 1999b, 2002) concerning death narcissism and the "white mourning" as well as his hypotheses regarding "the negative" and his specific investigations on borderline patients opened up new paths for my clinical and theoretical investigations.

Freud's theory, as well as the contributions of some of his followers, exclusively describe the vicissitudes of the mind's "contents"—the unconscious, preconscious, or conscious representation of thing, inner object fantasy, identifications in the ego and the superego, and so on. When we conceive the hypothesis that a mind may function in a deficient way due to its failure to "contain" the contents that it tries to think, we are able to observe transferential phenomena from a different perspective. These observations lead us to a psychoanalytic truth (Lutenberg, 1998) made evident by the defects in the psychic matrix that determines the mental void.

Whenever we suspect the existence of the clinical phenomenon of mental void, we should be very cautious and, at the same time, very creative. We can never expect the patient's associations to indicate or suggest the technical method we should use to recognize the existence of the problem as it happens when we investigate the relationship between "repression" and "resistance".

Mental void and borderline structures

Over the last 30 years, psychoanalytic research has given the borderline structure an increasingly sharp theoretical and clinical entity. This has enabled us to distinguish these problems more accurately during the regular sessions and, consequently, to be of greater help to our patients. Otto Kernberg (1975, 1995a), Herbert Rosenfeld

(1965), and André Green (1973, 1983, 1986b, 1996) have undoubtedly made a substantial contribution to the clinical and psychopathological discrimination of these patients whose psychopathology lies between neurosis and psychosis.

I have established that people suffering from a structural mental void generally *stabilize their tendency to fusion and confusion* through the borderline structure. This balance remains stable while the fusional links are kept in the outer and inner world. Persons, institutions, neosexual practices, and different degrees of addiction are the usual recipients of such symbiotic links. In the inner world the secondary autistic defences (Bleger, 1967b, Tustin, 1990) are the ones that stabilize these defences.

The developmental processes of each personality and separations of different sorts distort these defences and give rise to a decompensation of borderline conditions, pushing them towards the pole of temporary psychosis. As a general rule, the death of relevant symbiotically linked figures (father, mother, sibling, grandparent, uncle, aunt, significant other) is followed by a long period during which the personality adjusts to the characteristics of the so-called borderline personality (Kernberg, 1975). Later on, sometimes after several years, there appear compensatory configurations that replace the borderline configuration.

Let us see an example that is relatively frequent in this type of patient. After their mother's death, some of her children (who had had a symbiotic link with her), instead of starting a normal mourning process, experience the tribulations of a symbiotic mourning. During it, they go through a varied period of borderline-type confusion; then confusion is replaced by a serious phobia that usually appears with panic attacks; or a serious depression with psychotic colouring.

This sequence of different psychopathological configurations is explained in terms of the mental void theory as follows:

1. The break of the symbiotic link, forced by the mother's death, generates a feeling of dread that is muffled and compensated for by the borderline structure.

2. Once the initial confusion settles, instead of a process of identification with the lost object typical of normal mourning (Freud, 1917e [1915]), what takes place is an attachment to the subject self of a portion of the lost symbiotic object self. When the symbiosis with the mother encompasses a serious phobia or depres-

sion of the latter, this pathological portion of the maternal ego settles in the child's self, imposing a behaviour that dominates its whole personality. It is like a "pacemaker": it imposes upon the relative's self its own rhythm and life logic.

3. The subject's self takes on the characteristics of the pathological feature of the lost maternal object. These are "phobias" or "depressions" alien to the subject that require quite a different, specific interpretation technique. Many transgenerational problems (serious phobias, panic attacks, and symbiotic depressions in particular) appear in this way in clinic practice.

From the psychoanalytic technique and clinical viewpoint, borderline patients are characterized by their high intolerance of frustration. Examples are numerous. However, considering the infinite alternatives offered by the approach variables, the analysis of the approach itself is a highly valuable empirical reference for firsthand observation of the tolerance or intolerance to frustration that the borderline patient shows in each session.

In general, it is not easy to interpret these problems to the patient. These are times when the analyst must choose between the operability of active silence, a statement, or an interpretation. As pointed out by Bleger (1967b), the analysis of the setting disturbs the psychotic part of the personality. When this happens, the technical premise—so useful for neuroses—of turning the unconscious into conscious is not valid.

After a mutative interpretation (Strachey, 1934), these patients do not respond with an insight. When faced with a regression in the setting, they respond with a de-structuring of the ego; this is the most hazardous point in the treatment.

Therefore, the personal modifications introduced by each psychoanalyst in the approach to each particular patient are of key importance for the success or failure of the treatment. Not seeing the analyst, for instance, causes in the patients a persecution anxiety that paralyses them. They need to see their analyst to avoid falling into an uncontrollable regression tinted by a single emotion: terror. Visual separation generates in them a feeling of anxiety that almost immediately gives way to terror: an emotional condition typical of the appearance of void in the transference. They know this sequence very well in spite of not being able to think it in words; that is why they defend themselves from regression.

This specific item gave rise to a fruitful discussion in our research team coordinated by Green. The prevailing idea was that the fact that whether the patient remains face to face or lies on the couch depends on many variables that differ in each specific case. We all agreed that it was not convenient to force the borderline patient to lie on the couch. As a general rule, seeing the analyst helps him/her to control the pathological regression that may start in a session.

I found it very convenient, in order to understand the most typical psychodynamic movements of the instability of the borderline structure, to resort to Bion's theoretical diagram, which divides total personality into a psychotic part and a non-psychotic part. This has allowed me to be present at the analytic session devoid of any conditioning, paying attention only to the particular configuration that the patient's personality acquires through the development of the transference and countertransference.

When the associations or behaviour manifested by the patient indicate a non-psychotic processing of the transferential development, I can technically participate with interpretations meant to establish a dialogue with the non-psychotic part. In those special moments it is understood that we share the same verbal code (Liberman, 1970–72).

A psychotic processing of the transferential reality often abruptly interrupts this dialogue. What has previously been said within a symbolic verbal code is automatically ignored, and the universe of possible exchange comes to be dominated by a psychotic metamorphosis of the transferential experience.

The same is characterized, according to Bion's theory (1965, 1967d), by a transformation of emotions and feelings into beta elements. These beta units—resulting from the aborted thought—are only suitable for composing an obscure collection that pretends to be a thought. But it is not, since it is not meant to denominate a frustration but to substitute it. By means of massive projective identification these beta elements are expelled from the mind and form a hallucination. The beta elements that constitute the hallucination "are" the reality of the psychotic part.

According to the approach that I usually agree on with them, patients can choose either to sit in front of me or lie on the couch; when they "need to", they can walk freely around the office and then go back to sit on the chair or lie on the couch. This conception of the setting for the display of the fantasies typical of transference makes it possible for me to see a huge variety of extra-verbal figures that give me the indications required to infer the quality of the psychotic process that is taking place. This is the setting for the approach of the psychotic transference described by Bion (1967d) as being rash, premature, fragile, and tenacious.

A look towards the window, a silence that exaggerates a noise coming from the street (such as a car horn or an ambulance siren), a sudden incomprehensible jerk, an unexpected jump out of the couch if the patient is lying down, a walk around the room if he/she is sitting, lying on the couch if seated, and so on, are all movements through which the body is used as a "thing in itself" that responds to an automatism proceeding from the psychotic part of the personality. This view has often permitted me to "play" during the sessions. The comic effect of the analysis and interpretation of these behaviours attaches a different significance to the shared therapeutic work and the patient's and the analyst's own insight.

As a general rule, these analysands always talk exclusively about what happens to them outside the session. This simultaneous viewing of transference dynamics is of great usefulness—almost indispensable—to me to understand the borderline structure within which the void structure becomes stabilized. I always found it scarcely operative and even dangerous—technically speaking—to rely on the signs and descriptions that show me the manner in which analysands behave in the outer world.

The shared rationalization of everyday life may generate in the analysands an over-adjustment that causes a different "illness" in them and, consequently, makes their lives duller. I am referring to the tendency to serious obsessive rationality. This opens up the risk of future suicidal fantasies, particularly when analysands realize that, in order to be "healed", they have to kill their originality and creativity.

If we admit that there is in the borderline structure a precarious limit between the inner and the outer world, between the intrapsychic and the objectal, between the singular and the social, we can better understand why these people, when talking about external events, about what happened to them yesterday with "Mr So-and-so", are talking about themselves. The analogies found in their references are usually childish or even bizarre.

These personalities structure from a bonding perspective like the characters in Pirandello's work: they are always "in search of an author" capable of putting "words" into and giving a "meaning" to their existence, which they find blurred and empty. From their reports emerge a multitude of anecdotes that tell us about what is happening in the—unconscious—privacy of the transferential fantasy.

I have witnessed that borderline patients lack the experience of privacy. Since they do not live inside themselves, they can never decode what the analyst can tell them with regard to the transference analysis, so they usually take the contents of an interpretation literally instead of symbolically.

Whenever I work with these patients, I systematically perform after each session a personal synthesis of all the transferential events that *I visualized but was unable to interpret. The transferential reading provides very significant elements that help me to attain a level of psychic truth that no other investigation source offers. It is one thing that the analyst understands what happens with the bond; what he is to interpret to the patient is a different matter altogether.*

It is in general vital that the analyst tolerate the regression in the bond with the patient without interpreting it. He must tolerate the regression in the privacy of his own self. Then he has to build up an interpretation including said contents in terms that may be understood by the patient. When the psychotic part prevails in the transference, we must try to rebuild the mental container without analysing the contents. The concept of the *"container–contained relation"*, typical of the analytic link (not just of the analysand's mind) is fundamental to evaluating each participation of the analyst.

My theoretical hypotheses about structural mental void

As stated above, it is my understanding that, to theoretically conceive of the mental void, we must previously admit that a person's overall psychic structure has the capacity of being split into different partitioned portions that are disconnected from one another. Inside each of said parts there is a mental logic that is different from those of the remaining parts: this logic is what gives psychic meaning to the autonomous operation of each portion.

Thus, there will be a part where the predominant activity results from the "normal" elaboration of the Oedipus complex, which recognizes and accepts the principle of reality; in another part the pleasure principle may prevail; in others, the reality principle; the psychotic part, the neurotic part, the symbiotic, autistic, or creative part.

According to this hypothesis, there exists in each of these parts a manner of "Oedipus complex burial" that differs from that present in any of the others. It implies the existence of a different psychic balance for the split-off portion. Besides, in addition to these psychopathological variations, there always persists in the psyche the "empty" part in a virtual state. This gives rise to constant and new personality imbalances.

I understand that when there appears in a person a sensation or conscious feeling of a void, one should not think that it is a straightforward manifestation of the underlying void. In general, the secondary defence that offsets it also conceals it from the symptomatologic point of view.

Structural void, as such, finds its clinical expression through a specific feeling: terror. The secondary defences that offset it give rise to a sort of shell that isolates the complex affective problem from the structural mental void. Therefore, the symptoms generated by the void adopt the clinical form (psychopathology) of the compensating defensive structure. However, the void is unveiled by the emotion underlying the defence: the nameless terror.

The compensating cover (secondary autistic, symbiotic, neurotic, and/or psychotic) can be functionally compared to that of a "container" that holds, as its contents, the structural void. If it were a neurotic defence, we would say that the defence "represses" the void, but since it is a different mechanism, we can infer—paraphrasing Bion—that the defence "engulfs" the void.

"Engulfment" is a binding structure that Bion (1967d), described and typified to explain the constitution and assembly of what he called "bizarre objects". I have given this hypothesis of Bion's a different dimension: I take it as a reference to explain a defence mechanism operating inside the split ego itself.

The contents expelled from a split portion through massive projective identification can end up at another split portion of the ego that acts as a depository, storing what has been deposited in it. It is an "engulfment" that operates dynamically inside the different portions of the split ego.

When we see in clinical practice that the ego appears alien to itself, as is the case with borderline patients, we must consider this possibility. It is a very different way of understanding the "ego-dystonic" problems—that is, the feeling of otherness before the decisions made by the ego, and that the person feels alien to such decisions.

Psychotic or neurotic rituals can be part of this type of constellation as well as some alterations of the sexual behaviour. Teenage suicidal attempts, in particular, may have such an origin. It is not the same to consider this type of "engulfment" between the different portions of the ego, and to consider the possibility of hysterical identifications.

It is not the same to consider that the personality bearing the mental void demonstrates "a psychic conflict", in the classical sense of the term, and to think that such structural mental void expresses a sectoral inability of the mind to settle in the psychic conflict dynamics and, consequently, in the evolution process. This freezing of the mental transformation process (Bion 1965) becomes quite evident as transference and countertransference develop in each session. Historically, people affected by such perturbation have always evaded their developmental crises, freezing the transformational movement that would lead them to a psychic change. Hence the special care they require from the analyst as regards the technique used by the latter when trying to enter the developmental transformation area of the patient's mind during the psychoanalytic process.

Some patients usually report that they feel real panic when they experience a developmental success of any kind. For instance, they usually feel certain that if they experience success, a dearly beloved person, such as a son or daughter, will die. Although Freud thoroughly analysed this problem in "Those Who Fail When They Succeed" (1916d) and "The Economic Problem of Masochism" (Moral Masochism) (1924c), this certainty of a beloved person's death originates in a different source.

It arises, on the one hand, from the projection of the terror experience typical of the mobilization or mental void defences, and, on the other, from the massive projective identification of experiences born from the unconscious separation–death equation typical of symbiotic links.

Bleger's hypotheses published in his book "Symbiosis and Ambiguity" have guided my research on the structural mental void. His clinical vision continues to amaze me because of its clarity and perceptive sharpness. (Bleger, 1967b, chapters IV, V, and VII).

I agree with the authors who maintain that when a baby is born, a "normal" primary symbiotic link with its mother is immediately created (Bleger, 1967b; Mahler, 1958, 1967, 1984; Searles, 1965). This link represents the extra-uterine continuation of the bodily, psychic, and mental bond they had shared from the embryo's gestation to the time of birth. Although we study this primary normal symbiosis from a psychic link perspective, we know it has deep somatic roots.

In his book *Touching*, Ashley Montagu (1971, Chapter 11) says: *"gestation actually comprises an intrauterine phase or uterogestation, and an extrauterine phase or exterogestation. . .* exterogestation ends when the baby starts to crawl . . . it would last as long as uterogestation" (nine months each). This onto-phylogenetic conception corresponds with the descriptions of several psychoanalytic authors in relation to mental evolution—particularly with those of Winnicott (1958, 1963, 1965), who speaks of the mental evolution that extends from the "subjective object" to the creation of the transitional space.

Taking into account those first nine months of postnatal life from an "extrauterine human gestation" perspective helps us to note the valuable contributions made by many psychoanalytic authors who have written on the subject, as well as to reconsider the significance of the psychic traumas occurring during these periods.

During the first few months of postnatal life, the mother's psychic structure plays the part—for the baby's psyche—of the "container" that holds as its "contents" the baby's changing psyche in full developmental creativity. As we can see, this containing function is quite similar to that of the anatomical uterus during the baby's biological gestation (or "uterogestation"). This is the reason why I have called "mental uterus" the peculiar maternal functions that typify the developmental period of primary normal symbiosis.

From a theoretical point of view, the link that distinguishes the "mental uterus" is configured through the indiscriminate fusion of the newborn's "id" with its mother's "id", plus the "ego–superego" structure of the latter. From this initial state of perinatal psychic undifferentiation on, the whole developmental process inscribed in the baby's genetic formula becomes spontaneously active; its complete development allows the gradual maturing of the baby into a subject different from both its parents (Freud, 1924d).

Starting from this original symbiotic link, there take place in the baby's psyche structural differentiations—that is, all the transformations that give rise to the "psychic tissue" that each person configures during his/her life history.

The father is also part of this primary symbiotic link from the start, but as a "virtual" member, since his factual and functional presence (the psychic structure of the baby) materializes its developmental efficacy from inside the mother, as part of the total link (somato-psychic and social) that exists between mother and baby.

It has been proved in every branch of human research (psychoanalysis, developmental psychology, anthropology, linguistics, sociology, genetics, medicine, and paediatrics) that for an adequate development of the genetic potential carried by a human being, the physical and psychic presence of another human being is indispensable. This simple truth, which should be universally understood in every society, is currently in crisis.

We know that at any time during the structural differentiation of the baby's psychic apparatus there may occur "developmental crises" caused by psychic traumas of quite diverse types. Many such crises are resolved by means of multiple defences of different categories that bear a relation to the intensity and specific qualities of objectal separation anxiety. Some of these crises are resolved through a different mechanism, which is directly related to the structural mental-void problem: the secondary symbiotic defence, which differs in nature from original symbiosis, the primary symbiosis, and secondary defensive autism (Tustin, 1990).

Whenever the secondary symbiosis and secondary autism operate in a defensive manner, a split core is generated in the ego (under development). This defence, which is extreme, is generated only when the emotion underlying the developmental separation is nameless terror (Bion, 1967d). Under such emotional circumstances, the other less radical defensive attempts—those that the incipient "ego" had already learnt to resort to (Klein, 1952b)—give way.

Terror is the typical experience of the ego "de-structuring" condition. It is an original experience, which reveals the absence of psychic tissue: the void. Terror is equivalent to the automatic anxiety experience, which, for Freud (1926d [1925]), has a phylogenetic origin.

The defensive operation that solves the chaotic emotional state (terror, nameless terror), precipitates into the secondary symbiosis structure. From such a defensive movement, the interrupted or aborted mother–child separation remains inside the "ego". This is also the conceptual node of secondary autistic defence (Bleger, 1967b, Chapters III and IV).

Beneath secondary symbiosis and autism there underlie—in an undifferentiated frozen condition—both the portion of the de-structured ego that was aborted in the course of evolution and the psychic remnants of the dismantled object that is thus caught in the fusional link. We can therefore state, from a theoretical point of view, that the first movement that conditions the whole mental activity to the void arises from a specific emotion: nameless terror.

For Bion, terror is an original emotion that only acquires destructive qualities for the baby's mind when the experience of the instant in which terror is felt indicates to it that its mother is not taking charge, as a depository, of the terror the baby is feeling. When it "perceives" that its mother shows indifference before its terror, the terror increases and gives rise to the emotion Bion calls "nameless terror".

Under such circumstances, the experience of bond-breaking is highly traumatic: instead of generating a "catastrophic change"— from which the structural transformation of the psyche is born—it generates a psychic "catastrophe", the central knot of psychic void. Secondary symbiosis also freezes this disastrous condition of the link with primary objects.

I also found very useful for formulating my hypothesis on the mental void the whole conceptual body of Winnicott's theory. Although the entire theory was a very valuable contribution, I wish to underline three concepts in this summary:

a. The first relates to his definition of "fear of collapse". Its theoretical specificity—as regards the topic under discussion—becomes meaningful within his general theory of the psychic apparatus. As he states in the paper "Fear of Collapse" (1982), Winnicott decided on the term "collapse" "because it is somewhat vague and may mean several things". In his subsequent explanations he informs us that said fear responds to the emotions underlying psychotic conditions and the "void".

For Winnicott the psychic mark left by the "fear of collapse" tells us that at some early point in the developmental process there actually was a *"collapse of the self-establishment as a unit"*. Since for him—theoretically speaking—the "death drive" is not conceivable (Freud 1920g), the "fear of collapse" represents the greatest chaotic and de-structuring experience the human mind can conceive and suffer.

b. The second nuclear concept relates to the division of the personality into a "true self" and a "false self". To this particular conception of the ego division is linked the theoretical concept of "subjective object" and "transitional space" (Winnicott, 1958, 1971a, 1975).

c. The third is the one corresponding to his peculiar conception of developmental continuity and/or lack of continuity between soma, psyche, and mind (Winnicott, 1949). For him, the developmental disarticulation among these 3 levels of human existence is the basis for the generation of the false self.

The concept of death drive and automatic anxiety theorized by Freud in his topological theory, the hypothesis on nameless terror and the psychotic and non-psychotic parts of the personality born from Bion's theory, Bleger's theory as well as Winnicott's view on a primal collapse from which the subject never recovered, are all key for my conception of the structural mental void. I found their theoretical complementarity convenient for explaining the complex psychodynamics of the sectoral crumbling of the architecture of normal narcissism.

The contributions made by Green to the "void" concept all through his vast works (1973, 1983, 1986b, 1999b, 2002) have been particularly enriching, as they opened up new perspectives of the problem. Since his hypothesis on "death narcissism", up to his recent theoretical and clinical descriptions of the "central phobic position", with his theory on "the negative" in-between, Green has gradually presented different perspectives of normal and pathological narcissism that are relevant to the conceptual core of borderline pathology.

Starting from his work entitled "White Psychosis", written with Jean-Luc Donnet, the "void" concept has gradually acquired for Green clinical, technical, and metapsychological specificity (Donnet & Green, 1973). His metapsychological view of pathological objectal separations, as synthesized in his description of white, black, and red mourning (Green, 1983), is part of a transcendental differentiation that helped me to distinguish symbiotic separations from those three varieties described by him.

White mourning is connected with void, not with the "symbiotic mourning" problem, which is so different from the three Green described. As he himself states, the white concept "derives from the English blank in the sense of *unoccupied space* (for example, not printed, space left for the signature, blank check, carte blanche); it is an empty space. This also refers us to the concept of "blank sleep", which is an empty sleep, without representations but with emotion.

According to Green, in white psychosis there occurs in the ego a stripping of representations that leaves the ego facing its own constitutive void. Thus, he grants the concept of void a precise metapsychological specificity: lack of representations and identifications in the ego—a perspective with which I fully agree. But he states that this void is the result of a defence against the object intrusion "the ego makes itself disappear before the intrusion of that which is too full, of a noise that must be reduced to silence".

In chapter III of his book on life narcissism and death narcissism (Green, 1983) he specifically deals with "The White", saying that upon the failure of the phallic identifications that sustain the language, a regression from the phallic level of language to another level of metaphoric quality takes place—that is, there is a going back to the "object" but from the body, not from the language.

Under such circumstances: "The failure of the phallic fixations supported by the language (a language that is also present in the mouth) leads the subject back to a metaphoric orality as materialized in the body. The chest invades the belly to occupy the empty space left by the representation. It is remarkable that anxiety does not become evident as such but rather as a void. A void established against the desire of invasion by the driving object that threatens the ego with disappearance."

I quote these comments because they open up a vast field of research on "non-neurotic" patients, based on the difficulties they have with free association. This view of the problems affecting borderline patients may be combined with the perspectives generated in our circle by three masters of Argentine psychoanalysis: Pichon Riviere, Bleger, and Liberman.

The most significant conceptual difference between Green's view and my perspective of mental void is the distinction I draw between emotional and structural mental void, particularly because I take as a starting point primary and secondary symbiosis and defensive secondary autism. In my opinion, the problem of the intense intrusive fear mentioned by Green would come later.

Green's most recent view of the unconscious problems of the borderline patient is expounded in his article entitled "The Central Phobic Position" (2000a). His peculiar definition of "position" opens up new paths in the investigation of the pathology evidenced by these patients. Their developmental paralysis is perpetuated by the continuous attacks on the mind binding function. I agree with his viewpoints stated therein, as well as with his overall view of current clinical practice developed in the Introduction and in chapters 4, 7, and 8 of his book *La Pensée Clinique* (2002).

According to my theoretical inferences, the key pathological process that determines the mental void specifically consists of an obstacle—in general one of a traumatic nature—that affects the natural psychic differentiation of the human infant with which it is genetically endowed.

When a mental catastrophe occurs too early in postnatal evolution, the genetic patterns that mark the roads of human evolution in a phylogenetic manner become inactive and "freeze". This is a sort of "sectoral encystment" of the embryonic developmental structure carried by the baby. We assume that the potential mental evolution of this individual has been precociously dismounted from its natural track.

By this I am saying that the mental void carried by a patient consulting us (infant, adolescent or adult) stores an unedited developmental potential that may be edited. The fundamental factor for making it possible to "edit the encysted genetic patterns" lies in the approach proposed by the analyst, his technique, the theories he acknowledges as valid, his "humanism", and the infinite shades of his personality.

It is the psychoanalyst who configures the analytic approach and the technical consideration of such phenomena, so different from those born from "repression". It is then essential to have a previous idea of the difference between the silence of resistance and the silence that expresses and objectifies the structural mental void at the session.

When, in our capacity as analysts, we hold this genetic hypothesis on mental void, we are betting on the possibility of generating, during the therapeutic process, together with the patients, a radical revitalization of the various psychic abortions that took place in the course of their historic developmental processes. Such abortions have been instated within the virtual structure of the void and the corresponding defences (symbiosis and secondary autism).

Secondary defensive symbiosis has elements in common with the original, although its nature is entirely different: primary symbiosis is spontaneous and natural and does not exclude any sector of the soma-psyche. It is the continuation of an intrauterine somato-psycho-mental relation that has ended as such to give rise to a new postnatal relationship. Based on this link there emerges a personality that gradually differentiates itself starting from the very fusional indiscrimination.

Secondary symbiosis is reactive and defensive and therefore pathological. Once it has been configured within the mother–child link, it stops the evolution of the baby's ego and superego in the split sector involved in it. In the psychic gestation of the structural mental void both the mother's and the baby's intolerance to separation occur. This is why I consider mental void as a bond problem in spite of the fact that the "psychic abortion" caused by the developmental occlusion pertains to the individual who suffers it.

When secondary symbiosis is an insufficient defence to neutralize the threat produced by the possible sudden appearance of terror, new different defensive structures are generated, such as psychosis or borderline conditions, to complete the "defence" against this underlying terror. Also the pathology of compulsive sexual practices (neosexualities—Joyce McDougall's successful term) is an effect of the defence against mental void (Lutenberg, 1997, 2001).

Another defensive alternative that fits into this latent terror experience is that of secondary defensive autism. It leads, together with the suppression of terror, to a complete withdrawal of the ego from the outer world; this ego withdrawal involves such ego sector as has been caught by the defence.

Bleger (1967b) and Tustin (1968, 1981, 1990) have developed the theory, the clinical application, and the psychopathology of this defensive pattern in relation to said structures defined by them.

Defensive secondary symbiosis

The newborn's first developmental processes always have, in the background, the support of a symbiotic link with the mother (normal primary symbiosis). Mahler (1958, 1967) calls this "original symbiosis". It is on the basis of this complete mother–child bond that the baby's full developmental differentiation gradually appears. The same presents very peculiar somatic, psychic, and mental facets. This view of perinatal symbiosis is natural if we take into account that the human creature is always prematurely born.

In my opinion, we can briefly say that a newborn baby's psychic structure is constituted by its own id plus the id, ego, and superego of its mother (and father, or the "dad mental function"). The original symbiotic link always acknowledges this virtual psychic triangle that underlies the bi-corporal link existing between mother and baby.

In chapter VIII of *An Outline of Psychoanalysis* (1940a [1938]), Freud makes a revision in which he updates his hypotheses concerning the relations between the psychic apparatus and the outer world. As regards secondary symbiotic defence, I would like to point out that he leaves open the problem of very early defensive operations occurring upon frustration. As I understand it, in this work he explains the new semantic turn he gives to the re-denial concept and its relation to the frustrations that take place in very "early childhood".[3]

This hypothesis is transcendental for interpreting, in a more extensive way, the meaning of precocious ego splitting. This conceptual turn of Freud's helps me to better understand the subsequent developments formulated by Bion, Bleger, Klein, Lacan, Mahler, and Winnicott, among others. I consider all these references necessary since they relate to the core of my mental void hypothesis.

The ontological core of my mental void theory can be summarized as follows: Mental void is a virtual structure included in the privacy of secondary symbiosis and secondary defensive autism.

I understand primary symbiosis to be the basis on which the whole psychic differentiation of the human being occurs. When very intense traumatic circumstances interrupt the normal symbiotic continuity between the mother and the baby, there occurs a *psychic abortion*, as described above.

For a traumatic event, proceeding from the "real-objective world", to acquire the value of a psychic trauma lasting through the mental void—that is, that brings about such psychic abortion—it must meet several conditions:

a.   to be reiterated in time;

b.   to have a certain traumatic intensity;

c.   to operate when the baby is living this particular period, which Bastock called extrauterine gestation or exterogestation add (Montagu, 1971).

With regard to the last item, I wish to point out that this period mentioned by Bastock corresponds almost entirely with Winnicott's studies concerning the genesis of the illusion space, the transitional space, the transitional object, and the passage from a "subjective object" to an "object link".

When a significant traumatic circumstance takes place during the extrauterine gestation period, the baby lives a serious threat to its existence (terror); this automatically subjects the psychic evolution reached so far to a crisis. It may only reconstruct and advance in its evolution—now sectoral—after the splitting of the ego. Once the ego parts are split, it may build a new defence, secondary symbiosis that freezes the mental evolution of such a part.

Secondary symbiosis may be established by means of substitution links with different objects. Once constituted, this structure is segregated from the rest of the ego; it survives as a frozen part, and no developmental psychic transformations occur inside it. But, instead of developmental changes, there appears a very specific non-developmental transformation mechanism: *that of object substitution, not one of mourning.*

This theoretical (hypothetical) view finds its clinical match when we meet with borderline patients who systematically produce during their lives factual changes in the objects with which they later create new symbiotic links. When they break the link with such objects, they soon replace them with others without any feeling of pain or mourning for the lost object (Freud 1917e [1915]). They quickly repeat the cycle after each separation.

Historic–experiential chronology of structural mental void

I will make a short synthesis of my hypotheses on the sequence of traumatic events (historic–experiential truth, according to Freud, 1937d, pp. 268–269) that give rise to structural mental void.

a. *Primary void experience.* There starts, as from the original primary symbiosis, a developmental process that is precociously interrupted by significant traumatic circumstances. This gives rise to a psychic experience of chaos and mental turbulence (Bion, 1976a) characterized by a specific affective state: nameless terror (Bion). On this basis, there arises a primary pathological void experience, parallel with and/or overlapping the same nameless terror—the affective experience corresponding to structural mental void. For the time being it is impossible for me to differentiate the nameless terror concept from that of the primary pathological void experience.

b. *Primary defensive reorganization.* The baby reorganizes itself from this catastrophic situation—typical of primary void—by means of specific defensive structures: secondary symbiosis and secondary autism. These secondary defensive structures house vast portions of the affected person's developmental potential.

c. *Developmental freezing: structural void.* The potential developmental capacity of an individual remains caught in said defences. There remains inside the individual, frozen and suspended in time, a transformational capacity typical of the "id". These portions (symbiotic and secondary autistic defences) persist in the adult and become true "psychic holes". Their "emptiness" relates to the missing representations and identifications.

The developmental psychosexual process is aborted—theoretically accounted for as follows: a portion of the id cannot be transformed into ego or superego because it remains caught or "engulfed" within the symbiotic and/or autistic defence.

The perpetuation of this process may be observed in the psychoanalytic clinical situation by paying attention to the predominance of beta transformations (Bion) occurring as from the total transferential experience produced by a patient in the session (Lutenberg, 1998, chapter VI). We can also consider that within both defences is stored what Winnicott calls "non-integration". This conceptual specificity of Winnicott's theory is useful for differentiating "non-integration" from "disintegration".

Mental void, secondary autism, and secondary symbiosis thus become a conceptual triad closely interrelated by a specific mental condition: the perpetuation of the very early psychic disaster of which no representational memories are left.

d. *Developmental structural coexistence.* As a general rule, secondary autism and secondary symbiosis attend the whole of an individual's evolution and coexist with the rest of the personality that goes along the "natural" developmental track. It is a true compensation of the structural mental void. Different developmental circumstances (adolescence, migrations) or involutional circumstances (serious social crises, terrorism) pertaining to the history of each individual may disrupt such an equilibrium. The adequate, successful structural balance of the mind, based on this condition, may also give rise to surprising sublimations.

e. *Decompensated condition.* When, on account of different circumstances (either traumatic or developmental) an emotional imbalance results that damages the secondary symbiotic defence (or the secondary autistic defence), a serious decompensation crisis may arise. Under these circumstances the entire personality takes on the form of the most critical psychopathological conditions.

These include utterly serious psychotic structures, borderline structures, psychosomatic crises, impulsive crises with a predominance of different massive, uncontrolled actings-out *that may be mistaken for manic crises* but are different in nature. There is also a great difference in the clinical course of an "acute psychosis" condition caused by such decompensation of the mental void.

These are "benign psychoses", since, instead of damage, they may leave mental evolution as a sequel of the psychotic crisis. It all depends on the "container" holding these scattered "mental contents" during such crises.

f. *Sublimation.* In my opinion, every individual maintains forever active an undifferentiated part of his original "id". As a general rule, this bond does not give rise to any psychic perturbation. By means of this syncretic bond with the outer world, each individual creates, all along his historical evolution, a natural continuity between the original symbiosis (normal primary) and his own entire culture. This view is consistent with the hypotheses described by Freud as "oceanic experience" in chapter I of *Civilization and its Discontents* (1930a [1929]). In my opinion, this syncretic bond, in a dialogue with the most singular part of the individual—that is, with his "ego–superego"—is the source of any human being's creative inspiration (sublimation).

Final remarks

Secondary symbiotic defence and secondary autism hold inside them the structural mental void. It is a "virtual structure" that is encysted inside these defences. There dwells in it an id portion that has not undergone psychic evolution. There is also situated therein, in a virtual state, nameless terror—a terror that arises when said secondary symbiosis or autism are broken.

When natural psychosexual evolution is affected by different traumatic events, its psychic structure splits. A portion thereof will follow the path of evolution through the known developmental drive stages (oral, anal, phallic). Another portion of the psychic structure will be caught inside these symbiotic links, thereby configuring the secondary symbiotic defence.

When the secondary symbiotic defence is broken, the mental void becomes evident, turning from virtual into real. The analytic process itself may induce the breaking of the secondary defensive autism or the abandonment of symbiotic links.

According to Freud (1923b, 1923e), the human being's developmental evolution takes place in stages that are genetically conditioned as regards both their appearance and their decline. This also implies a developmental differential transformation of the id into ego and superego. The secondary symbiotic defence erases the entire developmental structure of the split psyche portion involved in the above alteration. As a result of the same defence, the structural identifications of the "ego–superego" are erased and returned to the id stage. Inversely to what happens in the psyche evolution, a passage from ego into id takes place.

The conclusion that confirms the symbiotic defence occurs when the split portion of the id fuses with the whole psychic structure of the "object" that accepts the proposed symbiosis. *The new symbiotic fusional link takes place as from the syncretic union of the "ids" of its components.* Several individuals may participate in this fusion.

As a matter of fact, this event occurs regularly in symbiotic families when structuring a "symbiotic magma" that stabilizes the defensive structure and aborts the potential evolution of its members. Its balance depends on the mutual fitting-in of the pathological configurations of all its members. Each of them contributes to the whole elements that are necessary for the "psychic balance" of all the members.

Singular sensitivity is cancelled. Nothing can be "felt" in accordance with one's own perception. Personal emotions and their corresponding transformations into thoughts (alpha transformations, according to Bion) are also confiscated by the defensive structure. On account of this, the portion involved in the secondary symbiotic defence does not learn from its everyday experiences. Thus, a sectoral "*living semantic aphasia*" is generated.

Said "aphasia" is dual: it has to do with understanding and expression; and, in addition, there is the inability to psychically inscribe the experience. I understand that, under the effects of secondary symbiotic fusion, there is no singular registry of the experience lived; the individual id involved in the syncretic magma never differentiates into ego–superego.

The severity of said "aphasia" depends on the amount of each subject's split portion abducted within said defence. Without the "family group", these persons do not exist as thinkers or as individuals capable of making decisions.

I have verified that in borderline patients, a particular type of resistance to analysis and insight derives from the virtual existence of this underlying fusional structure. They are analysands who show at each session to what extent their affectivity is engaged in extra-analytic relationships and links that constantly capture their whole interest.

When during the session they relate to the portions of their ego that are not involved in secondary symbiosis, they may attempt to start the elaborative work typical of the insight; otherwise, nothing is left from the analytic experience.

The marriage and/or moving elsewhere of a member of the family defensive alliance may set off a serious decompensation that expresses itself as a borderline condition. This decompensation may be the prelude to a psychosomatic or psychiatric illness, hence its clinical importance. But in a decompensated family, the different psychopathological figures may take turns among the members of the fused family group.

When symbiotic links are broken, the primitive portion that was paralysed (fusional id) is released in many members of the family fusion. This breaking up gives rise to a wide range of secondary compensations: neurotic, neosexual, borderline, psychopathic, or psychotic. The determining factor of the final structure of such secondary compensatory figures lies in the varying combinations that result from the union between this non-integrated primitive portion and other more integrated portions of the ego; new "objects" may also be added.

Notes

1. Within the concept of edition during analysis we can include a large number of elaborative and structural processes that occur during the psychoanalytic session, the common denominator of which is the gestation of a container and a structural mental web that had not existed previously. We can say in brief that it applies to the task of constructing new unconscious representations and identifications (Freud, 1915d, 1923b) based on the "id", or turning the emotional experiences the analysand lives through without being able to signify them into alpha elements (Bion, 1967d, 1970).

2. In chapters IV and V of *The Ego and the Id* (1923b) Freud theoretically develops the economic problem that occurs in sublimation and in the economic process connected with the construction of identification in the ego and the superego. He states that the drive disconnection (Eros–death drive) releases a part of the death drive. A part of this binds with the superego structure (masochism) and another remains "free". In my opinion it is the latter that generates the unbinding of the links and gives rise to a plurality of de-structuring processes.

3. "Fetishism should not be deemed to constitute and exception with regard to the ego splitting. *Quite frequently it appears in the situation of self-defence against an outer world warning felt as painful, and this happens through the denial of the perceptions that notify such claim from objective reality.* These denials come up quite often, *not only in fetishists . . .*" (Freud, 1940a [1938], Book XXIII, p. 205; italics added).

5

Transference and countertransference management with borderline patients

Otto F. Kernberg

At the New Orleans IPA Congress in March, 2004, I presented a preliminary, informal report on the main conclusions of the IPA-Research-Committee-sponsored research group. Although not finalized and formally approved by our research group, this report was presented in agreement with the principal investigator and group leader, Dr André Green. This research team, organized and directed by Dr Green from 2000 to 2003, met twice a year for two or three days each in Paris and New York. Its members were Drs André Green and Jean-Claude Rolland, from Paris; Drs Jaime Lutenberg and Fernando Urribarri, from Buenos Aires, Drs Elizabeth Spillius and Gregorio Kohon, from London, and Drs William Grossman and myself, from New York. In presenting my personal conclusions and reflections on what I believe were consensus viewpoints that emerged in the course of the work of that Committee, I also offer critiques of these viewpoints and include in my formulations conclusions stemming from the recent findings of a major, randomized controlled trial studying a psychoanalytic psychotherapy for borderline patients at the Personality Disorders Institute of the Weill Cornell Medical College (Clarkin, Yeomans, & Kernberg, 1999; Clarkin, Levy, & Schiavi, 2005).

The IPA Research Group represented adequately, I believe, major currents of contemporary psychoanalytic thinking, including the ego-psychological view particularly prevalent in the United States; the British, Kleinian, and Independent approaches as represented by the London colleagues; the Argentinean modification and developments of Kleinian thinking, as well as their absorption of French psychoanalysis, as represented by our Argentinean colleagues. The fact that each member of the group presented a personal approach rather than simply a certain theoretical school, and the fact that alternative views, such as the American Relational approach and Self psychology, were not represented, was openly acknowledged. While it might be argued that the group's composition set limits from the outset to the scope of the investigation, it was, in fact, difficult enough to bring together the quite different traditions that emerged in our meetings. We struggled simultaneously with these differences in theoretical approaches, as well as with the differences in diagnostic and therapeutic approaches to borderline patients that emerged from the start.

Our major tasks included the following: (a) to summarize the present "state of the art" regarding borderline patients as reflected in the prevalent contemporary thinking within the psychoanalytic community; (b) to propose, if possible, a consensus statement for consideration of the IPA Research Committee; and (c) to summarize major unresolved controversies and open questions that require further research in the future.

We explored clinical material presented by the group participants and attempted to clarify, in the process, our theoretical concepts in approaching these patients, our methods of assessment, the consequences we drew from assessment for the indicated treatment strategy, and the actual treatment approach pursued by the members of the group. It needs to be said that Dr Green's energetic, tactful, yet strong leadership kept the group together and productive throughout our work.

What follows is a summary of areas of agreement, areas of disagreement, and areas that we recommended should be focused upon as the next step in the process of consensus development. For each of these tasks, I shall first present my view of the consensus that evolved in the group, followed by my critique and conclusions at this point. This approach will, hopefully, make it possible for the reader to assess the extent to which our group work influenced my viewpoints and the extent to which research findings and further reflections modified these viewpoints.

I. Major areas of agreement

1. *The nature of the pathology*

There was general agreement in the group that borderline patients, however one defines this entity, are characterized by primitive, premature transference developments and have difficulty in accepting the usual psychoanalytic treatment frame. Whatever the underlying descriptive, structural, and psychodynamic features might be, these common clinical characteristics present immediate challenges to psychoanalytic treatment and require the analyst to think about either modification of the treatment with parameters of technique, or a shift into psychoanalytic psychotherapy, with implicit controversial questions about the boundaries between psychoanalysis and psychoanalytic psychotherapy. The fact that it took the group quite some time to reach this agreement indicates how many uncertainties there remain presently within the psychoanalytic profession about the nature of and best practice with borderline pathology. While there was general agreement regarding the large number of these patients whom we do see nowadays, we had to recognize that the psychoanalytic profession seems to still be far from consensus regarding the delimitation of this patient group beyond the clinical characteristics referred to.

While our research group focused, from the onset, on the nature of transference and countertransference developments with these patients and agreed implicitly that these developments reflect some fundamental underlying pathology of their personality organization, the group did not pay sufficient attention, I believe, to the general clinical characteristics of these patients beyond their specific developments in the psychoanalytic situation. I believe that this corresponds to a general trend in traditional psychoanalytic thinking: to focus on the dynamics of unconscious conflicts without sufficient attention to the structural consequences of these dynamic conflicts—namely, the defensive characterological structures that, in their specific configurations, are reflected in the personality disorders of contemporary clinical psychiatry.

There is, I believe, great distrust and potential bias within the psychoanalytic community against the findings of descriptive, phenomenological psychiatry, a bias that tends to ignore important findings that are not incompatible with psychoanalytic thinking and which, if integrated into psychoanalytically based approaches, would strengthen the power of clinical psychoanalytic interventions. It has been stressed throughout the psychoanalytic literature that psychiatric nosology tends to be excessively determined by surface manifestations of behaviour that fail to recognize the internal relations signified by different facets of behaviour. Such surface grouping of symptoms are mechanically arrived at on the basis of statistical analyses. However, if those findings are re-examined and reorganized in the light of psychoanalytic understanding, a new dimension of depth may be achieved, linking unconscious dynamics specifically with structural characteristics of the personality.

At the Personality Disorders Institute of the Weill Cornell Medical College we have been studying personality disorders from a psychoanalytic perspective for the past 25 years, and have reached the conclusion that the degree of severity of personality disorders corresponds to three types of personality organization: neurotic personality organization, borderline personality organization, and psychotic personality organization (Kernberg, 1984, pp. 197–209, 275–289). The neurotic personality organization corresponds to the moderately severe personality disorders, or character pathologies, that are usually amenable to psychoanalytic treatment, presenting the usual developments in transference and countertransference that standard psychoanalysis has illuminated. Borderline personality organization corresponds to the severe personality disorders that are typically subsumed in the diffuse use of the term "borderline" and includes patients whose pathology and treatment were the focus of our IPA research group. While neurotic personality organization corresponds to most of the hysterical, obsessive-compulsive, and depressive-masochistic personality disorders, borderline personality organization includes the histrionic or infantile, narcissistic, paranoid, schizoid and schizotypal, antisocial, and borderline personality disorder proper (the latter one as defined in descriptive psychiatry). Psychotic personality organization refers to patients with atypical forms of psychosis, a characteristic loss of reality testing, that, strictly speaking, are no longer part of the overall realm of personality disorders.

The key differential characteristic between neurotic personality organization and borderline personality organization is the presence of normal identity integration in neurotic patients, in contrast to the syndrome of identity diffusion in borderline patients. Normal identity refers to the integration of the concept of self and significant others, while identity diffusion refers to the lack of integrated self and other object representations. Identity diffusion is characterized by a stable split of intrapsychic representations of self and objects into an idealized segment of experience and a persecutory one, with corresponding severe distortions in the characteristic interpersonal experience of their relationship to love and sex, work and profession, and social life. The fact that descriptive psychiatry has found a 60% co-morbidity of several of these severe personality disorders included under borderline personality organization strengthens the Cornell studies finding of the commonality of the conditions included under identity diffusion. In addition, identity diffusion is intimately linked with a predominance of primitive defensive operations derived from splitting mechanisms, rather than repression and related mechanisms, as is the case of neurotic personality organization (Lenzenweger, Clarkin, Kernberg, & Foelsch, 2001).

From a clinical standpoint, the syndrome of identity diffusion explains the dominant characteristics of borderline personality organization. The predominance of primitive dissociation, or splitting, of the idealized segment of experience from the persecutory one is naturally reinforced by primitive defensive operations intimately connected with splitting mechanisms, such as projective identification, denial, primitive idealization, devaluation, omnipotence, and omnipotent control. All these defensive mechanisms contribute to distorted and chronic disturbances in interpersonal relations, thus reinforcing the lack of self-reflectiveness and of "mentalization" in a broad sense, decreasing the capacity to assess other people's behaviour and motivation in depth, particularly, of course, under the impact of intense affect activation.

Lack of integration of the concept of the self interferes with a comprehensive integration of one's past and present into a capacity to predict one's future behaviour and decreases the capacity for commitment to professional goals, personal interests, work and social functions, and intimate relationships. Lack of integration of the concept of significant others interferes with the capacity of realistic assessment of others, with selecting partners harmonious with the individual's actual expectations, and with investment in others. While all sexual excitement involves an aggressive component (Kernberg, 1995b, pp. 15–31), the predominance of negative affect dispositions of borderline patients leads to an infiltration of the disposition for sexual intimacy with excessive aggressive components, determining, at best, an exaggerated and chaotic persistence of polymorphous perverse infantile features as part of the individual's sexual repertoire and, at worst, a primary inhibition of the capacity for sensual responsiveness and erotic enjoyment. Under these latter circumstances, severely negative affects eliminate the very capacity for erotic response, clinically reflected in the severe types of sexual inhibition that are to be found in the most severe personality disorders.

Lack of an integrated sense of self and of significant others also interferes with the internalization of the rudimentary precursors of internalized value systems, leading to an exaggerated idealization of positive values in the ego ideal, and to a persecutory quality of the internalized prohibitive aspects of the primitive superego. These developments, in turn, foster a predominance of splitting mechanisms at the level of internalized value systems or superego functions, with excessive projection of internalized prohibitions, while the excessive, idealized demand for perfection further interferes with the integration of a normal superego. Under these conditions, antisocial behaviour may emerge as an important aspect of severe personality disorders, particularly in the syndrome of malignant narcissism, and in the most severe type of personality disorder, namely, the antisocial personality proper, which evinces most severe identity diffusion as well (Kernberg, 1984, pp. 197–209, 275–289). In general, normal superego formation is both a consequence of identity integration, and, in turn, protects normal identity. Severe superego disorganization, in contrast, worsens the effects of identity diffusion.

The choice of treatment for personality disorders, as we have found at Cornell (Clarkin, Yeomans, & Kernberg, 1999), depends, in great part, on their severity, reflected in the syndrome of identity diffusion. The presence or absence of identity diffusion can be elicited clinically in initial diagnostic interviews focused on the structural characteristics of personality disorders. The dimensional aspects— greater or lesser degrees of identity diffusion—still require further research. From a clinical standpoint, the extent to which ordinary social tact is still maintained or lost is the dominant indicator of the severity of the syndrome. The diagnosis of identity diffusion and of normal identity, in short, acquires fundamental importance in the clinical assessment of personality organization.

At the Personality Disorders Institute we have conducted a series of empirical studies evaluating the general hypothesis of the differentiation between neurotic and borderline structure on the basis of the syndrome of identity diffusion that, together with other contributions from the psychoanalytically oriented research literature on personality disorders, strengthen the diagnostic power of the concept of identity diffusion and the related diagnosis of borderline personality organization (Lenzenweger et al., 2001). More importantly, our development of a specific modification of standard psychoanalysis geared to the treatment of borderline personality organization has now been empirically studied and its efficacy demonstrated in comparison to other treatment approaches (Clarkin, Levy, & Schiavi, 2005). From a clinical standpoint, the possibility of a psychoanalytic assessment of the predominant structural characteristics of the patient, as well as the predominant dynamic hypotheses established in the initial interviews, facilitates the selection of the treatment—that is, standard psychoanalysis or modified psychoanalytic approaches— a point to which I shall return.

2. Salient clinical features

A general consensus emerged in our IPA group relatively easily, in contrast to the discussion about establishing the limits of this patient population, regarding the following features that were considered as typical of them: These patients have difficulties in experiencing and verbalizing preconscious fantasy, and with symbolic thinking. They have difficulty in establishing a representational frame for their affects and tend to displace intense affect states or express them in the form of somatization and/or acting out, rather than in the experience and communication of affectively invested representations. There was general agreement that a primary task in the psychoanalytic approach to borderline patients was to translate, interpretively, somatization and acting out into affective experience in the transference as an important early step in dealing with these manifestations.

We also agreed on the importance in these cases of fragmentation of free association as an expression of the prevalence of splitting mechanisms affecting cognitive processes. This fragmentation was observed originally by Bion (1967d), and recently developed further by André Green (2000a) in his concept of the "central phobic position"—that is, the defensive fragmentation of the patient's associative process to avoid his/her fear of fantasized traumatic consequences of undisrupted free association. One technical implication of this clinical fact is the need for the psychoanalyst, regardless of the modality of psychoanalytic approach, to interpret rapidly and systematically the patient's fragmented communications, thus fostering the development of eventual continuity in the interpretively formulated understandings, rather than passively expecting the fragmentation to resolve itself spontaneously or by gradual emergence of a dominant theme throughout the non-interpreted flow of the material.

I would add that, in our experience at Cornell, the fragmented flow of communication and kaleidoscopic behaviour of these patients is based on the activation in the transference of shifting unconscious object relations, with rapid "exchanges" between the patient's enactments of the respective self or object representations, while the reciprocal representations of object or self are projected onto the therapist. Primitive dissociation, or splitting, manifests itself as disjunction between verbal communication, nonverbal communication, and countertransference, determining a confusing experience for the therapist even when there seems to be a certain continuity of the verbal content from the patient. Primitive dissociation, in other words, may take the form of dissociated or fragmented verbal communication, or of dissociation among the various channels of communication in the transference.

We have learned from experience that the optimal way to explore the patient's material analytically is to attempt to diagnose the transference developments moment to moment (Clarkin, Yeomans, & Kernberg, 1999). The therapist must take a very active role in such rapid diagnosis and interpretive interventions, paying attention simultaneously to all three channels of communication (verbal, nonverbal, and countertransference) and describing in a metaphorical way the dominant object relation activated in the transference. This permits the therapist gradually to assess which pair of opposite internalized object relations (each pair being a dyadic self-representation–object-representation unit) is serving the function of defence and which represents the corresponding impulse being defended against. Analysis of the rapidly shifting transference dispositions gradually reveals a rather small repertoire of dominant object relations activated in the transference. These can gradually be sorted out into object-relations dyads with defensive functions and those with impulsive functions. Although these functions may be rapidly interchanged, the dominance of the same pair of object-relations dyads remain stable—what one might think of as the chronic transference dispositions.

The interpretive elaboration of the unconscious meanings in the here and now of each internal object relation activated in the transference, with a gradual sorting out of self from object representations and the dominant affect linking them, permits the patient to achieve the strategic goal of eventually integrating mutual split-off, idealized, and persecutory internalized object relations.

The consistent attention to transference and countertransference developments, the implicit split of the therapist into one part that is included in the transference/countertransference bind, and one part that remains as an "excluded other" carrying out the analytic task, and, symbolically, thus consolidating the triangular oedipal relationship over time and resolving the regressive dyadic enactments complements this technical approach. Our approach is essentially analytic, in terms of the management of the transference by interpretations alone, the maintenance or analytic reestablishment of technical neutrality as needed, and a maximal focus on the analysis of the transference rather that a supportive management of it. This approach developed in our Personality Disorders Institute, I believe, is commensurate with the major currents of object relations theories and reflects an integration of aspects of Kleinian, British Independent, and ego psychology approaches (Kernberg, 2001).

3. The use of countertransference

There was agreement in the group that consistent monitoring of the analyst's countertransference reactions to borderline patients was an essential—indeed, indispensable—aspect of the technical approach, because it is a window into the patient's internal world. The group started with an implicit agreement on the contemporary concept of countertransference as comprising: (a) the analysts' moment-to-moment emotional reaction to the patient, both in concordant identification and complementary identification experiences, and (b) the diagnosis and elaboration of countertransference developments into a specific chronic countertransference disposition towards a particular patient. There was agreement regarding the need to incorporate countertransference analysis into interpretive interventions, rather than communicating them directly to the patient, and to tolerate significant regression in the countertransference while the analyst maintains himself strictly in role—but not in a "robot-like" affective distance from the patient. It was also agreed that a firm and secure treatment frame was indispensable for this full tolerance to prevent acting out of the countertransference. Partial countertransference acting out, however, needs to be honestly acknowledged, without undue personal revelations by the analyst.

I find myself in essential agreement with these conclusions. I would only want to add two points regarding the countertransference consequences of the severe acting out and affect storms of borderline patients and regarding the difference between acute and chronic countertransference developments in terms of their implications and management. It may seem quite obvious that, given the dramatic, at times life-threatening tendencies of these patients towards acting out outside as well in the course of the psychotherapeutic sessions, a very intense countertransference reaction of the therapist may ensue, with the risk of partial acting out, particularly of aggressive countertransference feelings unconsciously induced in the therapist by the patient's projective identification expressed in highly provocative behaviour. To decide when limit-setting is indicated for objective reasons, or when such pressures in the therapist may reflect his/her acting out potential can become a major challenge at certain points in the treatment of these patients. A clear set of principles determining the protection of the therapeutic boundaries, what should be tolerated and what not, may be very helpful for the therapist to keep in mind at such difficult moments.

The acute shifts in countertransference experience from moment to moment, corresponding to the shift in the patient's fragmented transference expression, are eminently useful in the therapist's analysis of the transference–countertransference constellation. In contrast, chronic countertransference dispositions towards a certain patient that, typically, may increase gradually over time and are often not perceived by the therapist in its early phases, may become an important inhibiting element in the treatment. Such countertransference developments are often a response to intense yet subtle devaluing features in the transference, or to the more radical "deobjectalization" that André Green has described as the typical manifestation of the death drive (Green, 1993). In these latter cases, the danger of gradually giving up on the patient may become a major threat to the treatment. If, however, the therapist is aware of this development in his countertransference, utilizes the time between sessions for analysing this development, tracing its sources, and then introduces his new understanding in the sessions with the patient, such analysis of chronic countertransference reactions may, in turn, become a useful therapeutic instrument, of quite crucial importance with some very regressed cases.

4. Interpretation in the "here and now"

There emerged a general agreement in our IPA group on the importance of interpreting the unconscious meanings of the transference in the present transference–countertransference development very fully before proceeding to genetic interpretations. In fact, tracing back present transferences to hypothesized past unconscious developments before a full transformation of present unconscious meanings into a conscious and preconscious integration by the patient has been achieved may lead to further chaos or meaningless intellectualizations—if not to new, presently unanalysable transference developments as a response to such premature efforts at genetic reconstruction. Furthermore, the interpretation of unconscious meanings in the here and now needs to incorporate (a) the "total transference situation," including (b) the implications of the transference for the understanding of the present external reality communicated by the patient, (c) any somatization occurring in the context of transference development, and (d) the relationship of the transference to distortion and fragmentation of the patient's use of language. The analyst should reformulate the patient's statements to a minor degree in order to convey the interpretive communication in a way that the patient would be able to follow, thus restoring his linguistic capability and facilitating a preconscious tolerance of the interpretation that, in a second phase, would deal with the transference to the object as well. Here, the Kleinian focus on the total transference situation; the ego psychological focus on the present unconscious; the British Independents' approach to anchoring the interpretation on the presently dominant affect in the transference; and André Green's emphasis on the dual expression of the transference towards the object and towards language, all converge in a strong agreement regarding the nature of required transference interpretations.

Here again I find myself in full agreement with the consensus that evolved in the group regarding transference interpretation in the "here and now". It needs to be stressed that, in contrast to the Relational or Intersubjective approach, the group felt that the interpretation of the transference should not limit itself to the present relationship, but attempt to analyse the reactivation of primitive object relations of the patient. The interpretation should permit a gradual deepening of the patient's experience of his intrapsychic life and open up new channels to his unconscious past, gradually dissolving the conscious and preconscious myths that borderline patients typically present at the initiation of their treatment. The inclusion of the therapist's countertransference understanding in his transference interpretation, rather than the direct communication of the countertransference *per se*, powerfully contributes to gradual deepening of the patient's focus on his/her intrapsychic experience rather than maintaining the interpretive focus defensively on the surface of the immediate interaction. The deepening of transference analysis follows the general principle, implicitly acknowledged, I believe, by the entire group, that the transference does not reflect simply the reality of the past, but a combination of past reality, fantasy, and defences against both (Melanie Klein, 1952a).

5. The nature of the predominant instinctual conflicts

There was general agreement in our group that borderline patients do not present exclusively "preoedipal" conflicts, but a condensation of preoedipal and oedipal conflicts that require careful attention to the moment-to-moment shift regarding which aspect of the same conflict would need to be approached first. This synchronicity of transference developments will shift gradually into an oscillation between synchronic and diachronic expression of conflicts, in which the interpretation of a narrative within a historical sequence might become a feasible aspect of the interpretive work. There was general agreement on the predominance, in these patients, of conflicts around early aggression, determining the configuration of both preoedipal and oedipal conflicts and their condensation, and that the degree of severity of primitive aggression might be summarized in the following way:

At developmentally more advanced levels, aggression is directed against the object and against language, as mentioned before. At more primitive and severe levels that aggression is transformed into disinvestment, leading, first, to disinvestment of language, then to a disinvestment of the object ("the object and the need for it do not exist any more"), and, at the most severe degree of primitive aggression, to the disinvestment and the denial of the existence of the self. It is under conditions of predominance of such disinvestment of object and self that it is reasonable to talk about the death drive as the most severe manifestation of primitive aggression, that, in fact, dominates the most severe borderline patients.

Again, I find myself in full agreement with the consensus that evolved in the group as summarized.

6. The focus on the dominant affect

As mentioned before, the approach to interpretation from the point of the "selected fact" centres on the dominant affect and the defences against conscious and preconscious tolerance of this affective state by the borderline patient. The interpretive task includes the provision of a representational frame for the patient's affect that will permit the integration of defensively fragmented affect states in severely schizoid individuals, the reincorporation of projected primitive affects at first only available in the analyst's countertransference, the transformation of acting out and somatization into affective representation, and the tolerance of representational framing of initially intolerable affect storms. The patient's capacity for the development of symbolic management of affectively charged object relations is the desired consequence of effective interpretive work. While significant disagreements persisted in our group regarding the theoretical view of the relationship between affects, drives, representations, and object relations, clinically those different theoretical approaches within the group came together in this assertion of the privileged nature of the focus on the central affect within each transference development.

Once again, in the light of our experience at Cornell, I fully endorse this general conclusion of the research group. I would add that, from a practical viewpoint, a major issue that emerges in the treatment of severe borderline patients is the management of affect storms in the course of the sessions. Borderline patients present us, in this regard, with two apparently opposite and yet complementary situations (Kernberg, 2004): The first is one in which an open, observable affect storm explodes in the psychotherapeutic setting, usually with an intense aggressive and demanding quality, but also at times, with what on the surface appears to be a sexualized assault on the therapist, the invasiveness of which reveals the condensation of sexual and aggressive elements. The patient, under the influence of such an intense affective experience, is driven to action. At this point any capacity for reflectiveness, cognitive understanding, and verbal communication of internal states is, for the moment, unavailable. Thus, the therapist now must depend mainly on observation of nonverbal communication and countertransference in order to assess and diagnose the nature of the object relation, the activation of which is giving rise to the affect storm.

The second situation, namely, long periods during which the patient's rigid, repetitive behaviour, along with a dearth of affective expression—in fact, a deadly monotony—permeates the session, seems almost the opposite of the first. The effect on the interaction between patient and therapist during such "dead" periods can be as powerful and threatening as that of the affect storms referred to before. The therapist may feel bored and paralysed to the point of despair, rage, or indifference, but he can, at least, recognize that an impasse has been reached. On realizing that the significant information is coming from these countertransference reactions and the patient's nonverbal communication, the therapist may attempt to analyse and interpret the nature of the scenario that is being enacted via the patient's behaviour. This regularly leads to the striking emergence of the violent affect that the rigid monotony had masked, often felt first in the countertransference and then rapidly materializing in the therapeutic interaction, once that countertransference is utilized as material for interpretation of the nature of the transference. In short, the analytic management of affect storms illustrates once more the importance of countertransference analysis and its inclusion into transference interpretations.

7. The controversial nature of "support"

All along there existed an implicit agreement in the group, that the optimal treatment for the entire borderline spectrum, regardless of where the limits of this spectrum were drawn, was a technical approach centred on transference–countertransference analysis to help the patient to integrate the dynamic unconscious into the conscious and preconscious ego as the best "support," in contrast to supportive psychotherapeutic approaches.

While I subscribe to this conclusion of the IPA group, I believe it needs to be acknowledged that there are patients who are unable to tolerate an analytic approach, be it standard psychoanalysis or psychoanalytic psychotherapy, and where a supportive modality of treatment, based on psychoanalytic principles, may be a second-choice alternative. There is no doubt in my mind that, whenever possible, an analytic approach would be preferable, but I believe that it is one of our tasks in taking responsibility for the treatment of a broad spectrum of very severe cases of personality disorder that further work be done to clarify both what the limits of an analytic approach might be and how, from a psychoanalytic viewpoint, we might maximize the effectiveness of supportive approaches. This is one of the tasks in which our Personality Disorders Institute at Cornell is involved at this time.

II. Major areas of disagreement

1. Value and nature of diagnosis

There were significant disagreements regarding the definition of the field of borderline conditions related to the wide range of degrees of severity of illness and dominant psychopathology of the patients presented to and discussed by the group. At the same time, the very effort to arrive at a consensus about the diagnostic entity or grouping represented by these patients proved to be highly controversial. There was a strong resistance to adhering to the descriptive, "psychiatric" diagnosis of borderline personality disorder, and even to the broader psychostructural entity constituted by borderline personality organization as equivalent to severe personality disorders in general. There was however, general agreement that a diagnosis could not or should not be arrived at on the basis of the dynamic aspects of the patient's psychopathology—that is, whether the conflicts were predominantly preoedipal or oedipal, oral or anal, etc.

The North American members of the group were inclined to make an initial diagnosis of the patient based on a combination of descriptive and psychostructural criteria—such as the presence or absence of the syndrome of identity diffusion, the predominance or absence of primitive defensive operations during the early assessment, and the general manifestations of ego strength or weakness. The European and Latin American members of the group questioned the importance of such efforts and stressed, to the contrary, the importance of the evaluation of the patient's capacity to accept a psychoanalytic frame for evaluating his unconscious conflicts, the capacity to participate in the development of a psychoanalytic process, the nature of the evolving transference/countertransference bind, in addition to the patient's motivation, secondary gain, capacity for insight, and collaboration with the analyst.

For the French members, the patient's capacity to develop a fantasy life that signalled the optimal operation of preconscious functioning seemed essential to carry out an unmodified psychoanalysis, in contrast to patients with very little capacity for symbolic representation of affect states and the tendency to express affects as acting out or somatization, who would require a psychoanalytic psychotherapy. Concern was expressed by the British members of the group, largely agreed upon by all others except the Americans, that a sharp focus on a descriptive and psychostructural differential diagnosis would run counter the development of an analytic frame and created the risk of distorting the technical neutrality of the analyst. In short, there was disagreement regarding the following areas: (a) the feasibility of making an initial diagnosis, rather than allowing the gradual emergence of diagnostic conclusions throughout the treatment; (b) the importance of making such an initial assessment; (c) what modification of the treatment situation might be required; (d) the diagnostic criteria; and (e) the extent to which an initial diagnosis, accurate as it might be, would be helpful or restrictive in the initiation of the treatment.

Behind these disagreements emerged a more general issue of whether psychoanalysis and psychiatry are mutually complementary sciences that may strengthen one another, or whether they are competing frames of reference that implicitly deny the other's methodology in their effort to obtain data specific to their tasks. This group was truly divided regarding this issue, probably reflecting a broader controversy within the psychoanalytic community.

I have mentioned earlier that I stand clearly on one side of this divide in the group: I think that psychoanalysis and psychiatry are mutually complementary sciences that may strengthen each other, and that the research findings stemming from descriptive, phenomenological psychiatric approaches may be integrated creatively into a psychoanalytic framework that considers deep structures of the personality as well as the specific dynamics reflecting the patient's unconscious conflicts. Character structure, identity, reality testing, and the constellation of defensive operations are such deep structures manifested as the constellations of surface behaviour of the patient. Psychiatric diagnosis can be significantly enriched and more sharply focused by the integration of our psychoanalytic understanding of these realms. The deep structures of the mind as revealed in behavioural manifestations may provide an immediate picture of the overall organization of the patient's intrapsychic life; and, by the same token, they may point to the potentially optimal therapeutic approach within a broad spectrum of psychoanalytically derived treatments, including standard psychoanalysis, psychoanalytic psychotherapy, and supportive psychotherapy.

A full discussion of this issue would exceed the limits of this presentation. From a practical viewpoint, however, the possibility of diagnosing, beyond the dominant type of personality disorder, the presence or absence of identity diffusion and reality testing, for example, clearly have implications for the indication of treatment and the prognosis with various types of treatment. There is growing evidence, from the early psychotherapy research project of the Menninger Foundation (Kernberg et al., 1972), to the randomized controlled treatment of 90 borderline patients at our Institute that strengthens the arguments for this approach. In practice, members of our IPA research group who would object to the use of descriptive diagnosis stemming from psychiatry still believe in differential structures that determine the indications for standard psychoanalysis or a modification in the psychoanalytic approach. Although they might prefer to reach their diagnosis on the basis of the analysis of transference and countertransference developments over time, they also were interested in reaching this conclusion relatively rapidly in order to structure an optimal treatment approach for each patient. I believe that in this regard we may be closer clinically than we are theoretically.

2. Definition and indications of modified psychoanalytic treatments

The tradition of the psychoanalytic culture and theoretical approach represented by the members of the IPA group seemed important in determining where members of the group stood regarding these issues. Thus, for example, the Kleinian tendency to carry out standard psychoanalytic treatment for practically all the patients they see and their tendency to rarely consider modification to standard treatment stands in contrast to the American ego psychology tradition of considering psychoanalytic psychotherapy a distinct modality of treatment, indicated for patients with severe psychopathology who would not be able to tolerate a standard psychoanalytic approach. The French tradition to be flexible with psychoanalytic technique, both regarding frequency of sessions and face-to-face treatment, incorporates technical approaches that, from a North American perspective, would be considered psychoanalytic psychotherapy rather than psychoanalysis proper. There appears to be similar flexibility with respect to frequency of sessions and face-to-face contact in the British Independent tradition. Probably clinicians from all psychoanalytic schools, when treating psychotic patients proper, would see such patients in face-to-face interviews.

We gained the impression in the group that the Argentinean approach, as influenced by both British and French traditions of not privileging descriptive psychiatric diagnosis, was also open to modifying, as needed, standard psychoanalysis to adjust the treatment to the needs of patients with severe psychopathology. In so far as both French and British Independent analysts are willing to modify their technique for patients in the borderline range to such an extent that, in their view, this constitutes psychoanalytic psychotherapy, there may be a development of an emerging implicit consensus regarding the need to arrive at a definition of that psychotherapeutic technique and its indications and contraindications. In fact, agreement about technical requirements in the psychoanalytic approach to borderline patients spelled out before may apply, I believe, specifically to this psychoanalytic psychotherapy. Some of these technical approaches may, however, also be included, as needed, with patients in standard psychoanalytic treatment under conditions of severe regression.

An additional perspective was opened up by the group regarding the extent to which borderline patients require a consistent technical approach, regardless of which treatment modality is being used, versus an approach that changes flexibly throughout different stages of the treatment. Representing the empirical research findings at the Personality Disorders Institute at Cornell, I have stressed both the importance and the possibility of an initial diagnostic assessment of patients based upon descriptive and psychostructural criteria, for the indication of a specific psychoanalytic psychotherapy, and the empirical evidence available for the efficacy of this psychotherapy. My position represented a minority position within our group, although it generated significant discussions that highlighted the agreements and disagreements that are being reported here.

The long-standing research on the psychopathology, diagnosis, and transference developments of borderline patients at the Cornell Personality Disorders Institute, including the findings of our latest randomized controlled trial of 90 patients distributed across Transference-Focused Psychotherapy (TFP), Dialectical Behaviour Therapy (DBT), and supportive psychotherapy based on psychoanalytic theory, has yielded significant findings. Of the three treatment conditions, only TFP showed an increase in reflective function after one year of treatment. Reflective Function is a measure of the patients' capacity to better understand their own mental states and that of significant others (Clarkin, Levy, & Schiavi, 2005). It is the capacity to think about one's experience in relation to the intentions and viewpoint of the other. On this basis, I feel strengthened in my view that transference-focused psychotherapy, as a specific psychoanalytic psychotherapy for patients with borderline personality organization, is an effective treatment for patients whom the large majority of psychoanalysts, in any place in the world, would, I believe, not accept for standard psychoanalytic treatment. The publication of this treatment approach in a manualized form, and research indicating that it can be applied in adherent and competent ways, constitutes, I believe, an important step forward in the scientific development of psychoanalytic theory and its derived techniques and adds a new dimension to the overall discussion about the diagnosis and treatment of borderline conditions (Clarkin, Yeomans, & Kernberg, 1999).

3. Neurotic, borderline, and psychotic structures

Does it make a difference? There were significant differences in the viewpoints of the members of the IPA group regarding specific defensive organization and transference developments that would differentiate those three overall levels of psychopathology. While, as mentioned before, there was a clear agreement regarding particular aspects of the transference and linguistic communication of patients in the borderline field, there were significant disagreements regarding whether one could systematize different defensive organizations and transference developments for neurotic, borderline, and psychotic patients.

The North American group members thought that these patients evinced significant differences in transference developments: for example, the predominance of primitive, split-off part-object relations reflecting identity diffusion dominant in borderline cases, in contrast to total or integrated object relations activated predominantly in the transference of neurotic patients, and the fused, undifferentiated self and object representations in the case of psychotic patients. European and Latin American members of the group felt that both transference developments and defensive organization were highly individualized features emerging in the course of the treatment of any and all patients and that, for example, the same transferences and defensive consolidations could be observed with neurotic and borderline patients. In other words, a majority felt that the structural consequences of individual dynamics were more important, by far, than common group features attributed to any diagnostic designation. In fact, this conviction did strengthen the majority's view regarding the advisability of using standard psychoanalytic approach with all patients, until or unless transference developments and the patient's incapacity to maintain himself/herself within an analytic frame would make necessary some modification in the psychoanalytic approach.

This controversy resonates with the earlier ones referred to before. I would only add at this point that if we all agreed that certain patients cannot tolerate a standard psychoanalysis, requiring a modification of technique, it can only be an advantage to be able to clearly diagnose this as soon and as objectively as possible. What is the nature of the patient's condition, and what is the optimal treatment for this condition? I believe that the mental health community and society at large are making demands on us for clearer responses to those questions, and in fact, to the entire field of psychotherapeutic treatments. I believe we can successfully respond to these expectations and that, in fact, psychoanalysis may be a most powerful instrument for progress in the general areas of psychopathology, normal and pathological development, and treatment indications and techniques with which psychiatry is struggling at this point.

4. Initial contract and limit setting

My presentation to the group of videotaped sessions of a severely regressed borderline patient who had been physically attacking the furniture of my office, and with whom I had set clear limits of what was and what was not tolerable in the sessions, raised questions about the extent to which such a controlled setting constitutes an "imprisonment" of the patient that significantly distorts the transference and limits the possibility of a psychoanalytic approach. In more general terms, the issue was raised of the initial contract-setting in the case of patients with severe, chronic suicidal and parasuicidal behaviour not linked to depression; patients with antisocial behaviour, drug and alcohol abuse and dependency; severe eating disorders; and patients with a history of physical and/or sexual attacks on their therapists. A majority of the IPA group objected to setting limits or making preconditions at the initiation of treatment or even in the course of the treatment itself, experiencing such limit-setting as detrimental to an analytic approach. However, there was general recognition that these were very ill patients who would probably not be able to be maintained in a standard analytic situation unless such limits were established; and a recognition that, in practice, different psychoanalysts were willing to see patients of different levels of severity, in part determined by the private outpatient setting in which most psychoanalysts work, in contrast to the broader possibilities opened up by psychotherapeutic settings in the context of psychiatric hospitals or clinics that provide additional safety and protection to patients and therapists.

There was interest as well as questioning of a psychotherapeutic approach that employs limit-setting and includes temporary abandonment of technical neutrality, followed by a gradual reinstatement of technical neutrality through clarification and interpretation of the reasons that motivated the therapist's departure from neutrality. A general question evolved that remained open—namely, regarding the extent to which our technical approaches and innovations are determined by the severity of the patient's illness, and the extent to which there is a natural selection process on the part of psychoanalysts of those patients who, they conclude, are still able to accept a standard psychoanalytic frame. Many practical considerations and circumstances may determine analysts' approach to diagnosis and to modalities of treatment and technique.

In general, the same members of the group who acknowledged that they select patients for whom they think psychoanalysis is the optimal treatment were those who questioned the specific techniques of psychoanalytic psychotherapy because they correctly felt that they were not typical of standard psychoanalysis. I believe they were implicitly acknowledging that psychoanalysis has limited indications for a specific kind of patient, whom an experienced psychoanalyst is able to select through evaluation of transference and countertransference elements. This selective process may exclude a large majority of patients coming for psychotherapeutic treatment these days and challenges the psychoanalytic community to develop approaches for those patients for whom the classical psychoanalytic method is not the treatment of choice. I am confident that our theories, our understanding of the dynamic unconscious and of human personality, and our treatment instruments do permit us to develop new approaches to help large segments of the population whom we cannot reach at present.

5. Contraindications and prognosis

While all members of the IPA group agreed in principle that there are patients within the borderline spectrum who are not analysable, there remained significant disagreement regarding whether relevant categories of patients might be defined on the basis of their prognostic evaluation rather than their evaluation by means of a therapeutic trial analysis. Again, those of us who stress the importance of an initial descriptive and structural diagnosis felt, for example, that one could diagnose the antisocial personality proper as presenting an absolute contraindication for any psychotherapeutic modality of treatment, while the majority of the group, critical about such a "psychiatric" approach to diagnosis, stressed the importance of letting this decision evolve in the course of the treatment.

This discussion evolve d into considerations regarding prognostic issues. While there was a general consensus regarding the negative prognostic implications of severely destructive and self-destructive transferences, there was less agreement regarding other patient features, such as secondary gain, limited intelligence, the preservation of object relations in external reality, and so on. A majority of the group felt that, ultimately, the nature of the countertransference would be crucial in determining the prognosis for the treatment—in other words, the extent to which some degree of a harmonious relationship between the personality of patient and therapist, and the tolerance of negative countertransference, combined in helping therapists to deal with apparently impossible situations.

Regarding the issue of contraindications and prognosis, here I believe the experience gathered at the Cornell Personality Disorders Institute over the past 25 years of treating a broad spectrum of both hospitalized and outpatient borderline patients, with treatments carried out by experienced and specialized psychoanalysts as well as psychoanalytic psychotherapists, is relevant. I think there is ample evidence that there are important prognostic features in the personality and the life situation of the patient that worsen the prognosis, regardless of the therapist's countertransference disposition. These include, first of all, the severity of antisocial features: The more severe the antisocial features, the worse the prognosis, especially when the diagnosis of an antisocial personality proper is done in strict ways, following the criteria developed by Robert Hare (Hare, Hart, & Harpur, 1991), Michael Stone (1993), and myself (Kernberg, 1984). Antisocial Personality proper is a contraindication for almost every psychotherapeutic approach—a conclusion that corresponds to an implicit consensus of clinicians from many orientations. Another significant negative prognostic factor is the secondary gain of illness of patients who have managed to develop a social support system that protects their incapacity and/or unwillingness to work and fosters a dependent and even parasitic lifestyle; and a general impoverishment of object relations over many years, leading to a severe progressive isolation of the patient, probably corresponding to the syndrome of "de-objectalization" described by Green. The underlying psychology of patients with severe, chronic self-mutilation, which may lead to loss of limbs and to death, in addition to chronic severe suicidal behaviour of a well-thought out, secretly triumphant type not linked with depression, may reflect most clearly the deobjectalizing drive.

6. The nature of the diagnostic inquiry

The controversy regarding the importance of carrying out a descriptive-structural diagnostic assessment of patients extended to the nature of the diagnostic instrument utilized to arrive at a diagnostic formulation. Those who attempt to achieve a combination of psychiatric/psychodynamic diagnosis would raise specific questions regarding a patient's present symptomatology, his present personality functioning, and his view of self and others, and would assess identity integration versus identity diffusion, the patient's capacity for reality testing, ego factors (such as, anxiety tolerance, impulse control, sublimatory functioning), the patient's capacity to function in work or profession, and his/her intimate relations and social life. In short, they would present the patient with a very structured interviewing process, including many specific, concrete questions. Those who felt that the most important issue was to assess analysability would, in contrast, utilize a modified form of free association, permit the patient to speak freely in order to observe the natural organization of his/her psychological functioning, and, in general, reduce the diagnostic assessment to one or a few sessions in which the patient's willingness and capacity to undergo a psychoanalytic process could be assessed.

French psychoanalysts would be particularly interested in the patient's preconscious functioning, his capacity for representation of affects, and his tolerance of a fantasy life, in contrast to discharge of conflictual material by acting out or somatization; perhaps some Argentinean psychoanalysts would be most open to taking patients into psychoanalytic treatment even if they evinced clearly psychotic symptoms during such an evaluative process. In any case, the assessment process for the majority of the IPA group would clearly focus on the extent to which the patient was able to evince some rudimentary capacity for free association and self-reflectiveness.

I believe that there are two different issues that were combined in the discussion of this point. One is the nature of the initial diagnosis, and the other is the assessment of the patient's analysability or, more tentatively, the patient's capacity to participate in an analytic encounter. Those who question initial diagnostic interviews geared to establishing a differential diagnosis, be it along descriptive or structural dimensions, are concerned with interference with the possibility of assessing the patient's capacity to participate in an analytic endeavour. For this group the focus is on the first hours of engagement rather than on specific types of inquiries.

Those of us who would focus on the importance of a diagnostic assessment, however, would not argue with the importance of evaluating the patient's capacity for an analytic encounter but would, rather, insist on the realistic possibility of combining an initial systematic evaluation of the patient's psychopathology, differential diagnosis, and potential treatment indication with a second stage of what might be called an analytic interview. This is, in fact, what in practice is implicit in transference-focused psychotherapy (TFP) (Clarkin, Yeomans, & Kernberg, 1999). I think that any clinician may confirm by his/her own experience that such a sequence of inquiry is perfectly feasible, and that the initial, highly structured interviews will not interfere with a later instruction to the patient to speak more freely about what his/her concerns are or to invite the patient to carry out a communication that will already give us some indication of a capacity for free association and self-reflection. In any case, I stand clearly on the side of carrying out such a bi-phasic approach.

III. Open areas for further exploration

1. Diagnostic criteria and assessment

We all agreed that it is important that the controversies regarding diagnosis, a clear delimitation of the field of borderline psychopathology, and its differential diagnosis be explored further, so that a meaningful clinical and scientific development in this field can be fostered. We were impressed by the degree of agreement we achieved regarding concrete interventions in sessions with borderline patients, the understanding and interpretation of the transference, and the nature and utilization of the countertransference. We evidently had a common core of clinical experience with these patients, which led to significant rapprochement in our technical approach throughout our meetings. We felt that we could build on this common core to explore further the issue of diagnostic assessment and its relationship to treatment approaches and prognosis, and to research on outcome. Behind this, however, were two additional controversies: the extent to which psychoanalysis and psychiatry are related, what the nature of their relationship should be, and the extent to which psychoanalysis should creatively participate in the present-day demand for empirically based treatments.

2. The boundaries of psychoanalysis

We all recognized that certain patients cannot tolerate a standard psychoanalytic situation and yet are able to benefit from a psychodynamic approach utilizing techniques of transference interpretation, countertransference analysis, and technical neutrality. This demands further study of the boundaries of psychoanalytic technique proper, the nature and boundaries of modified or applied forms of psychoanalytic technique, and their indications and contraindications. As a practical reality, psychoanalysts are effectively treating a broad spectrum of patients with whom they apply analytic understanding and ways of intervening that may depart from and yet are intimately rooted in psychoanalytic technique proper. The description, analysis, and expansion of this field, broadly to be called "psychoanalysis and its derived technical modalities", seems of utmost importance for the reality of the present-day practice of psychoanalysts in all three regions and a potentially crucial contribution of psychoanalysis to mental health, beyond its traditional application with individual patients.

3. Dominant psychodynamic constellations

While a general agreement regarding the nature of the transferences and the importance of countertransference analysis and its incorporation into transference interpretation evolved in this group, we also realized that there is a great need for continuing to study particularly frequent dynamic constellations that borderline patients present. We need to develop further the findings to which authors from various schools have contributed, such as André Green's (1986b) clarification of the psychodynamics of the "dead mother" and of negative narcissism and de-objectalization; and the specific contributions of the Kleinian school, such as Bion's (1967d) description of the attack on language and the characteristics of regressive transferences of borderline patients, and Herbert Rosenfeld's (1987) contributions to narcissistic resistances; and Winnicott's (1960b) analysis of the false self, and of the relationship between transitional phenomena and fetishistic developments.

4. "Preoedipal" and "oedipal" dynamics

We all agreed that in the last 20 years there had been a tendency to relate borderline psychopathology to the developments in the first few years of life and, concomitantly, within ego psychology, the centrality of the mother–infant relationship during the period of separation-individuation. In a parallel way, the focus on the first year of life in the Kleinian school had reached a similar focus within a different conceptual model. All of this implied, the IPA group agreed, a certain neglect of the earliest manifestations of the oedipal conflict, the primary induction of unconscious sexual urges and conflicts already contained in the triangular aspects of the mother/infant relationship—in other words, the archaic oedipal conflict as described by French authors. The importance of unconscious conflicts around sadomasochism and the related early normal or abnormal condensation between aggressive and erotic strivings seems fundamental regarding the borderline field and needs to be studied more systematically. There was agreement that very deep and primitive sexual conflicts, condensed with aggressive strivings, were an important dynamic feature of borderline pathology that needed to be focused upon much more than what many clinical cases in the literature would indicate.

5. The criteria and limits of analysability

There was a general agreement that further research regarding the treatment of borderline conditions would be of enormous help in clarifying further indications, as well as limitations, for standard psychoanalytic treatment, thus enriching our present criteria for analysability.

* * *

In conclusion, regarding the overall work of our research group, what was achieved and what was not achieved, and where we need to go from here, I believe that there were significant points of clarification of where the entire psychoanalytic field stands at this point regarding borderline conditions, what the major issues are that need to be clarified, the controversies to be resolved, the place of clinical experience and research in all these processes, and what, in general, the psychoanalytic community can take from our explorations of borderline conditions. It is clear that we all struggle with patients for whom the standard psychoanalytic technique is contraindicated and who tend to induce in the therapist the tendency to abandon the treatment, or to avoid such patients altogether and refer them elsewhere, or to apply some degree of modification in technique, whether this is called an individually modified psychoanalytic technique or parameters of technique or a psychoanalytic psychotherapy. Most psychoanalysts feel comfortable taking one of these roads, with an internal conviction that they are still applying psychoanalytic understanding to the situation and to their decision-making regarding how to conduct the treatment. There is also agreement that these patients show remarkable differences from the standard psychoanalytic case in their transference–countertransference developments, their linguistic communications, and the complications that emerge in their treatment, and that all these characteristics have to do with deep structural conditions that differentiate them from neurotic patients. Evidently, the degree to which such a differentiated patient population can be diagnosed from the very onset of treatment or only in the course of an exploratory analytic approach is still highly controversial, as referred to before, and remains an area that needs further dialogue. Finally, the IPA group illustrated the ongoing controversy within the psychoanalytic community as to the extent to which it needs to relate to psychiatry and, implicitly, to other neurobiological and social-psychological sciences. I trust that my own conviction, viewing psychoanalysis as a basic science that does need to be related consistently to its boundary sciences in the neurobiological and social psychological area, has been expressed consistently throughout this discussion.

6

Reflections on a group
investigating borderline personality

William I. Grossman

The establishment of an international group of psychoanalysts to consider the nature of and psychoanalytic treatment of borderline personality disorders presents a window into the problems of clinical–conceptual research in psychoanalysis. The discussions exploring various aspects of psychoanalytic experience and problems in treating borderline patients were rich, stimulating, and illuminating for clinicians. However, in this chapter, I do not attempt to summarize the findings, agreements, and disagreements of the group members regarding what we learned about "non-neurotic" patients and their treatment. Instead, I present some reflections on the issues and problems involved in this kind of team effort. The fact that I focus on problems should not be taken as disqualifying the work that has been done but, rather, as something that has been learned through our work together. The progressive increase of mutual understanding of our points of view promised deepening of the exploration of key issues if time had permitted. It seems clear that research of this kind requires a considerably greater period of time for the realization of its potential.

Our group included eight people from four different countries and at least six different points of view, theoretically and clinically.

Sadly, Dr Grossman died before he was able to read his chapter in print.

Some members of the group were bi- and trilingual, so that the matter of translation between the languages of nations was relatively easy to manage, compared with the translation of psychoanalytic usages and points of view.

We had six weekend meetings over a two-year period. The intended format for our work was the presentation of borderline patients by different members of the group, one per meeting. The presenting members also distributed clinical notes and brief essays describing their points of view. This chapter focuses on two presentations of borderline patients with very different clinical features. Psychotic patients and patients with neurotic and narcissistic character disorders were also presented. Only three of the treatments had a recognizably psychoanalytic frame. The resulting discussions and exchanges of views were rewarding and, as I mentioned above, could reasonably be expected to lead to important clarifications of the understanding and treatment of borderline patients that could emerge, given sufficient time.

There are obviously a number of different kinds of issues to be considered in a group project having the goal of using clinical reports for research purposes. Similarities and differences in background and orientation to clinical material influence the discussion of basic issues such as the meaning of diagnosis, the timing of diagnosis, the kind of classification of patients, and the relevance of diagnosis and classification to treatment decisions. Similarly, the interpretation of clinical material engaged similarities and differences of theories and clinical orientations. Since the goal was to study and develop a psychoanalytic approach to the "non-neurotic" patient, some clarification of what various members meant by a "psychoanalytic approach" and "psychoanalytic psychotherapy" required consideration. One relevant issue was the question of whether psychoanalytic work is possible when the frame/setting of the treatment was different from the traditional setup. There were the usual questions having to do with the importance of frequency of sessions, the use of the couch, and the question of how much variation and flexibility regarding these factors was helpful or an interference within a given treatment, and in general. The point of these discussions was not to arrive at authoritative pronouncements on these issues. The goal was to understand the influence of these factors on analytic processes in both analysand and analyst. Among the important features of an analytic process would be the recognition of the subjective aspects of the experience as distinct from the exploration of environmental instigators.

An area for consideration related to the above is the group of issues having to do with the requirements of research and the kind of research that can be done with clinical presentations. The problem is stated in the title of André Green's (2000d) paper: "What Kind of Research for Psychoanalysis?" There were differences in the group regarding the requirements for any kind of research as well as the question of whether research with clinical material is possible or is, possibly, incompatible with it.

These questions are intimately related to the question of the extent to which psychoanalysis can be, or can be considered to be, a science, and if so, in what sense? This often-examined problem cannot be pursued here, but some aspects need to be considered if generalizations about clinical material are to be meaningful. While clinical thinking is not research-oriented thinking, careful description and some degree of objectification are common to both. One of the features of clinical thinking that presents particular problems for reproducible results involves the use of the self-observed and self-observing subjective processes of the analyst. An advantage of a group effort is that the interchanges offer multiple reflections on the presented clinical dialogue. This allows for and promotes further reflection by the treating analyst and often results in the further elaboration of the clinical material. These processes permit extended consideration of the relations between observations, interpretations, and the development of concepts.

Some problems of communication

Some of the problems of communication involved the differences of terminology related to different theoretical frameworks. While these present considerable difficulty, they are perhaps not the main problem. It may be that the use of the same terminology to describe or conceptualize different phenomena is more difficult to manage. Such misunderstandings are frequent and not always easy to resolve. In some ways, the effort to understand others speaking the same language resembles the problem of understanding the patients we are discussing. Their use of our common language may be idiosyncratic and belong to a system of thinking different from our own.

During our meetings, we had some useful discussion of these problems. We did not always resolve them, but the discussions served to clarify important aspects of our terminology and the kinds of intrapsychic and intersubjective processes these terms address. An important result of our discussions was to increase our mutual understanding in a way that, if such discussions were more common and more extensive, some of the controversies in our field would benefit.

Some of the confusions concerned relatively simple terms. For example, the word "action" had different meanings for different members of the group. In that connection, some people preferred a concrete sense of the word that could be used to distinguish physical action from the use of language and speech as action in which they were used for their effect on others rather than to convey meaning. Since there are other ways to express the latter functions, these kinds of usage issues were clarified and placed in their respective conceptual frameworks.

Another example is the use of the terms "observe" and "observation" to describe the analyst's activity. For some analysts, this is a departure from subjective and intersubjective orientations currently favoured by some groups. The choice of such language suggests to them to reflect a claim to an "objective" attitude of the analyst with all the associated connotations of positivistic, scientistic, and authoritarian orientations. A similar issue arises with the use of the term "object relations", which, for some, implies relationships of subject and object rather than the relationships between two subjects. The term "subject relations" has been suggested as an alternative (Green). Along similar, but not identical lines, the term "self" was, some time ago, introduced to escape the objectifications that some analysts thought the term "ego" implied. It is my impression that these problems are a modem continuation of the existentialist critiques of Freudian psychoanalysis as expounded many years ago by Binswanger and others. I also believe that the creation of entities or the recourse to sometime neglected entities—self, subject—cannot escape the "objectivity" of such entities, and that the desired closeness to the clinical material is not really achieved in this way. However, our discussion brought out the fact that there are overlapping meanings to the terms "ego", "self", and "subject", but that each of these terms is centred on different aspects of the person.

A related issue is the creation of new terms to refer to complex issues. My own impression is that a careful description of what is meant is preferable to new terminology. In any case, the description is required to clarify terminology, and the problem gets shifted to the discussion of the meaning of terms. As is well known, this readily becomes a further basis for controversy.

The meaning and value of diagnosis

Another example of differences of usage, and not the most profound, is the issue of diagnosis. Various members of the group had different ideas about what is implied by the idea of diagnosis and, therefore, what is to be done with it. That we need some kind of diagnostic evaluation as an organizer was clear, since, for the sake of brevity in discussion, broad diagnostic terms were constantly used on the assumption that everyone knew what was intended by hysteria, borderline, psychosis, and so on. The difficulty of understanding borderlines, the features responsible for it, and the manifestations of that range of problems were recognized by everyone. Some kinds of differentiation among patients had already begun with the designation "non-neurotic", something more than just borderlines, and the fact that people could agree on some characteristics of the patients we were alluding to. Clearly, a diagnostic process was at work.

Nevertheless, the question of diagnosis raised conflict in the group, and the question of the value of diagnosis, how it should be made, and when it should be made remained controversial to some extent throughout the meetings. The use of systematic diagnosis according to the DSM was generally regarded as not helpful in itself for evaluating the patients available for one kind of treatment or another since it does not adequately describe those features of the borderline patient that are relevant to treatment.

Broadly speaking, there were two ideas about diagnosis. One view was that speaking of diagnosis necessarily implied a formal classification like the DSM's, therefore implying rigidity and the early commitment to a particular formulation. Those with this view were concerned that this kind of diagnosis would lead to premature conclusions about the patient. They were also concerned that any efforts to formulate the dynamics and issues of a case early on would necessarily bias thinking about it, and that having formulated early, one would be so attached to the formulation that only what was expected would be observed. That is, the analytic mode of listening would be replaced by the investigative, diagnostic one. No doubt this is a possibility, though not inevitable. Perhaps a psychoanalytic model is that the art of listening resembles the art of the fugue.

Psychoanalytic treatment requires the recognition of psychoanalytic parameters, conceptions, and features that are relevant to issues of treatability and analysability. In contrast to the psychiatric diagnosis based on combinations of characteristics and traits, therefore, the psychoanalytic diagnosis involves utilizing description to formulate features of psychic structure. This conception of diagnostic process also includes an ongoing evaluation of specific conflicts involving management of affects and drive impulses, conflicts of identity and identifications, evaluations of issues such as object relations, capacity for free association, self-reflection, symbolization, and impulses to action. These come closer to psychoanalytic ideas of what it is important to evaluate but require more complex conceptualization. Fom this point of view, a diagnosis is the same as increasing understanding. These considerations are closer to what Kernberg considers to be a structural diagnosis as distinguished from dynamic diagnoses such as those formulated in terms of libidinal phases.

It seems to me that careful consideration of descriptive and structural conceptions of diagnosis suggests that they are not incompatible, either conceptually or practically. It is possible to do both types of evaluation in interviews that are not greatly structured. In either kind of diagnosis, diagnosis need not necessarily be fixed and rigid. Rather, diagnosis can be regarded as an ongoing process, as it were, in the background of thought. However, we need to take care not to be trapped in particular early impressions. If one thinks of diagnosis as a process, it may be both a preconception and something arrived at after the facts.

We can arrive at a diagnosis in interviews by means of the patient's response to interpretation, which permits us, for example, to differentiate neurotic and borderline from schizophrenic patients. Where are the small breaks in the first interview? What are the self-contradictions and inconsistencies that are accepted by the patient? Of course, content is informative. In this way we build up our picture of psychic structure and its associated conflicts and thus continuously tune our diagnosis. It is a spiral that evolves throughout a process and, in a sense, a process that constantly evolves throughout treatment.

A goal of the diagnostic process concerns the possibility of describing personality types whose transferential elaboration of their subjective experience takes expectable forms. This implies that the initial interviews can provide information about ability to associate freely, experience and contain affect, tolerate interpretation, and possibly other requirements of psychoanalysis.

Even if this is accepted, there are still questions about whether these observations are correlated with any kind of descriptive diagnostic categories and whether such categories can be used to predict significantly something about the response to some form of psychoanalytic treatment. It is also a question of whether the understanding of subjective experience gained in individual psychoanalyses can, in turn, eventually lead to uncovering features observable in initial interviews that will in some way predict the future unfolding of treatment to some extent. Many outcomes can come from the starting conflict, and contingent events play a role in the transformations of conflict. The setting and the interpretive style and content of interpretation are among the contingencies.

However, this approach requires consideration of the kinds of things that we notice that go into evaluations of affects, drives, identifications, capacity for symbolization, and object relationships. The goal is to find the basis for our own preconscious judgements. We need to consider not only the patient's relation to language (usage, value placed on it) but also our own use of language.

My own impression is that people generally do both kinds of diagnosis, although their attention to their ongoing formulations may be lacking and their formulations may be out of awareness. In any case, it seems possible to formulate provisionally without an unshakable commitment to the formulation. Again, this is an area calling for an attention to the details of our individual and group modes of thinking.

Since the analytic diagnostic evaluation involves some interpreting of the meaning of the clinical material, as might be expected, there were differences in interpretation that reflected differences of theoretical orientations. However, it may be that it is personal differences and idiosyncrasies in the use of terms that are the real issue. In those efforts, the role of clear and detailed description, as distinguished from using formulation of meaning as a form of description, was blurred. This points to a problem long recognized in psychoanalytic reports and theory: there is a ready move from observation to metapsychological formulation in which the formulation becomes the description.

The differences in approach of various members could provide more lines of exploration leading to integration of their points of view in clarifying the understanding of these patients. The format of shifting to other patients did not allow for the pursuit of the many questions opened by any one case. Given the constraints of our project format, those problems could have been explored in a detailed comparison of two cases. I compare some features of two of the case presentations, but before doing so, I mention some other issues relevant to considering them.

Psychoanalysis, psychotherapy, and the psychoanalytic state of mind

The idea of psychoanalytic consideration of particular features of mental function is also related to differences of opinion about the need for a distinction between psychoanalysis and psychoanalytic psychotherapy. One view holds that there is a way of thinking psychoanalytically even if certain features of the setting, such as frequency of hours and the use of the couch, are altered. André Green discusses this state of mind with some care in his paper on the central phobic position and elsewhere. The question of what promotes the psychoanalytic state of mind in psychoanalyst and patient requires exploration greater than was actually possible for our group. It is recognized that this state of mind is not possible for the borderline patient at the outset. It develops as a consequence of the treatment process. The question is, therefore: What promotes this development and what interferes? In other words, we need to determine to what extent we can develop ideas or a theory about technique that help to promote psychoanalytic thinking and emergence of unconscious fantasies in psychotherapy. Put differently, we need to use our psychoanalytic understanding to devise methods to promote psychoanalytic thinking. This requires greater attention to the features of the setup as well as interpretation and interaction. It seems evident that in psychotherapy some unconscious thoughts and fantasies can achieve consciousness with benefit under suitable conditions. It remains to be determined how the development and interpretation of the transference function under different conditions. In other words, it is necessary to discuss further the basis for the effects of transference interpretation in analysis and in psychotherapy, since such interpretations may have the implications of oracular pronouncements when the reasons for them have been insufficiently developed and understood by the patient. Of course, there are other issues that cannot be further discussed in this brief review.

It was generally agreed that one of the difficulties of dealing with these patients is that their aim is, in a certain sense, to act on the therapist and to elicit responses, affects, and actions. An associated question is, therefore, what conditions support psychoanalytic thinking in the therapist. A straightforward example was Elizabeth Spillius commenting on the difficulty of thinking fast enough to respond to a particular psychotic patient's comments. There are evidently differences in the conditions that analysts require for their functioning, just as different patients respond differently to the various aspects of the setting.

According to one point of view, whether the treatment was psychoanalysis or psychoanalytic psychotherapy depended almost entirely on the analyst's thinking psychoanalytically. This was not a view shared by all, and the issue was not resolved. While some people may consider the question unimportant, the considerations involved are relevant to the question of what kinds of observation and clinical experience contribute to a psychoanalytic understanding clinically and in research. This has been an ongoing debate in our field (see, for example Sandler, Sandler, & Davies, 2000; Wolff, 1996a, 1996b, 1998).

Research in psychoanalysis

All of these issues have a bearing on the nature of our research effort and our understanding of what research means for psychoanalysis. The group was organized to do research by means of detailed clinical presentations. The goal was to arrive at some consensus on features of the patients' mental function and their responses to various kinds of psychoanalytic interventions. The detailed comparison of patients and various treatments could presumably disclose the relative effectiveness of various ways of thinking psychoanalytically about the material. Then, some consensus about the nature of the problems of "non-neurotic" patients and possibly ideas about useful interventions and ways to validate understanding of these patients might be reached. With some agreements on these issues arrived at by people from different points of view, we would have some valuable research findings derived from some specifiable basis. With this kind of outcome, we would have some well-developed basis for the often repeated view that valid psychoanalytic knowledge exists even without the scientific research methodology employed in other fields.

The data in such research would be obtained via the use of psychoanalytic thinking in the process of gathering clinical observations. The material would be organized according to psychoanalytic conceptions of treatment process and psychoanalytic outcome. Consequently, the research would be a specifically psychoanalytic research. Of course, such an undertaking would, even under the best of circumstances, be demanding, difficult, and time-consuming.

As mentioned in the last section, the subject of psychoanalytic research involves the question of the value for psychoanalysis of other kinds of observations about people, other kinds of clinical, developmental, psychological, linguistic, social science, and neuroscience observations and concepts. We might go further and ask not only about the relevance of such observations and ideas, but also whether they may, in fact, be necessary for the development of psychoanalysis. This important and controversial issue cannot be explored here.

In the present context, the immediate question was whether the presentation of the treatment of psychotic patients and psychoanalytic psychotherapy of "non-neurotic" patients is relevant to a psychoanalytic understanding of "non-neurotic" borderline patients. To approach this and related questions mentioned earlier, we can discuss two presentations at our meetings and the group process they entailed.

Two case presentations

André Green and Otto Kernberg each presented a patient and offered material that was rich in content and conceptualization. These can be described in terms of the kind of presentation, the conceptualization of the treatment, the setting of the treatment, and the content of the presentation. My goal is necessarily limited to contrasting two different approaches, the kinds of information obtained, and their impacts on the research group. A deeper exploration of the treatment process and formulation in each case would be a truly worthwhile undertaking, which this group unfortunately could not pursue.

Among the points to be compared here are:

> differences in patients belonging to the same general diagnostic group;
> the method of treatment, including the treatment setup;
> the use of interpretation, the basis of interpretation;
> the relevance of modalities other than speech;
> the role of language and understanding of language;
> the conception of research;
> the way material was presented;
> utilization of data obtained by different methods.

André Green's presentation consisted of his paper, "The Central Phobic Position: A New Formulation of the Free Association Method" (Green, 2000a), plus detailed clinical material from two sessions occurring four years apart in a long treatment. His description of features of his patient, generalized, are easily recognized and generally accepted descriptors of borderline functioning. The patient was evidently someone who could use the conventional psychoanalytic setting. Therefore, the treatment had the format and conduct of a classical psychoanalysis employing the couch, an effort to promote free association and to use interpretation as the primary modality. He was able to manage his life, although self-destructively, in ways that interfered with the smooth conduct of the treatment. The patient's difficulties with free association were similar to those found in other borderline patients, and considering them was informative.

In a dramatic contrast, Otto Kernberg's presented a patient at another place on the borderline spectrum. The woman was suitable for neither the conventional psychoanalytic setting nor procedure. She, like André Green's patient, had been in prior treatments. However, whereas Green's patient had been terminated by his previous analyst because of the silences and stagnation of the treatment, Kernberg's patient's treatment was characterized by impulsive and violent action. She was a patient who would have been difficult to manage in the private office setting, and the treatment was conducted in a hospital. Kernberg's case was, therefore, different in many respects. After an introductory overview of the case history, rather than presenting process notes, Kernberg's presentation provided two hours of video observation of therapist and patient plus a transcript of the sessions. These tapes were part of a research project studying Kernberg's transference-focused psychotherapy technique (Clarkin, Yeomans, & Kernberg, 1999; Kernberg, Selzer, Koenigsberg, Carr, & Appelbaum, 1989). This is a psychoanalytically based psychotherapy for borderline personality organization as developed and manualized by a team of psychoanalysts, psychoanalytic psychotherapists, and researchers. In contrast to the patient presented by André Green, Otto Kernberg's patient was among the more disturbed group of patients, not suitable for even modified psychoanalytic technique. She was at times violent and difficult to manage. The patient was seen twice a week and was not on the couch. The treatment was characterized by action, at times violently directed at the office furniture, and refusals to leave the treatment-room. Her speech was emotionally expressive and forceful, infrequently reflective.

It is evident that these two presentations offer a contrast of two conceptions and methods of treatment. As research, each has advantages and limitations, and again, I am merely pointing to an interesting and complex subject that cannot be explored in depth here. These were markedly different patients who differed in the manifestations of their disorders, in treatments that differed in their settings and in the way they were conducted. The diagnoses were obtained by different methods: Green's by analytic interviews, Kernberg's by structured interview.

André Green's work was based on the idea that psychoanalytic research consists in exploring detailed case material for comparison with other similar material (Green, 2005). The material for this comparison is derived from psychoanalytic treatment. Of necessity, any group of such treatments would have a number of differences that would depend on specific problems owing to particular circumstances in each case. It would, of course, be very time-consuming to do such work on a significant scale, and to my knowledge, it hasn't been done.

Otto Kernberg's work is based on a manualized method of treatment and team discussion of taped interviews. Accordingly, interpretation is based on different kinds of material, and the role of active interventions is different. The significance for the patient of the observation and recording was the subject of much discussion regarding Kernberg's case. Kernberg's work has led to the development of structural diagnosis and criteria of borderline personality structure. A pivotal point in his formulations is the syndrome of identity diffusion. His systematic research over many years has led to a systematic treatment that can be taught to a number of other therapists and compared with other treatments, including non-psychoanalytic therapies. Ideally, arriving at a synthesis of the findings using the two approaches would be a worthwhile task to pursue. How this can be worked out remains to be seen. It requires a careful comparison of the details of the processes in the two types of research.

Research as process

In both types of research, the attitudes and responses of the therapist–researchers influence the collection and evaluation of the data. The factor of presentation to a group places the group in a similar position in relation to the presenter and the presentation. In effect, the emotional reactions of the group take part in the selection and evaluation of the observations on which generalizations are based. The mode of presentation, case report or videotaped sessions, plays a role.

What is the position of the group in each type of presentation? A case presentation is the account offered by a participant-witness to a relationship extending over a considerable time. It is this feature that makes the presentation analogous to the reports of witnesses to any historical event or crime. The presenter is a kind of historian, and the present writer is one as well, relying in part on the reports of observers. Of course, the conditions of observation during treatment are significantly different from these other situations in a number of ways. However, in the telling of the events, there are important similarities. These have to do with the purpose of the telling and the relation to the intended audience. Accordingly, and inevitably, the material is selected with the intent to influence the listener.

Every presentation is an invitation to the listener to allow the evocation of an understanding from the presenter's point of view. This is similar to a patient's account of relationships with other people and elicits what may be thought of as a kind of countertransferential response—such as identification, counteridentification, identification with the narrator's object, and so on. These are inevitable and contribute to our understanding of both therapist and patient, as they do in treatment. The important point is that with a case presentation, the listeners' relationship is with the presenter, even if the listening involves a degree of detachment. As is well-known, who the listener is and the presence of a group of listeners influences both the presenter and the listeners.

The group reacts to the experience of the presenter. The situation is familiar, since it is similar to listening to a case in supervision. This is not unlike listening to a patient. For these reasons, the identifications with the presenter or the subject of the presentation result in some processes parallel to the treatment. Further reflection is needed before the process can be clarified in a psychoanalytic state of mind. In our research group, the group appeared to have a sense of familiarity with André Green's presentation. We recognized the patient in the sense that we have seen patients like this one in our private offices. We have encountered the problems and can understand Green's approach, whether or not we felt at one time or another that we agreed or disagreed with it. It was in a familiar framework. The discomforts the patient might elicit at one time or another were familiar too.

The presentation of videotaped sessions faces the group with a different kind of presence. Otto Kernberg's patient and the treatment elicited strong feelings. The patient was less familiar, as was the institutional setting. The observational procedure was felt by some to be so intrusive as to distort and render impossible any kind of psychoanalytic inference or understanding. When the patient complained that being in this treatment was like being in prison, some members of the group felt that the patient was right. Some members felt that it was difficult to distinguish transference from actuality. Various members of the group felt that they would not want to treat, or could not treat, a patient of this kind. It was evident that observers were thinking about what it would be like to be the therapist and the patient.

However, despite the feelings aroused while viewing the presentation, after re-reading the transcripts, reactions were apparently modified by reflection. Some members of the group did, in fact, offer interpretations of the patient's conflicts and offered suggestions regarding treatment. As André Green then remarked, "even if the advisor is himself unable to follow the advice he provides, that's what we are here for". Otto Kernberg's presentation itself was, from one point of view, a physical intrusion into the group process, just as the video and the other research people might be seen as an intrusion into the treatment—a kind of third. The members of the group are witnesses to a scene, as though it were a drama on a stage. In this case, perhaps, it was more like watching a violent scene on the news with one of the participants present. Everyone reacts to the scene on the tape as well as to the person who participated in it and presents it. In this kind of situation, considering the significance of the material is affected by this situation. After all, viewing can be upsetting, and the presenter has done something to the witnesses.

These two presentations and their discussion suggest a possible direction for future work. The selection of pairs of cases for comparison along a number of dimensions of technique and conceptualization would be the beginning. With sufficient time to explore these issues in depth with each pair, a more systematic view of the significant factors could be formulated, along with the relevant observations.

Concluding thoughts

Clearly, this type of quasi-analytic thinking about process itself is subject to considerations similar to those being applied to the group reactions to presentation. It is a personal account of some participant-observations viewed from a personal perspective. In a sense, it involves considerations that are relevant to any kind of research involving the observation of people of any age, from infant to seniority. It is an attempt to look at the study of people both within the perspective of the research or treatment, while also taking a more distant look at the relationships of experimenter or therapist and subject or patient. I believe that both perspectives are necessary. Furthermore, it seems to me that this is an important part of involvement in psychoanalysis and psychotherapy where the patient's perspective on relationships must be understood on its own terms while maintaining a therapist's perspective, and in psychoanalysis a psychoanalytic perspective.

Taking this line of orientation a step further, I believe it is necessary to see psychoanalytic thought from within in the comparison of the multiple current viewpoints, comparing them with one another with a variety of methods. At the same time, it is necessary to see psychoanalytic thought in a wider perspective as a specific kind of contributor to understanding mental function. Other ways of studying "mind" need psychoanalytic contributions to point to aspects of mental life not arrived at in any other way and requiring study by the methods of other disciplines. At the same time, in contrast to some of our colleagues, I believe that psychoanalytic thought has much to gain from other fields, both clinically and theoretically. This is certainly not to say that psychoanalysis should end up looking like neuroscience, social science, or infant observation. Careful psychoanalytic observation and conception has specific things to offer that, as Freud said a long time ago, cannot be obtained in other ways. However, all this is a matter for another discussion. My point here is that our discussions of "non-neurotic" patients have not only brought out some further understanding of these patients but have also served to highlight some features of research by means of interaction.

7

The analyst's psychic work
and the three concepts of countertransference

Fernando Urribarri

"How does the contemporary analyst's mind work?" That was the key question that defined the research conducted by our group.

One of the most original and interesting features of our research was therefore the two-tier, heterogeneous, yet complementary exploration of contemporary psychoanalytic thinking. At a first level, our research explored the way of thinking of a group of psychoanalysts from different psychoanalytic orientations and cultures, both in terms of their personal opinions and, to a certain extent, as representatives of their respective currents. At a second level, the topic of "countertransference (with borderline patients)" focused on the specifics of analytic work from this side of the couch, in the analyst's mind—particularly with non-neurotic patients, who push the limits of analytic resources. At the intersection of those two levels is our goal, as set forth in the title and purpose of our research project: identifying points of consensus and disagreement among different theoretical and cultural perspectives.

A remarkable point of consensus in connection with our topic was summarized by André Green's statement (in our third meeting) that: "the research became an investigation on ourselves". Therefore, one of the most significant conclusions of our study is that—despite major differences of opinion—all colleagues in the group share a common historical concern: the need to overcome (theoretical and clinical) impasses linked to the crisis of post-Freudian models. This major "negative" consensus was accompanied by a certain convergence in the attempts to understand and find creative answers to this issue through an increasingly complex vision of the analyst's psychic work.

The experience of the crisis brought about by the reductionism of post-Freudian models is one of the axes defining the contemporary analyst's position and historical context. The awareness and elaboration of that crisis, and of the challenges and possibilities it implies, are precisely what defines a psychoanalyst as contemporary. In that sense, our group has been profoundly contemporary, our research being an exploration of common issues and of the different answers each one attempts to give. At the same time, such attempts provide us with a map of contemporary psychoanalysis and its two main currents: one aimed at updating and refreshing post-Freudian models, the other attempting to create a specifically contemporary model.

A historical and conceptual framework is therefore required for the results of our research to be understood and elaborated on. In this chapter I aim to provide such a framework and a context for the contributions of our group to a contemporary conception of analytic listening and countertransference. I will thus focus on psychoanalytic work, on the psychoanalyst's mental functioning in the session, and on the decisive changes experienced during the last thirty years (the results of which are now more clearly perceived). I would like to summarize that historical transformation, following the thread of substantial modifications in the theoretical conception and technical role of countertransference.

Briefly, tracing back the theorization on countertransference, I will refer to three historical phases—Freudian, post-Freudian, and contemporary—in the evolution of the analyst's activity, focusing particularly on the transition from a "totalistic conception" of countertransference (Kernberg, 1967), which includes the analyst's total functioning and is at the core of the post-Freudian clinical model, towards an "integrated conception" of countertransference within a wider, more complex contemporary vision of the analyst's psychic work—where the notions of frame and "internal frame" are central and countertransference is subordinated to the analyst's work on representation.

Three movements, three models

A historical perspective is required in order to understand the trans-formations undergone by the conception of the analyst's psychic work and countertransference. In providing such a historical back-ground, I intend to summarize and develop André Green's idea (Green, 1975) that, in the parallel evolution of psychoanalytic theory and practice, three consecutive historical movements can be distin-guished: Freudian, post-Freudian, and contemporary, each related to a specific theoretical and clinical model.

Those specific models should not be confused with the theories and great works (and great authors) they are legitimately based on and inspired by. As scientific paradigms described by Kuhn (1962), those models combine the two dimensions included in the term "paradigm": the institutional dimension, based on the discourse and vision shared by a scientific community, and the technical dimen-sion, represented by the "paradigmatic case or example" that illus-trates and validates the instituted discourse. As psychoanalysts, it is easy for us to understand that the paradigm plays both a cognitive and an identificatory role. Models, as paradigms, are also a mixed product, combining theory with institutional ideology and ideals. Thus, one of their fundamental aspects is their formulation of an im-age and an ideal of the analyst. In that sense, the three conceptions of countertransference to be described are not just three different conceptual definitions: they also embody and express three different visions—three ideals and three images—of the analyst's work.

The Freudian model:
free-floating attention and countertransference as an obstacle

The first movement is contemporaneous with the Freudian era. Con-ventionally, it extends from 1900—the date when Freud ordered his *magnum opus* to be printed—to the Second World War. Theory, marked by the discovery of the unconscious, focused on the intrapsy-chic conflict between sexual desire and defences. Clinical practice was governed by the analysis of transference and resistances accord-ing to the rules of the psychoanalytic method empirically set forth by Freud. Transference psychoneuroses constitute the clinical case of reference—the paradigmatic example (Kuhn, 1962) that illustrates and confirms the model.

In a clinical field limited to transference neuroses, the analytic process was based upon the logical articulation of the infantile neurosis/transference psychoneurosis/transference neurosis tripod. From a metapsychological perspective, transference is an intrapsychic process determined by unconscious mechanisms: it is a "false link" between an unconscious incestuous representation and the figure of the analyst. The Oedipus complex is considered to be the core complex in the neuroses, defined as "the negative of perversion". Both in his writings and in his practice, Freud posited that the analyst's position in transference is always predominantly paternal.

From a clinical standpoint, transference was conceived as a middle ground between illness and reality (Freud, 1912b), where the relationship between them can be modified. Dreams and their interpretation—"the royal road to the unconscious"—constitute an implicit model of reference: of the patient's compromise formations and their elucidation by the analyst, as well as of the analytic situation itself (the suspension of motility, the almost complete shutting-off of perception, object inaccessibility, the redirecting of psychic energy towards representation, which is thus over-invested). Relationships between unconscious (thing) representations and conscious (thing and word) representations are at the core of psychic functioning and constitute the axis of the talking cure.

The cure, defined as the resolution of transference neurosis, is achieved by means of a laborious, sustained working-through process in accordance with the rules of the analytic method. Technical rules are aimed at establishing asymmetrical and complementary patient–analyst dynamics. Patient and analyst are prescribed, respectively, free association and free-floating attention, abstinence and benevolent neutrality. *Countertransference is seen as an obstacle*, the analyst's unconscious and inadequate reaction to the transference, a neurotic residue to be resolved through his own analysis (Freud 1912b).

This position is not lacking in epistemological consistency, since the Freudian model is an individual model, focused on the individual psychic apparatus, where causality is defined by intrapsychic conflict. Thus, if countertransference is experienced by the analyst (like a "symptom"), it is logical to attribute its psychic causality to the analyst himself. Such logical argument—characteristic of the positivist scientific model—explains why Freud prioritized the role of drives and did not theoretically elaborate the role of the object or, metapsychologically, the analyst's psychic functioning, his work being restricted to applying the rules of his interpretative art.

The analyst was likened to a mirror or a surgeon: he communicates without showing his personality; he interprets with cool, calculated technical precision. Like Oedipus facing the Theban Sphinx, the psychoanalyst must solve riddles. He is the active interpreter of the transference (the translator of hieroglyphs of unconscious desire) rather than its object. The father role played by the analyst when interpreting and his management of the transference reinforce his position as an authority figure, reflected in military metaphors (battle against resistance, "*in effigie*") and in references to chess. Faithful to the ideals of his time, the Freudian analyst (like his contemporary, Sherlock Holmes) identifies himself with the rationalist ideal of scientific objectivity: the researcher's subjectivity is, by definition, excluded from the research process.

It is well known that, with the institutionalization and dissemination of the official myth of "classical analysis" (retrospectively attributed to an imaginary Freud) and the promotion of an "orthodox" analyst figure, the Freudian model came to be stereotyped, even caricatured. The best-known (and most criticized) image was that of the "mirror–analyst": a cool, distant analyst, anonymous rather than neutral, somewhat authoritarian, who cultivates an artificial silence and gives oracular interpretations. Moreover, from a theoretical perspective, the model was rightly criticized for its solipsistic reductionism.

Comments on free-floating attention and Freud's open-ended work

It is worth mentioning, as pointed out by Laplanche and Pontalis in their work *The Language of Psychoanalysis* (1967), that, despite its outmost significance as one of the pillars of the analytic method, free-floating attention was barely conceptualized by Freud. The Table of Contents of the *Standard Edition* shows that Freud examined this notion in only two texts (Freud 1912b, 1923a[1922]), and in neither of them did he provide an in-depth theoretical conceptualization. When studying the analytic method, Dora's psychoanalyst focuses on the patient's free association and on the rules of the interpretative art, as well as on how they're applied by the analyst as a "surgical" method. Without hiding his surprise, Freud himself acknowledges in *Constructions in Analysis* (1937d) the sparseness of the conceptual elaboration of the analyst's work (the second of those two "localities" where "the work of analysis" is carried out[2]). Up to that point, he says, it had been nothing but a "fact", known but not conceptualized.

On the two occasions where Freud does deal with free-floating attention, he repeats the same brief practical prescriptions (mostly negative: not to consciously focus on the material, etc.) and provides descriptions that are metaphorical rather than conceptual. Such brevity does not prevent two different perspectives or lines of thought on free-floating attention and the analytic work from overlapping (and, later on in the history of psychoanalysis, unfolding). In one of them, he explicitly linked listening to *Nachträglichkeit* [deferred action, "*après-coup*"], stating that it should not be overlooked that, in most instances, "the analyst has to listen to words whose meaning he will only understand later" [*nachträglich*] (Freud, 1912b). This line of thought locates the analyst's work in a specific, indirect, non-linear, complex temporality, where the analyst's "unconscious memory" acts as a mediator in the repetition–interpretation–memory–working-through process. The second line of thought was marked by the powerful image that likens the analyst's mind to a telephone headset that allows a direct unconscious-to-unconscious communication ("capturing the patient's unconscious through his own": Freud, 1912b). This difference corresponds to another pointed out by Donnet (1973) as regards Freud's interpretative model: on the one hand a slow, sustained process defined by the working-through and, on the other, a symbolic interpretation, with immediate effect. A certain ideal of immediacy (inspired by the second line of thought) was one of the symptoms of the illusion of direct access to the unconscious that would re-emerge in post-Freudian psychoanalysis (in some regions as a direct, "deep" interpretation of fantasy, in others as a play of signifiers and mimesis of the unconscious "style").

Moreover, having introduced the second topography and the second instinctual dualism, Freud would not revise or update the analytic technique as a whole (or present a new clinical case). He would openly discuss the limits of the "talking cure", of the power of words against the deadly repetition compulsion. In "Constructions in Analysis" (1937d) he discusses the limits of interpretation (to unlock infantile amnesia) and proposes "construction", where the analyst's contribution is even greater than in interpretation. At the same time, he explicitly acknowledges for the first time that "the work of analysis consists of two quite different portions, that it is carried on in two separate localities" (Freud, 1937d): their minds. These and other open-ended issues were later taken up, in diverse, divergent ways, by post-Freudian and contemporary analysis. Martin Bergmann (2000) states that, when looking back at these developments, it is necessary to acknowledge that Freud left us with a much more incomplete, open-ended psychoanalysis than he thought. Therefore, he concludes that a debate as to who is "Freud's true heir" is a "theological debate" that is unworthy of a group guided by scientific values.

The post-Freudian movement: totalizing countertransference

In the second—the post-Freudian—movement, the focus of interest shifted to object relations, giving rise to a predominantly intersubjective perspective. At the same time, a new conception of countertransference was at the core of a new technical model, whereby the analyst's image and work were redefined. In this new model, clinical work with children and psychotic patients was taken as a new focal reference point, as a paradigmatic example.

Linked to a valuable expansion of the clinical field, post-Freudian psychoanalysis, through its different currents, acknowledged and theorized the importance of the object, which Freud had neglected (Balint, 1937; Bion, 1959; Bouvet, 1956; Bowlby, 1958; Fairbairn, 1952; Klein, 1921, 1932; Winnicott, 1971a). Through a predominantly "genetic" or "developmental" perspective, the movement studied (and prioritized) the role of the primary object in the constitution and functioning of the early psyche. It introduced a kind of "third topography" focused on the relationship between the "self" and the object. Within that framework, the role of the object in clinical practice was re-evaluated, bringing about a change in the technique and an exploration of the maternal dimension of transference (and countertransference). Theory and practice would be marked by a new dual scheme (referring to the early, dyadic mother–infant relationship).

Through dialectics similar to those whereby transference was discovered and theorized by Freud, countertransference was no longer seen as a mere obstacle: it was redefined positively as a fundamental *tool* in analytic work (Heimann, 1950; Racker, 1948). It was considered as the analyst's emotional response, which was triggered by the patient's transference—rather than the analyst's neuroses or blind spots. It then became an affective way through which the analyst could have an unconscious understanding of the patient's unconscious. Thus redefined, countertransference would cover the analyst's entire mental functioning, giving rise to a "totalizing" conception (Kernberg, 1975; Urtubey, 1994).

Transference was then understood as a repetition of a past object relation, based on a predominantly intersubjective (rather than intrapsychic) axis. A "two-bodies psychology" emerged. Transference was considered an essentially projective process (based on the self–object axis), where the mechanism of projective identification was highlighted. Discovered by Melanie Klein, projective identification is the first intersubjective defence mechanism posited in psychoanalysis. Bion later expanded its definition, considering it also as a primitive (intrusive) preverbal way of communicating non-symbolized drives and affects. Such expansion would have major technical consequences.

The analysis of the psychic container, as well as of the (manifest/latent) content, emerged then as a major theoretical and clinical contribution. It was posited that projective identification is perceived by the analyst through countertransferential affects, which he contains and symbolizes, in the way the mother does with her infant's drives and preverbal communication ("maternal reverie"). Projective identification (likened to transference) and countertransference constitute a key axis in the post-Freudian model. Based on this axis, the analytic process would be understood as an alternating cycle of projections and introjections in a progression towards psychological "growth" (or maturing). The shift from an intrapsychic to an intersubjective axis was accompanied by the pre-eminence of the notion of "insight": awareness becomes a *vision of*—and *into*—the inner world (of what is no longer transferred–projected onto the object, to be introjected–internalized by the Self).

Another important change was introduced from a singular technical perspective, initiated by Ferenczi and Rank in 1924 and continued by Balint and Winnicott. According to this perspective, the patient's emotional experience is the key to certain treatments. Interpretation and the object relation with the analyst were considered to be the two therapeutic agents of the analytic technique, and in the treatment of severely regressive patients the latter is the most reliable and beneficial one. The idea that the analyst should refrain from interpreting so as to allow for regression to go as far back as necessary to enable a "new beginning" to emerge spontaneously (Bergmann, 1993) was then fostered, together with controversial changes to technique and frame.

In the analytic process, the archaic dimension of the transferential object relation and an infraverbal primitive communication were pre-eminent. As regards aetiology, particular emphasis was placed on early trauma as a trigger of destructive drives (and/or "primary attachment"), on early anxieties (separation, abandonment, fragmentation, etc.), and on primitive defence mechanisms. Analysis was aimed at overcoming pregenital fixations and even the psychotic core that was then thought to underlie various clinical conditions, including neurosis.

By applying to analysis in general the technical innovations introduced for the treatment of children and psychotic patients, interpretation became an interpretation *of* the transference "here-now-with me". The totalizing conception of countertransference radicalized the idea of unconscious-to-unconscious communication: countertransference was "guided" the analyst's understanding and was used (more or less explicitly) in the interpretation. There was a tendency to liken the analyst's work to the maternal role (according to the dual mother–infant scheme). In the projective identification–countertransference axis, the technical ideal was that of the analyst as a "container".

Comments

From expansion to reductionism. The Post-Freudian movement brought about a process of great scientific development and international institutional expansion. The theory of object relations and the notion of countertransference became key concepts that redefined the vision and language of psychoanalysis within the IPA.[1] Unfortunately, the expansion and institutionalization of the post-Freudian movement was accompanied by institutional bureaucratization and dogmatism, leading to the establishment of a reductionist scheme, whereby theory was simplified and encoded and technique was applied mechanically.

When the post-Freudian model was instituted as a dogma, it became reductionist, and, rather than establishing a dialogue or

articulation with the Freudian model, it had a tendency to exclude
it and replace it. Thus, the object replaced the drive as a pole of
conceptual reference. The self replaced the ego. Destructiveness prevailed over sexuality, anxieties over desire, early anxiety over castration anxiety, affect over representation, the preverbal over language,
the dyad over the triangle, the archaic over the oedipal. Neurosis became blurred by references to psychosis. The mother figure eclipsed
the (structural) importance of the father. A genetic, developmental
perspective ignored the structural by erasing the dialectic between
synchrony and diachrony. (Baranger, Baranger, and Mom, 1982, criticize the equating of psychoanalysis to the natural sciences and the
extrapolation of models from developmental psychology.)

The discovery of countertransference as a tool resulted in the
concealment of its dimension as an interference with and an obstacle to analytic listening. The radicalization of the idea of unconscious-to-unconscious communication turned countertransference
into an immediate guide to understanding (and interpreting) that
prevailed over the patient's discourse—the totalizing countertransference eventually substituted free-floating attention (Bollas, 2000).
In its most mechanical and extreme forms, the analyst ceased to be
likened to a decoding agent and became a psychic medium who can
"cross over" beyond words. Countertransferential affect understood
as information from a direct unconscious-to-unconscious communication gave rise to an immediacy[2] criterion that combines in a single
instance the reception, elaboration, and use of such "information".
The immediacy of countertransference eclipsed the articulation of
the listening-analyst's unconscious memory–*nachträglich*–interpretation. Similarly, the systematic interpretation of the transference
(here and now) eclipsed the construction (of historical truth), and
even the interpretation of the "there-and-then-with someone else".
The role of language (and the specifics of the analytic dialogue) was
impoverished by a "simultaneous-translation"-style "militant interpretation" (Bollas), or even by a lack of trust in interpretation.[3]

As regards technique, a certain phenomenological turn was also
criticized (Urtubey, Guillaumin), as the manifest meaning of the
affect experienced by the analyst was usually interpreted literally,
as an unconscious impulse—such has been the role of Grinberg's
concept of projective counteridentification—and attributed to the
patient. The use of a pre-established symbolic code in interpretation
has led a post-Kleinian analyst, Elizabeth Bott-Spillius, to point out

that "certain disciples (of Klein) have made—and may be continuing to do so, if less often than before—their interpretations of verbal
exchange and the behaviour of patients in a symbolic, rigid way"
(Bott-Spillius, 2001).

Anti-dogmatic openings

Historically, in a reaction to the dogmatism and reductionism of the
post-Freudian movement, three *anti-dogmatic movements* emerged. In
England, the Middle Group was opposed to Anna-Freudian and
Kleinian militantisms. Its historical role (apart from its conceptual
contributions) seems to have been to open up a transitional space,
where a new freedom of thought, creativity, and exchange of different ideas was legitimized. In that historical sense, Winnicott may
be seen as one the most influential—or inspiring—figures of contemporary psychoanalysis.[4] A singular—though equivalent—process
took place in France, where Lacan began to criticize the tendency to
forget Freud and reductionism (mainly in the United States), only
to reproduce later the typical post-Freudian movement: creating his
own reductionist model, turning it into a dogma, mechanizing a
specific technique, and becoming the charismatic leader of a militant current.[5] That is why, by the mid- to late 1960s, Lacan's main
followers (the most prominent analysts of the third generation) had
broken with him. Authors such as Laplanche, Pontalis, Aulagnier,
Anzieu, and Green, among others, advocated a renewed, deeper
reading of Freud and welcomed an exchange with other currents,
aiming at overcoming the deadlocks of Lacanian and post-Freudian
reductionism in general. In Argentina, we find a pluralist Freudian movement that questioned, both from within and from outside
the Argentine Psychoanalytic Association, the Kleinians' reaction-
ary dogmatism. At the APA, the movement was led by Willi and
Madeleine Baranger, and by Mom—and was also supported by historical figures such as Garma. In 1974, the movement brought about
an advanced democratic reform at the Psychoanalytic Institute and
instituted a pluralist Freudian model: this was the first psychoanalytic
institute where a pluralist canon was taught (based on the works of
Anna Freud, Melanie Klein, Winnicott, Bion, Lacan, as well as those
of contemporary authors, such as Otto Kernberg, André Green,
Jean Laplanche, Christopher Bollas, etc.). These three movements
gave birth to a contemporary perspective that has today, after over

thirty years, reached full maturity. [Again, it is interesting to note in this respect that the historian and psychoanalyst Martin Bergmann designates 1975 as the end of the Hartmann Era—that is, the post-Freudian Era, F.U.—as it was in that year, at the London conference, that Leo Rangell and Anna Freud, heirs of the Hartmann group, made the final effort to defend it. On the other hand, André Green challenged such vision with his own personal psychoanalytic ideas a new model firmly based on Freud, Lacan, Winnicott, and Bion (Bergmann, 2000).]

Contemporary psychoanalysis: an integrated countertransference

The third movement is contemporary psychoanalysis. It emerged as an attempt to overcome the deadlocks of the post-Freudian model and what, rather vaguely but expressively, is usually referred to as the "crisis of psychoanalysis". Two main contemporary orientations emerged from the acknowledgement of such a crisis. One of these seeks to update some variants of the post-Freudian model, while the second aims at developing a new model. It is the latter that we refer to as a "contemporary model". Schematically, in our group, the former orientation was diversely represented by Elizabeth Bott Spillius, Otto Kernberg, Bill Grossman, and Jaime Lutenberg, while the latter was represented by André Green, Jean-Claude Rolland, and Gregorio Kohon.

In a first approach, the contemporary model may be said to be based on three axes: a new reading of Freud (defined by Jean Laplanche as "critical, historical, and problematic"[6]) that re-values Freudian metapsychology and method as a principle of psychoanalysis; a critical and creative adoption of the major post-Freudian contributions (in a dialogue with contemporary authors of different currents), and an expansion of clinical practice to include predominantly non-neurotic cases. It is worth noting that Freudian vocabulary becomes the language, the "lingua franca", of this instituting movement and its new pluralist disciplinary matrix (Kuhn, 1962).

In the contemporary model, mental functioning is theoretically conceived as a heterogeneous process of representation that binds and symbolizes the intrapsychic dynamics and the relations between the intrapsychic (focused on the drive) and the intersubjective (focused on the object). The Freudian concept of representation is expanded and becomes more complex, covering body and affect as well as thinking. Within the dynamics of the oedipal structure, propelled by erotic and destructive drives and co-determined by object relations, representation is defined as the basic function of the psyche. A psychoanalytic variation of complex thinking (Morin, 1977), the contemporary metapsychological perspective emphasizes the heterogeneous, the process, and the poiesis or creativity.

Clinically, borderline pathologies constitute the new paradigmatic cases. This promotes the exploration of the conditions that make analysis possible and the limits of analysability. The concept of frame is introduced, with clear metapsychological principles, a methodological (and epistemological) role, and possible technical variations. The importance of the analyst's internal frame is thus highlighted, as well as its complex multiple functions in a session: the analyst's psychic work becomes a conceptual axis that articulates different elements, dimensions, and operations. In this context, countertransference is redefined, giving rise to the conception of *integrated or framed countertransference* .

* * *

Borderline patients thus become the paradigmatic clinical reference. This seems to be linked to a social–historical change,[7] reflected in the predominance of borderline cases over neuroses (now usually called "classic") in clinical practice. There is a simultaneous development of the study of the specifics (and variety) of borderline structures, considered to occupy an intermediate position between psychosis and neurosis, sharing elements with both while remaining distinct (Kernberg, Searles, Bergeret, Green, Anzieu, McDougall, Paz).

In borderline cases, the existence of a dual (simultaneous and split) conflict is posited: on a first level, a conflict of drives, between the ego and the id; on a second level, an identification conflict, between the ego and the object(s). Caught in such a crucible, the ego is particularly affected in terms of its narcissistic structure and its capacity for symbolization ("going blank" and feelings of emptiness are two of its symptomatic expressions). In a failed oedipal triangulation, the incestuous object of unconscious desire and the object of primary identification are insufficiently differentiated. Consequently, castration anxiety is coupled with separation and intrusion anxieties, thus provoking a paradoxical functioning. Sexual drives (with pregenital fixations and a functioning much closer to that of the Id than that of the Unconscious) play a fundamental role, which distinguishes borderline cases from psychoses (and the contemporary model from the post-Freudian[8]). On the other hand, what distinguishes them from neuroses is that destructive drives and primitive defence mechanisms (splitting, denial, etc.) are more pre-eminent in the former. Thus, in contrast with the post-Freudian predominance of object relations and destructiveness, the traumatic dimension of sexuality is recovered and renewed,[9] as well as the consideration of the traumatic potential of the object (particularly in connection with narcissism).

As regards non-neurotic structures (although with a wider scope), one of the main theoretical and clinical changes emerges from the critical review of the dualistic or dyadic post-Freudian scheme. Kohon (2005) writes:

> By now, most of us have heard it many times: if it is true that there is no such thing as an infant without a mother, then it is also equally true that there is no such thing as a mother and baby without a father, imaginary or real. The analytic encounter itself cannot be understood in terms of *just* the mother and baby relationship. Mother and baby can only exist in the context of a third term, which does not need to be physically present in order to be *there*. The third term (albeit not the only one) of all analyses, which regulates the relationship between patient and analyst, is defined and made present by the *psychoanalytic setting*.

On a similar note, specifically in connection with non-neurotic patients, André Green writes: "The issue is not the passage from two to three, from the dyad to the triad, but the transition from potential thirdness (where the father is present only in the mother's mind) to actual thirdness."

Practice in the middle ground of non-neurotic structures (borderline, narcissistic disorders, addictions, psychosomatic disorders, etc.) allows for the exploration of the limits of analysability, promoting a dual elucidation: the metapsychological foundations of frame and the Freudian method on the one hand, and the possible technical variations for the treatment of non-neurotic structures on the other.

In contemporary psychoanalysis (particularly influenced by the critical and creative adoption of Lacan's work in this respect), revisiting the Freudian method puts language at the core. In the expanded

Freudian representation theory the Unconscious is not structured like (or by) language; however, as Freud always posited, language becomes, by means of free association, "the royal road to the Unconscious". There is an irreducible heterogeneity between unconscious representations (unconscious thing-representations and affect representations) and word-representations, but they are also compatible, and an articulation between them is possible: these conflicting relations define the essence of psychic work. In clinical theory, the specifics of the functioning of language as determined by frame are established: the dual prescription of saying it all and not doing anything brings about transference onto words, and not only onto objects. Jean-Claude Rolland (2001) expresses this contemporary vision in his definition of the analytic situation as an "inter-discursive situation". As regards the technique, the principle of referring to the patient's discourse as a condition (though not a sufficient one) for psychoanalytic listening, dialogue, and interpretation to be possible is re-established. In his presentation, André Green introduced a contemporary revision of the concept of free association (and free-floating attention): he defined it as an arborescent process of creation of meaning that determines a dual movement of "retroactive reverberation and anticipatory implication (regarding what will follow)" in psychoanalytic listening. This polysemic virtuality of analytic communication can be potentially traumatic in non-neurotic structures: the central phobic position (Green, 2002b) is an example of a defence against such a possibility. In André Green's technique, the transitional and dialogic dimension of psychoanalytic work is emphasized, sometimes adopting the form of what I suggested calling "a verbal squiggle" oriented by (and towards) the representative movement of the patient's discourse.

An important innovation was the introduction of the concept of frame (Winnicott, Bleger, the Barangers). Frame is distinguished from the mere physical situation and is conceived as a function that constitutes both the encounter and the analytic process (forming a dialectic pair with it). Being the institution and *mise en scène* of the analytic method, the frame functions as a transition between social reality and psychic reality. It has a triple dimension: a physical dimension (weekly sessions, physical setting), a symbolic dimension (the fundamental rule of free association), and their articulation, which creates and contains the imaginary space (the "as if") characteristic of analysis. The frame institutes the analytic space or field

(Viderman, Baranger), a third space where patient and analyst's psychic spaces can get together and separate (become discriminated), thus avoiding collusions, regressive fusions, and being trapped into the mirage of duality. Providing contention and distance, the frame delimits the intermediate space where analytic communication is possible. The concept of frame is both clinical and epistemological: it is the condition for the analytic object (Green) to be constituted, a third object distinct from the patient and the analyst, an output of the communication of each particular analytic pair.

The introduction of the concept of frame inaugurates a triadic scheme (frame—transference—countertransference) of understanding the analytic process: if transference and countertransference are the engine, frame is the foundation (Bleger). In its dialectic relationship with the process, the frame is "mute" and "invisible", while the former flows normally. The frame becomes "audible"—even noisy—whenever there is a deadlock in the process. In the contemporary model, listening to the noises of the frame is not limited to a pre-established scheme (mother–infant, container–contained, etc.), nor is its interpretation limited to the idea of "attacks on the setting" and "acting-out". That is only one of the possibilities. In this new triadic scheme, the frame is polysemic, including different logics in the listening process: the logic of the unit (narcissistic), of the pair (mother–infant), of the intermediate (the logic of illusion, of the transitional), of the triangular (of the oedipal structure).

During one of our meetings, Green posited that the frame becomes a diagnostic tool. The possibility of using—or not using—the frame as a potential analytic space, where the fundamental rule is to be applied, allows for an evaluation of the possibilities and difficulties of representative functioning. Thus, in the case of non-neurotic patients, changes to the frame (such as less frequent sessions, face-to-face positioning, etc.) are justified in order to set up the best possible conditions for representative functioning. In contrast with the official—"classic" and post-Freudian—idea that psychoanalytic psychotherapies are simpler and more superficial variants of analytic work, these are recognized in their specificity, complexity, and difficulty.[10] From the analyst's perspective, special psychic work is needed so as to render those psychic conflicts on the limits of analysability imaginable, thinkable, and analysable. In both cases—psychoanalysis and psychotherapy—the aim may be said to be the same: the constitution of an internal frame (or an internalization of the frame), whereby the—intersubjective—dialogic core of analysis becomes a reflexive intrapsychic matrix (Urribarri, 2005).

At the same time, these works bring about significant theoretical and technical changes. Transference is seen as an output of the analytic situation, instead of a mere repetition of the past: in it, there is room for innovation, creation, or neo-genesis (Baranger & Baranger, 1967; Castoriadis, 1969; Laplanche, 1987; Viderman, 1970). Interpretation is not just decoding, but also poiesis, creation of meaning. With borderline patients, interpretation combines the logic of deduction (taken from the Freudian model) with the logic of induction. The conjectural dimension becomes explicit in the formulation, in which conditional modals are used to allow for the patient to accept or reject an interpretation. Technically, there is a shift from the (systematic) interpretation of transference to the interpretation *in* the transference. The "here-now-with me" dimension is thus articulated with the "there-then-with someone else". The Freudian *Nachträglichkeit* (the afterwardness, the *après-coup*, that defines the specific temporal dimension of psychoanalysis) recovers a central role, being elaborated on in a dual way: as an essential dimension, inherent to the representation process, and as a key to psychoanalytic work. Construction and "historization" become key dimensions in the analytic work (Aulagnier, 1984; Baranger, Baranger, & Mom, 1984; Faimberg, 2005; Laplanche, 1986).

In this context, a new concept is developed: that of *integrated (or framed) countertransference*. Countertransference as a phenomenon is thus integrated into the triadic scheme of the analytic process (frame–transference–countertransference). It is no longer defined as a symmetrical reflection of the patient's transference, but as an output of the analytic situation, conceived as a dynamic field (Barangers[11]). Transference and countertransference may be said to be an effect of the frame, while at the same time being the common cause of the constitution and dynamics of the analytic field. As regards analytic listening, countertransference is also framed in a renewed, wider, and more complex conception of the *analyst's psychic* work. It constitutes a part of the analyst's internal frame.

The contemporary revision brings about a distinction between different levels (or types of processes) within countertransference. In a formulation that is both personal and representative of such revision, Pontalis posits that a distinction should be made between: (a) a *countertransference of origin*, or pre-countertransference, that motivates and nourishes the analytic practice; (b) *countertransferential movements*—that is, the responses refracted by our phantasmatics to the analysand's transferential movements, which are part of the analytic process and may facilitate it; (c) *countertransferential positions*, assigned by the patient's phantasmatic *mise en scène*, moving away from which is difficult but possible and necessary for the analytic process; (d) the *countertransferential influence*, which renders the analyst paralysed, passive, humiliated, and unable to analyse, thus creating a critical situation.

Most contemporary authors highlight three situations in which countertransference plays a fundamental role: the construction of preverbal traumas; the representation of the non-represented, of conflicts on the limits of symbolization (in connection with the body, affects, etc.); and the listening (and translation) of turbulence, impasses, and break-ups in the process and the frame. Moreover, they clearly differentiate three logical phases of the "countertransference work" (the expression coined by Urtubey): reception (predominantly unconscious, integrated in the analytic listening as a "countertransferential resonance", accompanied by ego-dystonic manifestations); working-through of countertransference (predominantly preconscious); and the utilization of countertransference through its translation into the "analyst's internal discourse" (Rolland, 2001). Countertransference guides the analyst's interventions but is not expressed directly, neither as a confession nor as an "interpretation".

Countertransference thus becomes independent from the post-Freudian scheme. It is no longer seen as a patient's creation, passively received by the analyst, nor is it exclusively or pre-eminently affective. On the contrary, it is an output of the analytic field that can be translated into affects, physical sensations, as well as in words or phrases, figurations (mainly visual), day phantasies, hallucinations, and so on (Botella & Botella, 2001; Cesio, 1972; Rolland, 2001). Nor is it seen as being caused by projective identification, through an intrusion that puts the analyst into the position of being a passive receptor (alien to its origin and content). The patient influences the analyst through discourse (loaded with affects and both words and thing representations). The analyst's subjectivity manifests itself in countertransference as a part of the analytic dialogue. Finally, countertransference is no longer understood according to the dual model of the mother–infant relationship, nor is it considered a direct unconscious-to-unconscious communication that can be used by the analyst almost immediately. Countertransference is a demand on the analyst's psychic work.

Contemporary psychoanalysis develops *the analyst's psychic work* as a tertiary conceptual axis, seeking to include free-floating attention and countertransference as partial and complementary dimensions of a complex process. Moreover, the importance of the analyst's imagination, which is particularly necessary when working on the limits of analysability, is emphasized. Thus redefined, analytic listening is wider than countertransference, and the analyst's work goes beyond its working-through and use, as not every movement of the analyst's mind is countertransferential: for instance, the role of the formal regression of the analyst's thinking is emphasized as a way of providing the patient with figurability for what is not represented (Botella). It is also referred to as "a psyche for two bodies" (Joyce McDougall): as a "chimera", a two-headed monster that stands as a metaphor of the analytic pair, intertwined in the conflicting psychic movement of the session (De M'Uzan).

In order to illustrate the analyst's psychic work (as an axis that articulates a series of complementary operations), it is worth mentioning a precise description by André Green. Discussing the post-Freudian model, and in particular the Bionian notion of maternal reverie as a model of totalizing countertransference, he writes:

> What does the analyst's listening consist in? First, in understanding the manifest content of what is said, a necessary precondition for all that follows; then, and this is the fundamental stage, in *imaginarizing* the discourse: not only imagining it, but also including in it the imaginary dimension, construing what is implicit in such a discourse differently, in the mise-en-scène of understanding. In the following step, the analyst will unbind the linear sequence of this chain by evoking other fragments of sessions: recent ones (perhaps of the last session), less recent ones (from months ago), and, finally, much older ones (such as a dream from the beginning of the analysis). The analyst has to be the archivist of the *history of the analysis* and search the records of his *preconscious memory;* to this end, he will call his associations to mind at all times. Such is the backdrop against which the analyst's capacity for reverie is developed. Such capacity grows in the final step, that of *rebinding*, which will be achieved by selecting and recombining the elements thus gleaned to give birth to the countertransferential phantasy, which is supposed to meet the

patient's transferential phantasy. [translated from Green, 1986a, pp. 416–417; italics added]

Within the contemporary model, free-floating attention is seen as leaning on preconscious functioning. This does not mean that the analyst's unconscious role is excluded: it is articulated, mediated, by the preconscious, which allows for its symbolization and technical usage. The role of the preconscious acquires a new relevance as a representative space for mediation, intersection, and interaction: internal transitional space, a pivot of the patient's free association (and the analyst's free-floating attention), the seat of working-through. It is in this context that the concept of the *analyst's internal frame* emerges as a preconscious representative matrix. Its optimum functioning is that of the tertiary processes (Green): the processes of binding and unbinding, union and separation, of heterogeneous elements and processes (primary and secondary, but also originary, archaic, semiotic, etc.) on which the analyst's understanding and creativity is based. In the working-through of the countertransference, the analyst's tertiary processes allow for the primary unconscious resonance to link, and thus to acquire figurability, so that it then can be signified and thought through language, for its ultimate rebinding with the intellection of the analytic situation. In line with the idea of the frame being polysemic and the diversity of logics at play, the analyst's position is multiple and variable; it cannot be pre-determined or fixed: neither as oedipal father, nor as a mother–container, nor as a narcissistic double, the analyst must play, in the sense of performing and in a ludic sense, according to the scripts deployed in the polyphonic singularity of the analytic field. The acknowledgement that the unconscious "speaks" in many dialects promotes an ideal of a "polyglot analyst".

So how does the contemporary analyst's psyche works? I have attempted to answer this question by showing how contemporary listening has been renewed under the framework of what may be defined as a new, tertiary model (Urribarri, 2001). Tertiary, not so much by virtue of its "third" position, from a historical perspective, or of the significance it attaches to the articulation of the two former models, but due to the key role of certain new, "tertiary" concepts. I expect the concept of integrated or framed countertransference to be seen as a paradigmatic example, which is, in turn, articulated with other tertiary or contemporary notions, such as: the frame, a third element, constitutive of the analytic process; the triadic scheme made up by the frame–transference–countertransference; the analytic object, a (third) object made up by the patient–analyst communication; the analyst's psychic work, a conceptual axis that encompasses free-floating attention, countertransference, and the analytic imagination in the analyst's internal frame; and the tertiary processes—the core of the analyst's psychic work.

Notes

Translated by Carola De Grief.

1. Due to the limited scope of this chapter, focused on countertransference, two significant post-Freudian currents that partially or totally rejected the notion of countertransference—ego psychology (including Anna-Freudism) and Lacanianism—are not specifically analysed here. Very briefly put, North-American ego psychology and British Anna-Freudism rejected the Post-Freudian notion of countertransference. But in the last few decades (mainly with the support, in the United States, of Otto Kernberg, Harold Searles, and Thomas Ogden and, in the United Kingdom, of Joseph Sandler) the validity of the notion was acknowledged (especially as regards its articulation with projective identification) and the term was adopted in the theoretical vocabulary. Lacan rejected both the problem and the term, opposing them to the idea-direction of "the analyst's desire".

2. For example, Money-Kyrle (1956), when referring to countertransference, mentions three factors and concludes: "Of course, all three factors may be sorted out in a matter of seconds, and then indeed the countertransference is functioning as a delicate receiving apparatus."

3. In spite of its evident differences with Ferenczi–Balint–Winnicott, it is not a minor paradox that, by shifting its focus from language (the symbolic) to the act (reality), Lacanian practice became a somewhat active technique where interpretation is relieved by scansion and the cut of the session (Rosolato, 1999).

4. It is worth noting that, in 1964, Winnicott pointed out that the totalizing expansion of countertransference caused it to become less meaningful and specific. He aimed at clarifying and specifying the important issue of the analyst's mental functioning by proposing that a difference be established between countertransference—in terms of unconscious interference and the "professional attitude": "The professional attitude is rather like symbolism, in that it assumes a distance between analyst and patient."

5. Let us note that Kohut went through a similar process in the United States, going from being an innovative, anti-dogmatic thinker to becoming the leader of a militant current.

6. Laplanche: "A theorization based on Freud, even pointing out at times essential differences, is only justified to the extent that it can account for its options from a triple perspective: *Problematic*, contradictions and difficulties cannot be bypassed, since they are linked to some characteristics

of the object. It is necessary to "put them to work" . . . in order to find, at a different level, a formulation that modifies the way the problem is posed. *Historical* and *Critical*, in the sense that options become necessary" (Laplanche, 1986).

7. In the Post-modern Era, anorexics seem to embody the discontent in civilization, as hysterics did in the Modern Era (A. Giddens). Similar conclusions on historical and social changes from the predominance of neurotic cases to the pre-eminence of borderline and narcissistic disorders can be found in the sociological works of Sennett (*The Fall of Public Man*, 1977) and Lasch (*The Culture of Narcissism*), in the United States; Lipovetsky (*L'ère du vide*, 1983), in France, and García Canclini (*Imaginarios urbanos*, 1997), in Argentina.

8. Elizabeth Both Spillius chose the eloquent title "Rediscovering Hysteria" for her presentation on the recovery of sexuality in her current analytic listening. She observed, with the sharpness and honesty characteristic of the British tradition, that "the diagnosis of hysteria has been virtually highjacked by the diagnosis of borderline personality".

9. In our group, Jean-Claude Rolland advocated the role of the "pleasure principle as a compass in the analyst's listening"—in a French-style contemporary Freudian perspective. Along the same lines, when presenting his clinical cases, he posited the need to "find the libidinal scene behind the trauma".

10. In contrast with the post-Freudian orthodoxy, which categorically opposes psychoanalysis to psychoanalytic psychotherapy, the second case and treatment presented by Rolland (of a patient with a neurotic structure, initially in crisis after the death of her father) is an example of the contemporary perspective, where both approaches are combined at different periods of the same treatment.

11. Willi and Madeleine Baranger posit that there is an (intersubjective) phantasy in the analytic field, which translates into the creation of a "front of resistance". It differs from (and is irreducible to) both transference (or projective identification) and countertransference.

CONTRIBUTIONS MADE
AT THE FINAL MEETING OF
THE IPA RESEARCH GROUP,
September 2003

8

Pulling it together

Elizabeth Bott Spillius

A summary of our individual views about the research

At the final meeting of the IPA Research Group, André Green asked each of us what we had thought of the research as a whole.

Otto Kernberg said that he had originally wanted our group to reach a consensus but realized the rest of us did not want to do this, and so he had listed our areas of agreement and disagreement. The list was quite complicated, with 9 points of agreement and 8 of disagreement (see chapter 5; I have also included them as an Appendix).

The nine points of agreement focused mainly on the intensity of the analyst–patient relationship. Of the eight points of disagreement the most important, it seemed to me, concerned the nature of the diagnostic process. Otto works in a psychiatric institutional setting where formal procedures of structural and dynamic diagnosis precede treatment. The rest of the members of the seminar thought that they too were engaged in diagnosis, but in a different way. I believe we thought that we make some preliminary diagnosis in interviews with the patient before the treatment begins and that once it has begun, diagnosis continues on a daily basis, more or less, but without being part of a formally structured process. I think we would have agreed, however, that our diagnoses were not as systematic as Otto's, perhaps largely because they were not conducted to determine the type of treatment. For the most part our treatments are psychoanalysis or psychoanalytic psychotherapy, whatever the diagnosis.

Bill Grossman thought that psychoanalysis is a way of thinking in which reciprocity between analyst and patient is a necessary feature. He made a distinction between static and process characteristics. He was impressed by the fact that the discourse between us had become more mutually understandable. He thought that things we often regard as disputes in psychoanalysis are actually multiple perspectives. He emphasized the complexity of psychoanalysis and said we need to have both global and singular views. He stressed the difference between knowing something and the experience of gaining knowledge—a very similar distinction to the one Bion makes in *Learning from Experience* (1962).

I (Elizabeth) talked mostly about research design and how, in spite of having two major variables instead of one, we had all nevertheless had a valuable experience of learning from one another.

Jean-Claude Rolland spoke at some length, some of which I was not sure I understood. His most striking statement, at least for me, concerned what he called *the borderline situation* as distinct from the borderline patient. He thinks of the borderline situation as a structure to which the borderline patient subjects the analytic process, so that the analyst is acutely affected emotionally. The borderline patient tends to use the analytic situation to promote a "real" relationship in analysis. In other words, I think Jean-Claude was saying that the transference with a borderline patient is different from the usual sort of transference, which recognizes an "as if" quality in the relationship. Jean-Claude ended with an example of a woman patient who talked about violent criminals and then, tangentially, about her father. Jean-Claude said that she was thinking of her father when she spoke of the criminals. She said that of course she knew that. However, she improved markedly after this interchange.

I could not think about this at the time because of taking notes, but afterwards I thought that this was the third time that Jean-Claude had said this: with the psychotic young man who said his doctors had given up on him, Jean-Claude had said, "You were thinking about your parents when you felt given up by your doctors"; when the neurotic woman patient whose husband had left her forgot her name, Jean-Claude had said, "You were thinking of the death of your father when you forgot your name"; and in this third example he said the patient was thinking of her father when she spoke of the criminals.

What does this mean, I asked myself. Is this a specially significant part of Jean-Claude's outlook, particular just to him? Or is he making the point that this is part of *everyone's* unconscious outlook, their expectation? Or is it specific to French psychoanalysis? (I still don't know.)

Jaime Lutenberg was impressed by the exchange of views we had had, and he stressed the idea of symbiotic transference in borderline patients, meaning a particular dependent relationship in analysis that is formed between a part of the patient and a part of the object. He also stressed the importance of ambiguity in the symbiotic relationship.

Fernando Urribarri made an important statement at the end, which he had not been able to make earlier because he did not present clinical material. He talked about the patient's preconscious and the analyst's preconscious and said that when talking about the borderline patient, we had been talking about a sort of patient who is at the limits of analysability. For Freud, neurotic patients had been the model, the typical patient, but now borderline patients were the typical patient, the model for contemporary analysts. Fernando was impressed by Jean-Claude's idea of the *borderline situation*—which he thought we had all used to locate our approach. He also suggested that we use Jean-Claude's idea of looking for the libidinal scene behind the trauma. He went on to say that borderline patients express two sorts of destructiveness, one against the subject's own functioning, and the other in attacks on the link with the object. We have been going beyond countertransference, Fernando continued, and what is larger than countertransference is analytic listening.

A lot more was said here by Fernando and others, but my notes are not detailed enough to do justice to the discussion.

André said we had had important thoughts in this discussion, and we all agreed. He also talked very seriously about his concern about the future of analysis, which we shared.

We went on to talk about the book (this volume) that would come out of our work.

We talked, too, of our wish somehow or other to continue our discussions. It was Gregorio Kohon who said, and I think we all agreed, that we were finding it difficult to say goodbye because we knew we had developed something good, and it was difficult to let it go.

APPENDIX
Otto Kernberg's view of points of agreement and disagreement
in the research group

Areas of agreement

1. There is a primitive intense transference in borderlines, which immediately activates an intense countertransference that threatens the frame (setting).

2. Borderline patients tend to defend themselves against the representational frame of affects by acting out and in somatization.

3. There is a splitting of free associations because borderline patients are afraid that their own free associations will lead to trauma. This means that in our technical approach there needs to be rapid intervention to deal with rapid changes in meaning.

4. Countertransference reactions are high. There is a moment-to-moment reaction to the patient. In Otto's view this is not only a matter of technique. Because of the splitting of associations, the neurotic can make links, but the borderline breaks links.

5. Interpretations are made in the here-and-now situation first rather than genetic interpretations. There is momentary somatization and acting out.

6. The work of Lieberman and Victor Rosen was discussed briefly.

7. My notes are not really clear here but I think they say that we are all agreed that, in contrast to the old ego psychological view, the unconscious conflict varies from patient to patient, and there is rapid change in focus from synchronic to diachronic.

8. André and Gregorio look for the dominant affect of the patient, which they regard as the selected fact. It is seen through the vertex of analytic experience of the total transference situation.

9. The analyst attempts to protect the frame.

Areas of disagreement

1. We differ on the value of *diagnosis*. We do not differ in our views of DSM4 and ICD (International Classification of Diseases). But we disagree on whether it is possible to make a dynamic diagnosis of the dominant conflict, and so on, and whether it is helpful to

make a structural diagnosis. Most of us agree that these patients
are stable in their instability.

2. There is disagreement about our position regarding psychosis.
   Should we try to influence this: should we try to modify the
   frame into psychoanalytic psychotherapy, or not? Is it necessary
   to modify the analytic frame? Are there limits distinguishing psychoanalysis and psychoanalytic psychotherapy? In French analysis
   there have been introductions of modifications without calling
   the results of these modifications by the term "psychotherapy".
   André Green wanted to introduce psychoanalytic psychotherapy
   into the training and was told no, our cases are neurotics; but
   now five years later there are so many examples of training cases
   who are not neurotics. Elizabeth Spillius thought the definition
   of agreement and disagreement on such matters depended very
   much on the local psychiatric and psychoanalytic culture.

   The French, Otto said, are more flexible than the Independents, the Kleinians, or the ego psychologists.

   Psychoanalytic psychotherapy, Otto says, ideally should not
   use supportive techniques.

   But psychoanalytic psychotherapy needs to define how it is
   different from psychoanalysis.

4. The extent to which we should link ourselves with psychiatrists.

5. The initial evaluation of patients. There is a disagreement about
   whether patients should be explored about acceptance of the
   frame, capacity to symbolize, and so on, in the initial consulta-
   tion. Some feel that full psychiatric diagnosis is helpful because
   it predicts a capacity to accept the frame. Others think that the
   psychiatric approach interferes with the understanding of the
   transference and that it restricts the analysis.

6. There is a sharp difference about transference. Some think it is
   the same as in neurotic patients, but Elizabeth and André agree
   that borderline patients are at the end of treatment whereas
   neurotics are at the beginning. Otto thinks that in neurosis one
   mostly gets projection of the object onto the analyst, whereas
   in borderlines it alternates between projection of the self and
   projection of objects.

7. There is disagreement implicitly about whether a contract needs
   to be set up between patient and analyst. André Green describes
   flexible changes in the frame. There are those, however, who

maintain a strict frame, the Kleinians, and it is implicit in Otto's psychotherapy.

8. There is disagreement regarding the handling of severe regression—whether it should be fostered or reduced. Kleinians would interpret. Independents would encourage regression. (Not always—Elizabeth, Gregorio.)

Controversies for the future

What are the limits of treatability, and how can they be defined? To what extent are countertransference developments an important indicator of treatability? Does the length of treatment depend on diagnosis? Should one undertake diagnosis to predict this?

9

On the relevance of the borderline situation

Jean-Claude Rolland

On the question of diagnosis

It seems to me unscientific to declare that the question of diagnosis is pointless and incongruous, as several of us were tempted to do during the discussion. Freud taught us to consider the establishment of a diagnosis as an essential part of psychoanalytic work, and André Green recalled that Freud had added to the existing nosological arsenal of his time by including the description of obsessional neurosis. Simply put, the diagnostic enterprise is inherent in the analytic situation and follows its course. It is included in the construction we build concerning our patients from the first interview that we have with them. These constructions are absolutely necessary for us to locate our patients' demands metapsychologically and then in order to decide on the patients' analysability.

But as we progress in our experience as analysts, these constructions refer less and less to considerations of structure in the nosological sense of the term: for example, to know whether we are in the presence of a psychosis or a neurosis, and what sort of neurosis. My diagnoses refer more and more to considerations of structure in the psychodynamic sense. We try in effect to represent what balance is achieved in this patient, between his drives and the organization of his ego: or, further, between what one could infer of his internal experience (the nature of his anxiety, the degree of his inhibitions, the dissociation that splits him) and the means by which he can articulate all this in order to verbalize it in the precise context of free association.

Furthermore, this diagnostic enterprise, which is appropriate to the analytic situation, undergoes, in relation to a traditional diagnostic enterprise of this psychiatric type, still another variation: we try to represent a history of the illness or the symptom that affects our patient and leads him to require an analysis. We seek to locate the traumatic event or events that led to it as well as the affective and genetic situation in which the patient finds himself at the moment—for example, whether the pathological situation was produced in childhood, in adolescence, or at the threshold of the adult world, and what was the familial context at the time when it was developing. But our diagnostic enterprise undergoes yet another development: it is not so much an objective story, a chronological story of his affliction, that interests us, but the way in which it tends to be re-actualized in the analytic enterprise that he seeks, the way in which the unconscious stake that supports "becoming ill" and the traumatic experience that underpins it are reproduced in the analytic situation itself. We try to establish by our construction the identity of the object the loss of which was counter-invested by the symptom, this object that he tries to re-find as reincarnate in the transference to the analyst.

The psychoanalytic diagnostic enterprise follows a complex development and proceeds in stages and is removed up to a point from the psychiatric enterprise. Its final purpose is the recognition of the transference, which is its finally achieved form, its conclusion. What characterizes it is that it goes from the most objective and the most social to the most singular and intimate. I refer here to the thoughts constructed by Gregorio: what he defines as the intimacy of the analytic situation. Otto has insisted, and not without good reason, on reiterating the need to establish, in the area of the analysis and of the analytic situation, a diagnostic structure that, because of its rational and objective character, contrasts with the ruptures of the intricate nature of the transference experience. We are obliged to ask ourselves about this: who is it for, and why? Such a procedure addresses itself to an imagined third party—society, for example—to which one would like to justify the enterprise that one has established, even though such an enterprise—the establishing of the analytic

situation—is only justified for the patient by an insistence on infantile desire (the vehicle of suffering and satisfaction) that has already
returned in his symptom or his illness, as well as in his demand for
an analysis. In the analysis is an echo and, in an asymmetrical way, a
desire to respond to this desire and to submit to it and dissolve it in
the transference experience.

The cure realizes a situation with two people who are cut off as
much as possible from the external world—not so much to exclude
it but to constitute it, to create an intimacy in transference–countertransference in which their psychic apparatuses assign a new place
to the unconscious experience that contributes to an interplay of
symbolic oppositions that are specific to the analytic process, in order to recreate, paradoxically, an external reality.

For certain patients—and one can tell more early on—the creation of this intimacy, even if not really impossible, stumbles nevertheless upon particular obstacles. For example the patient finds out that
he has someone close to him who has contacts with the analyst, or he
opposes the analytic rule, or he has difficulty in timing or in making
payments. Or he might manifest a very distant presence, talking of
himself as if he were someone else, like a stranger, who only partici-
pates in a mediated way in a process whose fluidity he also blocks.

For my part, I make use of the category of borderline in facing
these difficulties. The representation for me is not so much a structural problem as a situation designating a certain type of development that certain patients undergo, reducing the analytic process
even while being engaged in it consciously without ambiguity.

The traumatic nature of the analytic situation

The analytic situation is traumatic. André Green has often reiterated
this. During the whole time of the session, during the whole time of
his analysis, the method based on free association and interpretation
is challenging, in the unpleasure of it, the balance that had been
established in the patient between primary and secondary processes,
between ego forces subjected to ideals and to the demands of reality and the claims of the unconscious formation revived by the
transference regression. Pierre Fedida, among the French authors,
was the one who best described the critical character of the analytic
experience. To underline this essential aspect of the analysis, he

spoke of the transference crisis which echoes, according to him, a countertransference crisis. The point of relevance in this conceptual system is not only that it accurately describes the clinical practice with borderline patients. It has the advantage of locating the analytic experience alongside crises that are produced at the moment of the emergence of the pathological event, and the illness that constitutes it freezes it as a defensive counter-investment. The crisis evoked in the transference–countertransference experience appears in this light as a repetition of the traumatic crisis that triggered in the patient, at the origin of his illness, a violent conflict, opposing a certain reclamation from the drives and the entreaties of the ego. Or also it opposes a "sacrificial" libidinal demise linked to a certain object relation to the patient's narcissistic integrity.

The analysand accepts facing the traumatic nature of this experience as well as the fear or inhibition it arouses because he gains the conviction (meaning that the patient listens to us) that we have the measure of the analytic frame and also because of our internal frame—defined by the freedom and accuracy of our constructions—that assures him of the containment of his experience, to take up one of Bion's words. Jean-Luc Donnet is the French author who has best captured the nature of the exciting function that the analyst, through his presence, provides the analysand when facing a critical ordeal. The image he gives, a "well-tempered couch", perfectly illustrates the opposition where the experience of the cure lies between the disquiet of the transference and the tranquillity of the experience of being held.

Generally, the analysand who is naturally endowed with a "sufficiently strong ego", an ego that is itself containing, is not reticent in confiding in his analyst. He spontaneously lends himself, perhaps projectively, a containing capacity and gives himself lightly to the experience, abandoning himself to it with ease: he gives himself room to have an internal and associative activity that guarantees a rebalancing of primary and secondary processes. He authorizes the analyst to proceed freely and fully in his interpretive function.

With other patients, on the other hand, one has to realize more-or-less quickly that this activity, called "perlaboration", essentially linguistic, is hardly produced at all. These patients are indifferent to the interpretive function of the analyst. They only seem to be concerned that their distress, rage, or passion evoked by the transference should be contained. They are very much attached to their analysis and find a real improvement, but the question of psychic change is not their immediate concern.

For the analyst it is, rather, a question of survival. We can define these analytic situations well by saying that the patient privileges a person-to-person relationship with the analyst rather than a transference to the analyst. Between these two situation there are infinitesimal, complex gradations. I propose that I play with this provisional conceptual opposition only to open the question of the difference in the nature between the neurotic transference and the borderline transference—a question that we should examine in minute detail. These are situations that we can characterize by referring to the conjunction of a strong analytic demand and a weak analytic process.

Such situations are undoubtedly difficult for the analyst to tolerate, for two reasons: because he can only partially use his technical capacity, and because it is a requirement that he should make a very active and strong affective and representational investment, which is nevertheless essentially unconscious. The analyst is always solicited in his function of keeping to the frame of the experience, and under-solicited in his interpretive function. The analyst is faced with a particularly powerful and alien countertransference. The unconscious involvement evoked by this extreme transference experience leads the analyst to perceive the patient in his most radical alien-ness (alterity). And to counter this, the analyst perceives himself in a way that is most unknown to him.

Faced with these borderline situations in terms of analysability I am led to refer to the conceptual category of borderline not to designate an individual structure, but to define a form of intersubjective relationship in which the other imposes himself on me as doubly other—other in the objective sense that he is not me, that he is my "*Gegenstand*" [object], the one who stands against and opposes me and reduces me thus to my pure subjectivity; he is other also in the sense that the mystery of his existence comes to meet me by altering me. What Freud on many occasions designates under the term "*Ich-veränderung*", this alteration of the ego to which our patients subject us, seems to me to be at the heart of the countertransference already described carefully and at length in *borderline situations.*

At the end of three years of an intense and fascinating piece of work achieved by our group, thanks to André's generosity I can reconcile myself fully to this concept, which initially I regarded with a certain reticence. Nevertheless it seems like a revolutionary concept that Freud did not have available. It adds to the analytic theory a tool that allows us to think and to unravel what the fundamental anthropological reality of subjectivity is—this "mass of two", to pick up the term used by Pierre Fedida. An archaic reality that only transference/countertransference regression evoked by the analysis of these patients is capable of manifesting, the analyst in recognizing the other in his suffering and is the only witness of his existence and must adopt and maintain this position that Freud in the *Outline* (1940a [1938]) identified with the figure of the "*Nebenmensch*". The term is difficult to translate if we want to obviate the religious slant that it contains, which is alien to Freudian thinking. The figure that suggests or comes near a concern about humanity, the one I need to become a humanizing influence, that is located in the opposition to the couple that he formed with the alienating and destructive figure of the *Urvater*—the primal father.

The position required from the analyst by his patients could be represented as the proximity of a subject that is already constituted to help another to constitute himself in a subjectivity. From the primal time of being a subject (subjectivation) it is certain that "borderline analysands" offer a representation that remains hidden in many ordinary analysands.

The reference to unconscious desire

It would be impossible for me to be an analyst if my ability were not based on the conviction inherited from the early Freud, the author of the *Studies* (1895d), of the *Psychopathology of Everyday Life* (1901b), according to which what determines the psychic activity that determines the dream, slips of the tongue, the psychoneuroses, is the realization of a hallucinatory satisfaction, the fulfilment of an unconscious desire. The often intense suffering, the real alienation of the relationship of the subject to his external world, which flows eventually from this type of account that we call irrational, can only be considered as the price to be paid for a regressive tendency of the psychic apparatus. It is an inadequate manifest plan that nevertheless underlines a rigorous finality in terms of the pleasure principle. Unconscious desire organizes psychic life in a structural conflict. Freud's summarizes the precarious economy of the conscious–unconscious balance of the ego and the id by the formula "satisfaction for one system, unpleasure for the other".

In order to represent the dynamic that leads a patient to engage in analysis, it is necessary to refer to a redoubling of this conflict. Gregorio Kohon, in his presentation, said something about it: the excess of suffering—of anxiety, for example, which we must remember only belongs to an instance of the ego as a "minority"—is never enough by itself to constrain a patient to renounce his neurosis. The satisfaction that he gains through the symptom remains his most precious possession. It is necessary in order for him to accede to a demand that there should emerge in him a cultural expectation that gives him the means to discern, even confusedly, the inevitably incestuous character of satisfaction. It is probable that because of the transference attraction, the encounter with the other who is the analyst is never reducible to a simple substitute for the primary object; the analyst awakens this civilizing movement as a suggestion towards renunciation.

10

Borderline traces
and the question of diagnosis

Gregorio Kohon

Psychoanalysis is an organized body of knowledge, acquired and developed through study and personal experience, the object of which
is the *psychic reality* of the human subject. Psychic reality, as understood by psychoanalysis, cannot be reduced to either the mental or
the physical; the psychoanalytic object is a different object of study,
with its own characteristics, categories, and laws (Gomez, 2005).
The psychoanalytic models and theories are based on fundamental
hypotheses and basic assumptions that have been arrived at through
a mixture of clinical experience and self-reflection, speculative intellectual activity and intuition, free-floating attention and deduction,
and the attribution of retrospective meaning and abstract representations. Since the psychic processes under scrutiny are unconscious,
there is no tangible or measurable method that would offer any
kind of evidence for the accuracy of hypotheses and assumptions
other than those offered by and from within the psychoanalytic
method and setting. This does not make psychoanalysis necessarily
inadequate or ineffective. Conversely, it challenges the very concept
of science, which is forced to confront the ontological status of the
psychoanalytic object of enquiry.
    André Green (2002a) has introduced the concept of *la pensée
clinique*, defined by a different, particular, and specific mode of cau-

sality, not reducible to other kinds of scientific forms of thought. The rationality of this form of thought is at the basis of the communication among psychoanalysts. Within the realm of psychoanalytic clinical thought, theories become validated when the individual subject recognizes the interpretations offered by the theory as his or her own. Every interpretation is tried out and tested, as it were, in every new situation in which it appears; it is then that theoretical ideas become personal knowledge. This is what makes research in psychoanalysis especially difficult.

Clinical research could be succinctly characterized by the recurrent comparison, contrasting, and evaluation of clinical material against theoretical models and ideas. This might lead either to a re-discovery and confirmation of psychoanalytic concepts, and/or to the new development of psychoanalytic concepts (Leuzinger-Bohleber & Bürgin, 2003). In the context of the present research group, it soon became clear to each member of the group that there were crucial and significant disagreements, which divided its members—at certain times—in seemingly irreconcilable ways. Theoretically, as much as technically, the differences themselves (once they became explicit in the discussions) seemed to become the object of study and research. For Urribarri (see chapter 4), the key question that ended up defining the object of research was, "How does the mind of the contemporary psychoanalyst work?" According to Spillius (chapter 1) it was an *exploratory* clinical research group; the emphasis, therefore, was on the exploration of hypotheses, rather than on the testing and proving of them.

From the beginning, the members of the group were confronted with the problem of whether the concept of borderline was a legitimate and justifiable diagnosis. In this contribution, I will address some of the issues concerning this challenging question.[1]

The term "borderline" appeared for the first time in the 1880s, in the work of C. H. Hughes (1884) and Irving C. Rosse (1890) (both reprinted in Stone, 1986). Although it described frontier states of madness, it did not constitute at the time a true diagnostic concept. In 1921, the term re-appeared in the work of T. V. Moore, in a paper published in the *Psychoanalytic Review*, "The Parataxes. A Study and Analysis of Certain Borderline Mental States". Freud used it once in the preface (1925f) to a book by August Aichhorn, *Wayward Youth*, when he spoke of "borderline and mixed cases". The concept of borderline only became nosologically defined with the publication in 1938 of Adolph Stern's article, "Psychoanalytic Investigations of and Therapy in the Border Line Group of Neuroses". Stern's aim was to establish the analysability of a certain group of patients who could not properly be diagnosed as psychotic and who yet could not be identified as neurotic. He described a number of symptoms in their clinical presentation which included intense narcissism and hypersensitivity, accompanied by severe insecurity and feelings of inferiority; intolerance of psychic pain; extreme anxiety; and difficulties in sustaining interpersonal relationships. The intensity of each and every one of these symptoms, Stern argued, made the psychoanalytic treatment of these patients particularly problematic. Today, seventy years later, most clinicians would describe similar symptoms in the presentation of borderline patients.

It was through the development and use, in the United States, of neuroleptics that the emphasis started to change. In a few years, the focus moved from the need to differentiate the borderline condition from neurosis to the question of its closeness to psychosis. This change of emphasis in the (originally) psychoanalytic diagnosis stirred American psychiatrists to become especially interested in borderline phenomena. Psychoanalysts, who worked within mainstream psychiatry and psychiatric teaching institutions in the United States, attempted to develop a more coherent clinical picture, a diagnostically precise approach to these patients. Otto Kernberg's 1967 paper offered the most integrative and systematic description of what he called a "borderline personality organization"—a separate and seemingly coherent structural diagnosis, a concept that Kernberg specifically differentiated from and opposed to the notion of "borderline states". He saw the diagnosis of borderline personality disorders as an encompassing diagnostic group under which other personality disorders would be subsumed. Kernberg's ideas were extremely influential and could be summarized thus: while the capacity for reality testing would distinguish the borderline from the psychotic, the possession of a sense of identity would separate the neurotic from the borderline.

Nevertheless, the attempt to establish the concept of borderline as a clear and well-defined semiological description was not fully accepted; contradictory views within the psychoanalytic community at large have since continued to coexist. In France, Laplanche and Pontalis declared that the term had "no strict nosographical definition. The variations in its use reflect the real uncertainty concerning the area to which it is applied" (1967). Ten years later, André Green (1977) wrote, "the limits are not all situated in the same places by the different writers, who nevertheless are supposed to be competent in this matter". In 1981, Widlöcher emphatically stated that the meaning of the concept of borderline has "become imprecise, confused, and even contradictory. In fact one could speak of a plurality of concepts which certainly cover a widely recognised clinical reality, but while using criteria so different that the definition of this new category loses its precision to the extent that the clinical studies, the etiological hypotheses and the psychopathological theories multiply themselves. It is therefore necessary *to speak of concepts, in the plural, of borderline states*" (Widlöcher, 1981, italics added).

While these controversies and disagreements were taking place on the international psychoanalytic scene during the 1960s and 1970s, British clinicians (W. R. D. Fairbairn, Michael Balint, Harry Guntrip, Hanna Segal, Betty Joseph, etc.) treated similarly disturbed patients but very rarely appealed to the concept of borderline. In fact, for a long time most British psychoanalysts ignored the word "borderline" altogether in their writings. It was only through the work of Herbert Rosenfeld and Henry Rey, towards the second part of the 1970s, that the British psychoanalytic establishment started to use the term as a psychoanalytic diagnosis. (It should also be noted that, at the time, they also avoided, without actively opposing, the use of medication for disturbed patients—a practice that, in contrast, developed more actively in other countries.)

By the mid and late 1980s, authors and clinicians made renewed efforts to question the homogeneity of the syndrome. Abend, Poder, and Willick (1988) argued that it is the presence of serious pathology in the area of the ego that identifies the borderline conditions but, in agreement with Meissner (1984), they did not believe that borderline psychopathology constituted a single diagnostic entity. They specifically opposed the definition of the borderline personality disorder offered by the DSM-III (American Psychiatric Association), which included potentially self-damaging impulsivity or unpredictability; a pattern of unstable and intense interpersonal relationships; inappropriate, intense anger or lack of control; identity disturbance; affective instability; intolerance of being alone; physically self-damaging acts; and chronic feelings of emptiness and boredom. These authors argued that while it might be clinically useful to keep the reference of "borderline" for a certain heterogeneous group of disturbed patients whose analysability is often questioned, they still doubted that they constituted a specific diagnostic entity; the illusion of a unified clinical entity offered by the DSM-III did not seem to account for the variety of clinical presentations. While Rangell (1988) questioned the usefulness of the term in the first place, Shengold (1995) emphatically declared that he found the diagnosis of borderline increasingly *less* useful.

As has also been the case with the diagnosis of schizophrenia, it became clear that the diagnosis of borderline depended largely on the theoretical background of the individual clinician. Nevertheless, for better or worse, in many psychoanalytic quarters there is a widespread belief that neurotic patients have steadily been disappearing from our consulting-rooms, making space for a plethora of those with personality and character disorders, both of these understood as belonging to the borderline spectrum. Some psychoanalysts believe that there is "broad agreement that neurotic problems, as Freud described them, are increasingly unusual in psychoanalytic practice . . ." (Fonagy, Target, Cottrell, Phillips, & Kurtz, 2002). While in a previous article, Fonagy (1991) stated that "Psychoanalysis and modern psychiatry take opposing approaches to the definition of borderline patients", he later appealed to the authority of the contemporary psychiatric classification systems to support his present position, claiming that the term *neurosis* is no longer a "legitimate" term in psychoanalysis (Fonagy et al., 2002).

Different disciplines may use the same words but with different meanings; sometimes, even within the same discipline, the use of one word can be understood in different ways. The concept of borderline states itself seems to occupy a borderline place between psychiatry and psychoanalysis, both disciplines having different methods and—at times—conflicting aims. Since psychology and psychiatry are scientific disciplines that are not necessarily connected with the object, the theories, or the methods of psychoanalysis, the descriptions of borderline patients offered by psychologists and psychiatrists, while not irrelevant, can be said to be extraneous to psychoanalysis. That which, to psychiatry, appears at a phenomenological level as a properly unified clinical syndrome may or may not be a specific type of pathology from a psychoanalytic point of view. In practice, from being a descriptive psychiatric category, the concept of borderline has become an explanatory concept. Given the specificity of the psychoanalytic discipline, there is a serious conceptual problem to be confronted.

The contemporary presentation of these patients appears to be very close to the clinical picture presented by Freud's hysterical patients. Inevitably, the argument is that Freud's patients were, after all, not hysterics but true borderlines. Nevertheless, many authors, myself included, have suggested in the past that this is not the result of a change in the population of patients but a consequence of a change in the theory of psychoanalysis (Kohon, 1984, 1999).[2]

I have argued that—as a consequence of the process of de-sexualization that took place in the development of psychoanalytic theory after Freud—psychoanalysis reverted to a simplistic theoretical "naturalism". As part of the changes in the theory, hysteria, for example, was turned into a defensive technique aimed at maintaining "at a distance and under control anxieties which are defined as *primitive, psychotic* and *not sexual...*" In other words, patients may be hysterics but *"since the theory looks for something else, it also finds something else."* Patients, who would have been considered hysterics in the past were now understood to be psychotic or borderline. (Kohon, 1984; see also Kohon, 1999). I have also put forward the idea that the subject is confronted, at a certain point in the Oedipal drama, with the choice between mother and father. This is a *hysterical stage*, a developmental moment characterized by what I called *divalence*: not being able to choose between mother and father as the primary sexual object. The hysteric might get stuck at this stage, moving simultaneously between two sets: in one set, he occupies the place of his mother and attempts to seduce the father. In another set, he is in aggressive rivalry with the father for the conquest of the mother. Unable to make the choice between one and the other, hysterics cannot define themselves as men or a women.[3]

Critical assessments of psychoanalytic theoretical concepts play a very important part in the development of psychoanalysis; they constantly re-address the clinical as much as the theoretical specificity of this discipline (above all, but not exclusively, the psychoanalytic understanding of sexuality as well as that of the unconscious). In fact, Christopher Bollas stated that, "As Gregorio Kohon writes, hysterics do not know their gender" (2000, p. 90). Nevertheless, in my writings I did not use the concept of "gender" but that of "sexual difference". The theoretical concept of sexual difference, which is specific to psychoanalysis, should not be displaced by a theory of the social construction of gender, nor can it be reduced to the biological differences between the sexes. Similarly, it cannot be substituted by a symbolic interpretation that would consider "sexual difference" as the result of historical contingencies. In any case, hysterics know fairly well the biological differences between male and female (the question of sex), as much as they are aware of the social construction that makes a human being masculine or feminine (the question of gender). Nevertheless, *from the point of view of the choice of a sexual object*, they simply do not know what to do with their knowledge. This is not the same for the patient in a borderline predicament, who, in contrast to the hysteric, never reaches this stage of choice; he is too confused to occupy any position in the Oedipal triangle.[4]

In 1997, André Green had also referred to the link between hysteria and borderline, stating that "Despite its legendary polymorphism, the concept of hysteria as it is understood and recognized by psychoanalysis forms a totality better defined, despite everything, than that designated by the vague expression 'borderline states'" (Green, 1997a).

A number of established opinions (Kernberg, 1967, 1975; Masterson & Rinsley, 1975; among others) have suggested the existence of a direct correlation between the presenting symptoms and specific developmental traumas. Nevertheless, the clinical evidence seems to be contradictory and not well defined; there does not seem to be an unequivocal and indisputable direct causality between a trauma and the emergence of borderline phenomena. After all, the true reality of an event in the life of a subject is not what determines its psychic traumatic effectiveness. If there was a trauma in the history of the borderline patient, it only became such because the event (real or imagined) escaped symbolization. In fact, it might never be possible to develop a theory that would definitely account for the origin of borderline states; the genetic factors appear to be varied, multiple, and even contradictory. In some patients, failures of the environment, emotional traumas, and psychic difficulties seemed to have appeared not in early childhood but much later in life. For example, borderline phenomena could develop and appear after an adolescent breakdown. Naturally, this would have aetiological determinants from childhood, but these would not necessarily have produced the breakdown. It is conceivable that the presence of borderline disturbance—even a fairly serious one—would be an indication, not of a regression to early stages, but of a certain discontinuity in development. Rassial (1999) has called it *panne*, a breakdown, a stop. He argued that it may not have amounted to an original, proper psychotic breakdown; it can be represented, rather, as a traumatic halt that poignantly punctuated a period of psychic strife. This is very close to Winnicott's ideas (1960b); he considered that there had been an actual traumatic arrest in the subject, caused by cumulative maternal failures—thus creating a false self. Yorke, Wiseberg, and Freeman (1989), while opposed to the notion of borderline disorders as a well-defined nosological entity (describing them instead as "non-neurotic developmental disorders"), particularly emphasized the existence in the subject of a faulty and vulnerable ego structure; as a consequence of this, it is argued, object constancy was not developed properly, the ego remaining in constant danger of fragmentation.

The characteristics observed in the so-called borderline might indeed not constitute a psychoanalytic diagnosis, but the unquestionable presence of these subjects in the consulting-room of psychoanalysts remains a true challenge to the analyst's offer of treatment. In the end, borderline states can only be defined according to the form in which they present themselves in the psychoanalytic setting. These different forms tend to "jump" onto—or, as it were, get a ride on—other neurotic and psychotic structures that then tend to disappear under their weight. The suffering of the borderline, which can never be confined to neurosis, psychosis, or perversion, nevertheless structures his subjectivity.

From a psychoanalytic point of view, we can identify a cluster of symptoms. Rather than symptoms, I would prefer to call them "marks" or "traces", which I—like many other psychoanalytic clinicians—have found present in a relatively large number of these non-neurotic patients. Each of these marks might appear as a single—although not unique—characteristic, or as a mixture. They are not even exclusive to this type of patients; they can also be found in neurotic and psychotic structures, although they seem to be more frequent and intense in those patients who present borderline states of mental functioning. They are not presented here in any special order.

As described originally by Stern in 1938, most contemporary authors agree that these subjects suffer from a narcissistic hypersensitivity, which makes their relationships extremely intense but, characteristically, chaotic and short-lived. Once in analysis, the subject develops a passionate and severe transference, which may change from a positive extreme to a negative one very rapidly. When positive, this excessive emotional involvement with the analyst might offer the necessary conditions for the treatment to succeed (see Kohon, 2005). The analyst might be subjected to suffering and abuse (love that kills, deadly love). If both analyst and patient survive these storms, extreme positive transference situations might help to dislodge and fight against the psychotic parental involvement, always so evident in the patient's internal world. Needless to say, when this "limitless" transference is negative, hope disappears, and not much can be saved from the wreckage; everything that may have been built by the patient and analyst is reduced to rubble.

There is confusion between love and hate. In fact, the subject seems to experience the object as *simultaneously* good and bad; thus, the object appears to be intrusive as well as distant and inaccessible at one and the same time (Green, 1975). One example of this confusion between love and hate has been described by Rosenfeld (1987), who talked about patients feeling phobic about their own mothers: they are terrified that they have to defend themselves against something extremely dangerous; for them, the physical experience of feeding (love) becomes in their minds confused with being poisoned (hate). Probably, the original nourishment that they needed for survival might indeed have been toxic (Eigen, 1999). Sometimes, after becoming aware in the treatment of hating the primary object of love, patients can develop a more tolerant, loving relationship with their objects.

In parallel to the subject's confusion between love and hate and the chaos that this confusion provokes in the subject's emotional life, the analyst finds himself responding to his patient in the countertransference with an equivalent form of "emotional chaos". At the beginning of the treatment, the analyst might feel seduced by a hysterical presentation of the borderline's self, but this is soon replaced by an actual feeling of being "mad", of not knowing what to think, of having had his clinical judgement warped (Viqui Rosenberg, personal communication).

In most cases, there is confusion between mother and father. At the same time, there is a specific and particularly intense guilt associated with the maternal figure, inevitably experienced whenever there is any hint of progress in the analysis. The feeling of guilt becomes more relevant and critical if and when the patient has been living out the mother's psychosis (as in the case described by Kohon, 2005). The resistance to the analyst's interventions can be persistent and, in many cases, chronic enough to cause the failure of the treatment. The analyst's interpretations threaten the subject's narcissistic identifications with his psychotic mother. Insight creates a conflict of loyalties.

The patient needs the analysis, but he experiences the psychoanalytic situation itself as a repetition of a trauma (Kohon, 1999). Due to his narcissistic vulnerability, he tends to experience interpretations as a source of great humiliation. The analyst, in trying to make sense of the patient's words and actions through his interpretations, enacts the original trauma; his communications to the patient become, in turn, traumatic; misunderstanding the analyst's interpretations is central to the patient's predicament (Bion, 1962). Britton, following Rosenfeld (1987), suggested that "the analytic method itself is felt by the patient to be a threat: its structure, its method, its boundaries" (Britton, 1998). The presence as much as the absence of the analyst is experienced by the patient as impingements.

Another malignant form of the transference situation is constituted by a sustained, prolonged, and unbroken impasse in the analysis (Rosenfeld, 1987). At times, this might be evident; at other times, a slow, rather imperceptible libidinal disinvestment takes place, first on the part of the patient, and then on the part of the analyst. Boredom gains the upper hand in the treatment, curiosity disappears, *jouissance* is a long-forgotten event. The patient does not know what he wants from the analysis, nor can he remember why he started the treatment. For the analyst, the sessions have become one more task to get through in the day, clocking time to earn his living. The patient creates an empty space in the analyst's mind, and the analyst experiences a sense of exclusion from the patient's internal world (Perelberg, 2003, 2004).

Some of these patients' capacity to symbolize appears to be impaired. I have called this *symbolic impoverishment* (Kohon, 1999). The analytic narrative—whether dreams, slips of the tongue, etc—are not a text to be deciphered and interpreted; in the patient's mind, they are a series of actions requiring a response, or the avoidance of a response. This is different from the phenomena described by Hanna

Segal as the symbolic equation in schizophrenics. In the case of symbolic impoverishment, the subject does not experience the "symbol-substitute" as the original object (Segal, 1957), confusing one with the other. Symbolic impoverishment is not as primitive; it does not entail a psychotic level of mental functioning. Instead, it creates very specific psychic conditions for the malignant misunderstanding of the psychoanalytic situation (as already mentioned above) and an incapacity to endure psychic pain.

These patients are closely linked to the thin- and thick-skinned narcissists described by Rosenfeld (Rosenfeld, 1987). Rosenfeld saw the thick-skinned narcissist as someone who is insensitive to deeper feelings, envy being a major obstacle to the analysis. By contrast, the thin-skinned narcissist is hypersensitive and easily hurt; this type of patient seemed to have been made to feel persistently ashamed, vulnerable, and rejected. Anthony Bateman (1998) suggested that the two groups described by Rosenfeld move between the thick-skinned and thin-skinned positions. Ronald Britton (1998) has also expressed similar views, holding that "inside every thick-skinned patient (there) is a thin-skinned patient trying not to get out", and vice versa. In a similar vein, Fonagy has suggested that the lack of consistency and safety in the subjects' early object relations has not helped them to develop the capacity to mentalize—defined as the capacity "to conceive of conscious and unconscious mental states in oneself and others" (Fonagy, 1991; see also 2000). Consequently, the fluidity of identificatory processes between positions and ideas, and between masculinity and femininity, is impaired (Perelberg, 1999a & 1999b).

A specific form of persecutory depressive anxiety is at the core of the borderline predicament, originating in contradictory feelings that do not achieve resolution (*neither yes nor no*, Green, 1977). Depression and anxiety are the most common reactions to the demands of reality, which is mostly experienced as an impingement. Intense anxiety attacks the subject's capacity to think. Other people might appear and re-appear as alien or intrinsically unknowable.

Loss seems unbearable (Steiner, 1979). It is as if the borderline subject was not able to accept and to negotiate the very loss inherent in the original object of need (Rey, 1979), as if he could not count on the symbolic tools that should have helped him to respond to this exposure. Afterwards, any future loss has become intolerable and the emptiness fixed. If it were at all possible to give words to his sorrow, there could be hope for reconciliation with the loss of the original maternal body—a possible outcome for a successful analysis.

Jean-Claude Rolland (personal communication) introduced an important distinction: while *not being alive* could describe the internal world of the autistic patient, *full of dead objects* would describe the borderline experience. In the most seriously disturbed cases, the dead objects have been "murdered" and are always threatening to return. Rosenfeld (1987) has argued that the deadness of these objects should remain "secret"; the secret is kept not just from others—that is, the analyst—but also from the subject himself: for example, the patient does not have any dreams. This is different from symbolic impoverishment. It is not so much a failure of the symbolic process; instead, it is the result of avoidance, thus connected to the phenomena described by the concept of the central phobic position (Green, 2002a).

All these marks or traces constitute and define the basic emotional instability of the subject, which is absolutely central to his psychic and emotional functioning. This ontological insecurity (Laing, 1960), arising from the fragility of his narcissism, materializes in paranoid anxieties whenever he has to negotiate the difference between the inside and the outside, thus, justifying the concept of "borderline". Paradoxically, and most pertinently, this instability offers the subject "some kind of stability of personality organization" (Rey, 1979). It organizes his life through the constancy of chaos.

In taking up permanent and static residence in their psychic refuges (Steiner, 1993), they not only find a form of narcissistic safety, however fragile, but also gain sadomasochistic satisfaction from the relationships they establish with their objects—however precarious the existence of these objects may be. The subject's state of mind cannot tolerate uncertainty, inconsistency, ambiguity, or contradiction. It is a mind that cannot play; there is only a frantic search for reassurance that is never fulfilled.[5]

Something in them turns into an internal tyrant, a terrorist, a *Mafioso*, who is idealized and to whom they gladly submit. This is especially relevant to the treatment of these patients because this scenario is projected onto the scene of the treatment and the figure of the analyst. The sadomasochistic relationship is, then, recreated in the process of the analysis, the analyst becoming the patient's sadistic persecutor. The borderline subjects feel that they have lost their freedom in and through the psychoanalytic treatment itself, that the analyst becomes the cruel tyrant and torturer who keeps them actually trapped; thus, they feel unable to escape from the analysis except through an explosive acting out or interruption.

In the end, the borderline patient will have to accept that his distorted idea of safety is completely illusory. This acceptance cannot be achieved without genuine psychic pain and arduous working through. He will have to recognize, like the rest of us, that paradise has not only been lost—it simply never existed.

Notes

1. My clinical presentation to the research group can be found in Kohon (2005).

2. In referring to my work, Libbrecht (1995) agreed with my own suggestion, that this theoretical switch represented an impoverished definition of Freudian psychoanalysis (Kohon, 1984).

3. For an application of the concept of divalence, see, for example, the clinical case of Mrs K, described by Maguire (1995). Furthermore, see also the use that Nitza Yarom (2005) has made of the same concept in her description of the matrix of hysteria from a theoretical and clinical point of view.

4. Juliet Mitchell (2003) has questioned "the current translation of 'sexual difference' as the more fashionable 'gender difference'", as exemplified by the work, among others, of Dana Breen (1993). Mitchell offered interesting and different reasons for this shift. A collection of papers on the subject of gender and sexual difference has been edited by Iréne Matthis (Matthis, 2004).

5. The impossible wish for an equally unattainable safe place has been described in the psychoanalytic literature, most prominently by R. D. Laing (1960) and Michael Balint (1968). An interesting article related to the confusion of boundaries and the individual's search for a safe place is Ann Speltz's *The Voyage Out* and Virginia Woolf's Struggle for Autonomy" (Speltz, 1987). Through the study of her writings, diaries and letters, Speltz describes Virginia Woolf's dependence upon circumscribed spaces for a sense of well-being.

REFERENCES AND BIBLIOGRAPHY

Abend, S., Poder, M., & Willick, M. (1988). A response. *Psychoanalytic Inquiry*, *8*: 438–455.

Anzieu, D. (1985). *Le moi peau*. Paris: Dunod. [English: *The Skin Ego*. New Haven, CT/London: Yale University Press, 1989.]

Anzieu, D. (1993). *El Cuerpo de la Obra: Ensayos psicoanalíticos sobre el trabajo creador*. Mexico City: Ed Siglo XXI.

Aulagnier, P. (1975). *La violence de l'interprétation*. Paris: PUF.

Aulagnier, P. (1984). *L'aprenti-historien et le maître sorcier*. Paris: PUF.

Balint, M. (1937). Early developmental status of the ego: Primary object-love. In: *Primary Love and Psychoanalytic Technique*. London: Tavistock, 1965.

Balint, M. (1968). *The Basic Fault: Therapeutic Aspects of Regression*. London: Tavistock.

Baranger, M. (1993). The mind of the analyst: From listening to interpretation. *International Journal of Psychoanalysis, 74*.

Baranger, W., & Baranger, M. (1959). La situacion analítica como campo dinamico. In: W. Baranger & M. Baranger, *Problemas del campo analítico*. Buenos Aires: Kargieman, 1969.

Baranger, W., & Baranger, M. (1969). *Problemas del campo psicoanalitico*. Buenos Aires: Kargieman.

Baranger, W., Baranger, M., & Mom, J. (1982). Proceso y no proceso en el trabajo analítico. *Revista de Psicoanálisis, 4*.

Bateman, A. (1998). Thick- and thin-skinned organisations and enactment in borderline and narcissistic disorders. *International Journal of Psychoanalysis, 79*: 13–25.

Bergeret, J. (1974). *La depresion et les états limités*. Paris: Dunod.

Bergmann, M. (1993). Reflections on the history of psychoanalysis. *Journal of the American Psychoanalytic Association, 41.*

Bergmann, M. (2000). *The Hartmann Era*. New York: Other Press.

Bergmann. M. (2001). La psychanalyse: Histoire et crise actuelle. *Revue Française de Psychanalyse, Hors Serie.*

Bion, W. R. (1957). Differentiation of the psychotic from the non-psychotic personalities. *International Journal of Psychoanalysis, 38* (Parts 3–4). [Also in: *Second Thoughts* (pp. 43–64). London: Heinemann, 1967.]

Bion, W. R. (1958). On hallucination. *International Journal of Psychoanalysis, 39.* [Also in: *Seconds Thoughts*. London: Heinemann, 1967.]

Bion, W. R. (1959). Attacks on linking. *International Journal of Psychoanalysis, 40.* [Also in: *Seconds Thoughts*. London: Heinemann, 1967.]

Bion, W. R. (1962). *Learning from Experience*. London: Heinemann. [Reprinted London: Karnac, 1984.]

Bion, W. R. (1963). *Elements of Psycho-Analysis*. London: Heinemann. [Reprinted London: Karnac, 1984.]

Bion, W. R. (1965). *Transformations*. London: Heinemann. [Reprinted London: Karnac, 1984.]

Bion, W. R. (1967a). Attacks on linking. In: *Second Thoughts* (pp. 93–109). London: Heinemann. [Reprinted London: Karnac, 1984.]

Bion, W. R. (1967b). Differentiation of the psychotic from the non-psychotic personalities. In: *Second Thoughts* (pp. 43–64). London: Heinemann. [Reprinted London: Karnac, 1984.]

Bion, W. R. (1967c). Notes on memory and desire. *The Psychoanalytic Forum, 2* (3). [Reprinted in E. Bott Spillius (Ed.), *Melanie Klein Today, Vol. 2: Mainly Practice* (pp. 17-21). London: Routledge, 1988.]

Bion, W. R. (1967d). *Second Thoughts: Selected Papers on Psychoanalysis*. London: Heinemann. [Reprinted London: Karnac, 1984.]

Bion, W. R. (1970). *Attention and Interpretation*. London: Tavistock. [Reprinted London: Karnac, 1984.]

Bion, W. R. (1976a). Emotional turbulence [Paper given at the International Conference on Borderline Disorders, Topeka, Kansas]. In: *Clinical Seminars and Four Papers*. Oxford: Fleetwood Press, 1987.

Bion, W. R. (1976b). On a quotation from Freud [Paper given at the International Conference on Borderline Disorders, Topeka, Kansas]. In: *Clinical Seminars and Four Papers*. Oxford: Fleetwood Press, 1987.

Bion, W. R. (1977). *Two Papers: The Grid and Caesura* [Originally presented as talks to the Los Angeles Psychoanalytic Society, in 1971 and 1975, respectively]. Rio de Janiero: Imago; London: Karnac, 1989.

Bleger, J. (1967a). Psychoanalysis of the psychoanalytic frame. *International Journal of Psychoanalysis, 48.* [Also in: *Simbiosis y Ambiguedad*. Buenos Aires: Paidos.]

Bleger, J. (1967b). *Simbiosis y Ambigüedad*. Buenos Aires: Paidos.

Bleichmar, S. (1987). *En los origenes del sujeto psiquico*. Buenos Aires: Amorrortu.

Bloom, H. (1994). *The Western Canon*. New York: Harcourt Brace.

Bollas, C. (2000). *Hysteria*. London/New York: Routledge.

Bollas, C. (2002). *Free Association*. Cambridge: Icon Books.

Botella, C., & Botella, S. (2001). *La figurabilité psychique*. Geneva: Delachaux & Niestlé.

Bott-Spillius, E. (2001). Developements actuels de la psychanalyse kleinien. *Revue Française de Psychanalyse, Hors Serie*.

Bouvet, M. (1956). La clinique psychanalytique: La relation d'objet. In: *Ouvres psychanalytiques, Vol. 2*. Paris: Payot, 1967.

Bowlby, J. (1958). The nature of the child's tie to his mother. In: *Attachment and Loss, Vol. 1* (Appendix). London: Hogarth, 1969.

Breen, D. (Ed.) (1993). *The Gender Conundrum: Contemporary Psychoanalytic Perspectives on Femininity and Masculinity*. London/New York: Routledge.

Britton, R. (1998). *Belief and Imagination: Explorations in Psychoanalysis*. London/New York: Routledge.

Castoriadis, C. (1969). Epilogomens. In: *Les carrefours du labyrinthe*. Paris: Editions du Seuil.

Castoriadis, C. (1989). *La institución imaginaria de la sociedad, Vol. 2*. Barcelona: Tusquest.

Cesio, F. (1970). Contratransferencia. *Revista de Psicoanálisis, 27* (2): 210.

Clarkin, J. F., Levy, K. N., & Schiavi, J. M. (2005). Transference focused psychotherapy: Development of a psychodynamic treatment for severe personality disorders. *Clinical Neuroscience Research, 4* (5–6): 379–386.

Clarkin, J. F., Yeomans, F. E., & Kernberg, O. (1999). *Psychotherapy for Borderline Personality*. New York: Wiley.

Deleuze, G. (1968). *Difference and Repetition*. London: Athlone, 1994.

De M'Uzan, M. (1977). Contretransfert et systeme paradoxal. In: *De l'art à la mort*. Paris: Gallimard.

Donnet, J.-L. (1973). Le divan bien tempéré. In: *Le divan bien tempéré*. Paris: PUF, 1998.

Donnet, J.-L. & Green, A. (1973), *L'enfant de ça*. Paris: Minuit.

Eco, U. (1979). *Obra abierta*. Barcelona: Ariel. [English: *The Open Work*. Cambridge, MA: Harvard University Press, 1989.]

Eigen, M. (1999). *Toxic Nourishment*. London: Karnac.

Etchegoyen, H. (1978). Las formas de transferencia. *Psicoanalisis, 2*.

Etchegoyen, H. (1982). A cincuenta años de la interpretación mutativa. *Revista Chilena de Psicoanalisis, 4*.

Etchegoyen, H. (1983). Insight. *Trabajo del Psicoanalisis, 2*.

Etchegoyen, H. (1986). Fundamentos de la técnica psicoanalitica. Buenos Aires: Amorrortu. [English: *Fundamentals of Psychoanalytic Technique*. London: Karnac, 1991.]

Faimberg, H. (2005). *The Telescoping of Generations*. London: Routledge.

Fairbairn, W. R. D. (1952). *Psycho-Analytic Studies of the Personality*. London: Routledge.

Fenichel, O. (1945). *Psychoanalytic Theory of Psychosis*. New York: Norton.

Fonagy, P. (1991). Thinking about thinking: Some clinical and theoretical considerations in the treatment of a borderline patient. *International Journal of Psychoanalysis, 72*: 639–656.

Fonagy, P. (2000). Attachment and borderline personality disorder. *Journal of the American Psychoanalytic Association, 48*: 1129–1146.

Fonagy, P., Target, M., Cottrell, D., Phillips, J., & Kurtz, Z. (2002). *What Works for Whom? A Critical Review of Treatments for Children and Adolescents*. New York: Guilford Press, 2002.

Foucault, M. (1964). *La historia de la locura en la época clásica, Vols. I & II*. Mexico City: FCE. [English: *Madness and Civilization: A History of Insanity in the Age of Reason*. London: Routledge, 2001.]

Freud, S. (1895d). *Studies on Hysteria. S.E.*, 2.

Freud, S. (1900a). *The Interpretation of Dreams. S.E.*, 4–5.

Freud, S. (1901b). *The Psychopathology of Everyday Life. S.E.*, 6.

Freud, S. (1905d). *Three Essays on the Theory of Sexuality. S.E., 7*: 125.

Freud, S. (1910a [1909]). Five lectures on psycho-analysis. *S.E., 11*: 3.

Freud, S. (1910d). The future prospects of psycho-analytic therapy. *S.E., 11*.

Freud, S. (1911b). Formulations on the two principles of mental functioning. *S.E., 12*: 215.

Freud, S. (1912b). The dynamics of transference. *S.E., 12*.

Freud, S. (1912–13). *Totem and Taboo. S.E., 13*: ix.

Freud, S. (1914c). On narcissism: An introduction. *S.E., 14*: 69.

Freud, S. (1914g). Remembering, repeating and working-through (Further recommendations on the technique of psycho-analysis, II). *S.E., 12*: 147.

Freud, S. (1915c). *Instincts and Their Vicissitudes. S.E., 14*: 111.

Freud, S. (1915d). Repression. *S.E., 14*: 143.

Freud, S. (1915e). The unconscious. *S.E., 14*: 161.

Freud, S. (1916d). Those wrecked by success. In: Some character-types met with in psycho-analytic work. *S.E., 14*: 311.

Freud, S. (1916–17). *Introductory Lectures on Psycho-Analysis. S.E.*, 15 & 16.

Freud, S. (1917d [1915]). A metapsychological supplement to the theory of dreams. *14*: 219.

Freud, S. (1917e [1915]). Mourning and melancholia. *14*: 239.

Freud, S. (1918b). From the history of an infantile neurosis. *S.E.*, 17.

Freud, S. (1919h). The uncanny. *S.E., 17*: 219.

Freud, S. (1920g). *Beyond the Pleasure Principle. S.E., 18*: 3.

Freud, S. (1921c). *Group Psychology and the Analysis of the Ego. S.E., 18*: 67.

Freud, S. (1923a [1922]). Two encyclopaedia articles. *S.E., 18*.

Freud, S. (1923b). *The Ego and the Id. S.E., 19*: 3.

Freud, S. (1923e). The infantile genital organization: An interpolation into the theory of sexuality. *S.E., 19*: 141.

Freud, S. (1924b [1923]). Neurosis and psychosis. *S.E., 19*: 149.

Freud, S. (1924c). The economic problem of masochism. *S.E., 19*: 157.

Freud, S. (1924d). The dissolution of the Oedipus complex. *S.E., 19*: 173.

Freud, S. (1924e). The loss of reality in neurosis and psychosis. *19*: 183.

Freud, S. (1925f). Preface to August Aichhorn's *Wayward Youth. S.E., 19*.

Freud, S. (1925h). Negation. *S.E., 19*: 235.

Freud, S. (1926d [1925]). *Inhibitions, Symptoms and Anxiety. S.E., 20*: 77.

Freud, S. (1927e). Fetishism. *S.E., 21*: 149.

Freud, S. (1930a [1929]). *Civilization and Its Discontents. S.E., 21*: 59.

Freud, S. (1933a [1932]). *New Introductory Lectures on Psycho-Analysis. S.E., 22*: 3.

Freud, S. (1937c). Analysis terminable and interminable. *S.E., 23*: 209.

Freud, S. (1937d). Constructions in analysis. *S.E., 23*: 257.

Freud, S. (1940a [1938]). *An Outline of Psycho-Analysis. S.E., 23*: 141.

Freud, S. (1940b [1938]). Some elementary lessons in psycho-analysis. *S.E., 23*: 281.

Freud, S. (1940e [1938]). Splitting of the ego in the process of defence. *S.E., 23*: 273.

Freud, S. (1950 [1895]). Project for a scientific psychology. *S.E., 1*: 283.

García Canclini, N. (1997). *Imaginarios urbanos*. Buenos Aires: EUdeBA.

Gazzano, M., & Sor, D. (1992). *Fanatismo*. Turin: Ananké.

Giddens, A. (1991). *Modernity and Self Identity*. London: Verso.

Gomez, L. (2005). *The Freud Wars: An Introduction to the Philosophy of Psychoanalysis*. London/New York: Routledge.

Green, A. (1973). *Le discours vivant*. Paris: PUF.

Green, A. (1975). The analyst, symbolization and the absence in the analytic setting (on changes in analytic practice and analytic experience). *International Journal of Psychoanalysis, 56*: 1–22. [Also in: *On Private Madness*. London: Hogarth, 1986.]

Green, A. (1977). The borderline concept: A conceptual framework for the understanding of borderline patients. In: P. Hartocollis et al. (Eds.), *Borderline Personality Disorders: The Concept, the Syndrome, the Patient*. New York: International Universities Press. [Also in: A. Green, *On Private Madness*. London: Hogarth, 1986.]

Green, A. (1983). *Narcissisme de vie, narcissisme de mort*. [Narcissism of life, narcissism of death]. Paris: Éditions de Minuit.

Green, A. (1984) Le langage dans la psychanalyse. In: *Langages*. Paris: Les Belles Lettres.

Green, A. (1986a). La capacité de rêverie et le mythe étiologique. In: *La folie privée*. Paris: Gallimard, 1990.

Green, A. (1986b). *On Private Madness*. London: Hogarth; Madison, CT: International Universities Press.

Green, A. (1990). *La folie privée*. Paris: Gallimard.

Green, A. (1992). La tiercéité. In: *La pensée clinique*. Paris: Odile Jacob, 2001.

Green, A. (1993). *Le travail de négatif*. Paris: Les Editions de Minuit.

Green, A. (1996). *La metapsicologia revisitada* [Metapsychology revisited]. Buenos Aires: EUdeBA.

Green, A. (1997a). Chiasmus: Prospective—borderlines viewed after hysteria; retrospective—hysteria reviewed after borderlines. *Psychoanalysis in Europe: Bulletin of the EPF, 48*: 39–42.

Green, A. (1997b). The intuition of the negative in *Playing and Reality*. *International Journal of Psychoanalysis, 78*: 1071–1084.

Green, A. (1999a). *The Fabric of Affect and Psychoanalytic Discourse*. London: Routledge, Kegan & Paul.

Green, A. (1999b). *The Work of the Negative*. London: Free Association Books.

Green, A. (2000a). The central phobic position: A new formulation of the free association method. *International Journal of Psychoanalysis, 81*: 429–451. [Also in: P. Williams (Ed.), *Key Papers on Borderline Disorders*. London: Karnac, 2002].

Green, A. (2002b). *La Pensée Clinique*. Paris: Odile Jacob.

Green, A. (2000c). *Time in Psychoanalysis: Some Contradictory Aspects*. London: Free Association Books.

Green, A. (2000d). What kind of research for psychoanalysis? In: J. Sandler et al. (Ed.), *Clinical and Observational Psychoanalytic Research: Roots of a Controversy* (pp. 21–26). Madison, CT: International Universities Press.

Green, A. (2005). The illusion of common ground and mythical pluralism. *International Journal of Psychoanalysis, 86*: 627–632.

Green, A., & Kohon, G. (2005). *Love and Its Vicissitudes*. London/New York: Routledge.

Hare, R. D., Hart, S., & Harpur, T. (1991). Psychopathy and the DMS-IV Criteria for Anti-Social Personality Disorder. *Journal of Abnormal Psychology, 100*: 391–398.

Heimann, P. (1942) A contribution to the problem of sublimation and its relation to processes of internalization. *International Journal of Psychoanalysis, 23*: 8–17. [Also in: *About Children and Children-No-Longer: Collected Papers*, ed. M. Tonnesmann. London: Tavistock/Routledge, 1989.]

Heimann, P. (1950). On countertransference. *International Journal of Psychoanalysis, 31*.

Hughes, C. H. (1884). Moral and affective insanity: Psychosensory insanity. *Alienist and Neurologist, 5*: 229–315. [Also in M. H. Stone (Ed.), *Essential Papers on Borderline Disorders: One Hundred Years at the Border*. New York: New York University Press, 1986.]

Jones, E. (1953–57). *Sigmund Freud: Life and Work* (3 vols). London: Hogarth.

Kermode, F. (1985). *Forms of Attention*. London: Verso.

Kernberg, O. F. (1967). Borderline personality organisation. *Journal of the American Psychoanalytic Association, 15*: 641–685.

Kernberg, O. F. (1975). *Borderline Conditions and Pathological Narcissism.* New York: Jason Aronson.

Kernberg, O. F. (1984). *Severe Personality Disorders.* New Haven, CT: Yale University Press.

Kernberg, O. F. (1995a). *Aggression in Personality Disorders and Perversions.* New Haven, CT: Yale University Press.

Kernberg, O. F. (1995b). *Love Relations: Normality and Pathology.* New Haven, CT: Yale University Press.

Kernberg, O. F. (2001). Recent developments in the technical approaches of English-language psychoanalytic schools. *Psychoanalytic Quarterly, 70* (3): 519–547.

Kernberg, O. F. (2004). *Aggressivity, Narcissism, and Self-Destructiveness in the Psychotherapeutic Relationship* (pp. 220–244). New Haven, CT: Yale University Press.

Kernberg, O. F., Burstein, E.D., Coyne, L., Applebaum, A., Horwitz, L., & Voth, H. (1972). Psychotherapy and psychoanalysis: The final report of the Menninger Foundation's Psychotherapy Research Project. *Bulletin of the Menninger Foundation, 36* (1–2).

Kernberg, O. F., Selzer, M. A., Koenigsberg, H. W., Carr, A., & Appelbaum, A. H. (1989). *Psychodynamic Psychotherapy of Borderline Patients.* New York: Basic Books.

Khan, M. M. (1974). The concept of cumulative trauma. In: *The Privacy of the Self.* London: Hogarth.

Khan, M. M. (1983). *Hidden Selves.* New York: International Universities Press.

Klein, M. (1921). The development of a child. In: *Love, Guilt and Reparation and Other Works, 1921–1945. The Writings of Melanie Klein, Vol. 1.* London: Hogarth, 1975. [Reprinted London: Karnac, 1992.]

Klein, M. (1932). *The Psycho-Analysis of Children. The Writings of Melanie Klein, Vol. 2.* London: Hogarth, 1975.

Klein, M. (1945). The Oedipus complex in the light of early anxieties. *International Journal of Psychoanalysis, 26.* [Also in: *Love, Guilt and Reparation and Other Works, 1921–1945. The Writings of Melanie Klein, Vol. 1.* London: Hogarth, 1975. [Reprinted London: Karnac, 1992.]

Klein, M. (1946). Notes on some schizoid mechanisms. *International Journal of Psychoanalysis, 27.* [Also in: *Envy and Gratitude and Other Works. The Writings of Melanie Klein, Vol. 3.* London: Hogarth, 1975. [Reprinted London: Karnac, 1992.]

Klein, M. (1952a). The origins of transference. *International Journal of Psychoanalysis, 33:* 433–438.

Klein, M. (1952b). Some theoretical conclusions regarding the emotional life of the infant. In: *Envy and Gratitude and Other Works. The Writings of Melanie Klein, Vol. 3.* London: Hogarth, 1975. [Reprinted London: Karnac, 1992.]

Klein, M. (1955). On identification. In: *Envy and Gratitude and Other Works.*

The Writings of Melanie Klein, Vol. 3. London: Hogarth, 1975. [Reprinted London: Karnac, 1992.]

Klein, M. (1957). Envy and gratitude. In: *Envy and Gratitude and Other Works. The Writings of Melanie Klein, Vol. 3*. London: Hogarth, 1975. [Reprinted London: Karnac, 1992.]

Kohon, G. (1984). Reflections on Dora: The case of hysteria. *International Journal of Psychoanalysis, 65*: 73–84.

Kohon, G. (1986). Introduction. In: G. Kohon (Ed.), *The British School of Psychoanalysis: The Independent Tradition*. London: Free Association Press.

Kohon, G. (1999). *No Lost Certainties to be Recovered*. London: Karnac.

Kohon, G. (2005). Love in the time of madness. In: A. Green & G. Kohon, *Love and Its Vicissitudes*. London/New York: Routledge.

Kohut, H. (1971). *The Analysis of the Self*. New York: International Universities Press.

Kristeva, J. (1980). *Pouvoirs de l'horreur*. Paris: Editions du Seuil.

Kuhn, T. S. (1962). *The Structure of Scientific Revolutions* (2nd edition). Chicago, IL: University of Chicago Press, 1970.

Lacan, J. (1967). *Écrits*. Paris: Editions du Seuil.

Lacan, J. (1977a). The agency of the letter in the unconscious or reason since Freud. In: *Écrits* (pp. 179–225). New York: Norton.

Lacan, J. (1977b). On a question preliminary to any possible treatment of psychosis. In: *Écrits* (pp. 179–225). New York: Norton.

Laing, R. D. (1960). *The Divided Self: An Existential Study in Sanity and Madness*. London: Tavistock.

Laplanche, J. (1986). La pulsion de mort dans la theorie de la pulsion sexuel. In: *La pulsion de mort*. Paris: PUF.

Laplanche, J. (1987). *Noveux fondament pour la psychanalyse*, Paris: PUF.

Laplanche, J., & Pontalis, J.-B. (1967). *The Language of Psycho-Analysis*. London: Hogarth, 1973. [Reprinted London: Karnac, 1988.]

Lasch, C. (1979). *The Culture of Narcissism: American Life in an Age of Diminishing Expectations*. New York: Norton.

Lenzenweger, M. F., Clarkin, J. F., Kernberg, O. F., & Foelsch, P. A. (2001). The Inventory of Personality Organization: Psychometric properties, factorial composition, and criterion relations with affect, aggressive dyscontrol, psychosis proneness, and self-domains in a nonclinical sample. *Psychological Assessment, 13* (4): 577–591.

Leuzinger-Bohleber, M., & Bürgin, D. (2003). Pluralism and unity in psychoanalytic research: Some introductory remarks. In: M. Leuzinger-Bohleber, A. U. Dreher, & J. Canestri (Eds.), *Pluralism and Unity? Methods of Research in Psychoanalysis*. London: International Psychoanalytical Association.

Leuzinger-Bohleber, M., Dreher, A. U., & Canestri, J. (Eds.) (2003). *Pluralism and Unity? Methods of Research in Psychoanalysis*. London: International Psychoanalytical Association.

Libbrecht, K. (1995). *Hysterical Psychosis: A Historical Survey.* Somerset, NJ: Transaction.

Liberman, D. (1970–72). *Lingüística, interacción comunicativa y proceso psicoanalítico, Vols 1–3.* Buenos Aires: Galerna.

Liberman, D. (1976). *Comunicación y Psicoanalisis.* Buenos Aires: Alex.

Liberman, D., & Maldavsky, D. (1975). *Psicoanalisis y semiótica.* Buenos Aires: Paidos.

Lipovetsky, G. (1983). *L'ère du vide. Essais sur l'individualisme contemporain.* Paris: Gallimard, 1996.

Little, M. (1951). Countertransference and the patient's response to it. In: *Transference Neurosis and Transference Psychosis.* London: Jason Aronson, 1981.

Lutenberg, J. (1985). Diálogo analitico. Censura-cesura. *Revista de Psicoanalisis de APdeBA, 10.*

Lutenberg, J. (1993). La asociación libre corporal. *Revista de Psicoanalisis de APdeBA, 15* (No. 2).

Lutenberg, J. (1995a). Clinica del vacio. El vacio mental y la angustia. Reflexiones clinicas y técnicas acerca del acting. *Revista Zona Erógena, 26.*

Lutenberg, J. (1995b). Simbiosis defensivas e identificaciones estructurantes. *Revista de Escuela Argentina de Psicoterapia para Graduados, 21.*

Lutenberg, J. (1996). La edición en el analisis. *Revista Zona Erógena, 31.*

Lutenberg, J. (1997). El vacio mental y la sexualidad humana. *Revista Zona Erógena, 35.*

Lutenberg, J. (1998). *El psicoanalista y la verdad.* Buenos Aires: Publikar.

Lutenberg, J. (2001). La créativité negative et l'hallucination negative de la parole. In: *Penser les limites. Écrit en l'honneur d'André Green.* Buenos Aires: Publikar.

Lutenberg, J. (2003a). La contratransferencia y la edición. *Publicaciones Oficiales del congreso IPA 2003.*

Lutenberg, J. (2003b). Male sexuality and mental void. In: A. M. Alizade (Ed.), *Masculine Scenarios.* London: Karnac.

Lutenberg, J. (2003c). Las modificaciones en la clinica psicoanalítica actual. *Actas congreso de Federación Latinoamericana de Asociaciones de Psicoterapia Psicoanalítica y Psicoanálisis, 2003.*

Maguire, M. (1995). *Men, Women, Passion and Power: Gender Issues in Psychotherapy.* London & New York: Routledge.

Mahler, M. (1958). Autism and symbiosis: Two extreme disturbances of identity. *International Journal of Psychoanalysis, 39.*

Mahler, M. (1967). *On Human Symbiosis and the Vicissitudes on Individuation.* London: Hogarth and The Institute of Psycho-Analysis.

Mahler, M. (1984). *The Selected Papers of Margaret Mahler, Vol. 2: Separation–Individuation.* New York/London: Jason Aronson.

Marucco, N. (1998). *Transferencia y cura analítica.* Buenos Aires: Amorrortu.

Masterson, J., & Rinsley, D. (1975). The borderline syndrome: The role of the mother in the genesis and psychic structure of the borderline personality. *International Journal of Psychoanalysis, 56*: 163–177.

Matthis, I. (2004) (Ed). *Dialogues on Sexuality, Gender and Psychoanalysis.* London: Karnac.

McDougall, J. (1978). *Plaidoyer pour une certaine anormalité.* Paris: Gallimard.

McDougall, J. (1982). *Théatres du Je.* Paris: Gallimard. [English: *Theaters of the Mind.* New York: Brunner Mazel, 1991.]

McDougall, J. (1989). *Theaters of the Body.* New York: Norton.

Meissner, W. (1984). *The Borderline Spectrum.* New York: Jason Aronson.

Meltzer, D. (1975a). Adhesive identification. *Contemporary Psycho-Analysis, 2.*

Meltzer, D. (1975b). *Explorations in Autism.* London: Karnac.

Meltzer, D. (1983) *Vida Onirica* [Oneiric life]. Madrid: Tecnipublicaciones SA.

Mitchell, J. (2003). *Siblings.* Cambridge: Polity.

Money-Kyrle, R. (1956). Normal counter-transference and some deviations. *International Journal of Psychoanalysis, 37.*

Montagu, A. (1971). *Touching: The Human Significance of the Skin* (2nd edition). New York: Harper & Row, 1978.

Montagu, A. (1981). *El Sentido del Tacto.* Madrid: Aguilar.

Moore, T. V. (1921). The parataxes. A study and analysis of certain borderline mental states. *Psychoanalytic Review, 8*: 252–275.

Morin, E. (1977). *La méthode.* Paris: Editions du Seuil.

Neyraut, M. (1974). *Le transfert.* Paris: PUF.

Ogden, T. (1979). On projective identification. *International Journal of Psychoanalysis, 60.*

Ogden, T. (1993) The analytic third: Working with intersubjective analytical facts. *International Journal of Psychoanalysis, 75.*

Ogden, T. (1994). *Subjects of Analysis.* Northvale, NJ: Jason Aronson.

Perelberg, R. J. (1999a). The interplay between identifications and identity in the analysis of a violent young man: Issues of technique. *International Journal of Psychoanalysis, 80*: 31–45.

Perelberg, R. J. (1999b). The interplay of identifications: Violence, hysteria, and the repudiation of femininity. In: G. Kohon (Ed.), *The Dead Mother: The Work of André Green.* London: Routledge.

Perelberg, R. J. (2003). Full and empty spaces in the analytic process. *International Journal of Psychoanalysis, 84*: 579–592.

Perelberg, R. J. (2004). Narcissistic configurations: Violence and its absence in treatment. *International Journal of Psychoanalysis, 85*: 1065–1079.

Pichón Riviere, E. (1951). Algunas observaciones sobre la transferencia en los pacientes psicóticos. *Revista de Psicoanalisis, 18.*

Pichón Riviere, E. (1968). *Clases de la Escuela de Psicologia Social.* Private publication.

Pontalis, J.-B. (1981). *Entre le rêve et la doleur.* Paris: Gallimard.

Prieto, L. J. (1967). *Mensajes y señales*. Barcelona: Seix Barral.

Racker, H. (1948). A contribution to the problem of counter-transference. *International Journal of Psychoanalysis, 34.*

Racker, H. (1949). *Transference and Countertransference*. London: Hogarth, 1968.

Racker, H. (1960). *Estudios sobre técnica psicoanalítica.* Buenos Aires: Paidos.

Rangell, L. (1988). The future of psychoanalysis: The scientific crossroads. *Psychoanalytic Quarterly, 57:* 313–340.

Rascovsky, A. (1960). *El psiquismo fetal.* Buenos Aires: Paidos.

Rassial, J.-J. (1999). *Le sujet en état limite.* Paris: Éditions Denoël.

Reich, A. (1951). On countertranference. *International Journal of Psychoanalysis, 32.*

Rey, J. H. (1979). Schizoid phenomena in the borderline. In: J. Le Boit & A. Capponi (Eds.), *Advances in the Psychotherapy of the Borderline Patient.* New York: Jason Aronson.

Rolland, J.-C. (2001). Le discours interne. In: C. Botella (Ed.), *Penser les limites.* Geneva: Delachaux & Niestlé.

Rosenfeld, H. A. (1965). *Psychotic States.* New York: International Universities Press.

Rosenfeld, H. A. (1987). *Impasse and Interpretation: Therapeutic and Anti-Therapeutic Factors in the Psychoanalytic Treatment of Psychotic, Borderline and Neurotic Patients.* London: Tavistock.

Rosolato, G. (1999). *Les cinq axes de la psychanalyse.* Paris: PUF.

Rosse, I. C. (1890). Clinical evidences of borderland insanity. *Journal of Nervous and Mental Diseases.* 17: 669–683. [Also in: M. H. Stone (Ed.), *Essential Papers on Borderline Disorders: One Hundred Years at the Border.* New York/London: New York University Press, 1986.]

Sandler, J. (1976). Countertransference and role-responsiveness. *International Journal of Psychoanalysis, 3.*

Sandler, J., Sandler, A.-M., Davies, R. (2000). *Clinical and Observational Psychoanalytic Research: Roots of a Controversy.* Madison, CT: International Universities Press.

Searles, H. (1965). *Collected Papers on Schizophrenia and Related Subjects.* London: Hogarth.

Segal, H. (1957). Notes on symbol-formation. *International Journal of Psychoanalysis, 38.* [Also in: *The Work of Hanna Segal: A Kleinian Approach to Clinical Practice.* New York/London: Jason Aronson, 1981.]

Sennett, R. (1977). *The Fall of Public Man: On the Social Psychology of Capitalism.* New York: Knopf.

Shengold, L. (1995). *The Delusions of Everyday Life.* New Haven, CT: Yale University Press.

Speltz, A. (1987). *The Voyage Out* and Virginia Wolf's struggle for autonomy. *Annual of Psychoanalysis, 15:* 311–334.

Steiner, J. (1979). The border between the paranoid–schizoid and the depressive positions in the borderline patient. *British Journal of Medical Psychology, 52*: 385–391.

Steiner, J. (1993). *Psychic Retreats: Pathological Organizations in Psychotic, Neurotic and Borderline Patients.* London/New York: Routledge.

Steiner, R. (2000). Introduction. In: J. Sandler, A.-M. Sandler, & R. Davies (Eds.), *Clinical and Observational Psychoanalytic Research.* London: Karnac.

Stern, A. (1938). Psychoanalytic investigation of and therapy in the borderline group of neuroses. *Psychoanalytic Quarterly, 7*: 467–489.

Stone, L. (1961). *The Psychoanalytic Situation.* New York: International Universities Press.

Stone, M. H. (1993). *Abnormalities of Personality.* New York: Norton.

Stone, R. (Ed.) (1986). *Essential Papers on Borderline Disorders: One Hundred Years at the Border.* New York/London: New York University Press.

Strachey, J. (1934). The nature of the therapeutic action of psycho-analysis. *International Journal of Psychoanalysis, 15.*

Tausk, V. (1919). On the origin of the "apparatus" in schizophrenia. *Psychoanalytic Quarterly, 2* (1933): 519–556.

Tustin, F. (1968). Autismo y psicosis infantiles. Buenos Aires: Paidos. *Autism and Childhood Psychosis.* New York: International Universities Press.

Tustin, F. (1981). *Autistic States in Children.* London: Routledge & Kegan Paul.

Tustin, F. (1990). *The Protective Shell in Children and Adults.* London: Karnac.

Urribarri, F. (2001). Pour introduir la pensée tertiaire [Introducing tertiary thought]. In: C. Botella (Ed.), *Penser les limites.* Geneva: Delachaux & Niestlé.

Urribarri, F. (2005). Frame and representation within contemporary psychoanalysis. In: F. Richard & F. Urribarri (Eds.), *Enjeux pour une psychanalyse contemporaine.* Paris: PUF.

Urtubey, L. de (1994). Le travail de contre-transfert. *Revue Française de Psychanalyse, 58.*

Viderman, S. (1970). *La construction de l'espace analytique.* Paris: Denoël.

Wallerstein, R., & Green, A. (1996). *Clinical and Observational Research: Roots of a Controversy.* London: Karnac.

Widlöcher, D. (1981). Les concepts d'etat limite. In: *Actualités de la Schizophrenie.* Paris: PUF.

Winnicott, D. W. (1949). Mind and its relation to the psycho-soma. In: *Collected Papers: Through Paediatrics to Psycho-Analysis.* London: Tavistock, 1958.

Winnicott, D. W. (1958). *Collected Papers: Through Paediatrics to Psycho-Analysis.* London: Tavistock.

Winnicott, D. W. (1960a). Counter-transference. In: *The Maturational Processes and the Facilitating Environment.* London: Hogarth, 1965. [Reprinted London: Karnac, 1990.]

Winnicott, D. W. (1960b). Ego distortion in terms of true and false self. In:

D. W. Winnicott, *The Maturational Processes and the Facilitating Environment.* London: Hogarth, 1965. [Reprinted London: Karnac, 1990.]

Winnicott, D. W. (1963). Fear of breakdown. In: *Psycho-Analytic Explorations.* London: Karnac, 1989.

Winnicott, D. W. (1965). *The Maturational Processes and the Facilitating Environment.* London: Hogarth. [Reprinted London: Karnac, 1990.]

Winnicott, D. W. (1971a). *Playing and Reality.* London: Tavistock.

Winnicott, D. W. (1971b). The use of an object and relating through identifications. In: *Playing and Reality* (pp. 86–94). London: Tavistock.

Wisdom, J. O. (1962). Comparison and development of the psycho-analytical theories of melancholia. *International Journal of Psychoanalysis, 43:* 113–132.

Wittgenstein, L. (1989). *Conferencia sobre ética.* Buenos Aires: Paidos.

Wolff, P. (1996a). Commentaries. *Journal of the American Psychoanalytic Association, 44:* 464–474.

Wolff, P. (1996b). The irrelevance of infant observations for psychoanalysis. *Journal of the American Psychoanalytic Association, 44:* 369–392.

Wolff, P. (1998). Response by Peter H. Wolff. *Journal of the American Psychoanalytic Association, 46:* 274–278.

Yarom, N. (2005). *Matrix of Hysteria: Psychoanalysis of the Struggle between the Sexes as Enacted in the Body.* London/New York: Routledge.

Yorke, C., Wiseberg, S., & Freeman, T. (1989). *Development and Psychopathology: Studies in Psychoanalytic Psychiatry.* New Haven, CT: Yale University Press.

Zac, J. (1964). El impostor. *Revista del Psicoanalisis, 21* (1).

Zac, J. (1968). Relación semana/fin de semana. Encuadre y acting out. *Revista del Psicoanalisis, 25.*

Zac, J. (1970). Consideraciones sobre el acting out y aspectos técncios de su tratamiento. *Revista del Psicoanalisis, 27.*

Zac, J. (1973). *Psicopatias.* Buenos Aires: Kargieman.

INDEX